EMBERS OF WAR

EMBERS OF WAR

*Letters from a Quaker Relief Worker
in War-torn Germany*

Grigor McClelland

British Academic Press
I.B. Tauris Publishers
LONDON · NEW YORK

Published in 1997 by British Academic Press
an imprint of I.B.Tauris & Co Ltd
Victoria House, Bloomsbury Square, London WC1B 4DZ

In the United States and Canada distributed by
St Martin's Press, 175 Fifth Avenue, New York, NY 10010

A full CIP record for this book is available from the British Library

A full CIP record is available from the Library of Congress

ISBN 1 86064 312 4

Typeset in Monotype Ehrhardt
by Lucy Morton, London SE12

Printed and bound in Great Britain by WBC Ltd,
Bridgend, Mid-Glamorgan

Contents

PART I   Work with Displaced Persons

v

Foreword

by Sir Geoffrey Wilson, KCB, CMG

Permanent Secretary, Overseas Development Ministry,
1968–70; Chairman, Oxfam, 1977–83

In 1945 I was a temporary civil servant in the Foreign Office, dealing with Eastern Europe, and was appalled, even at second hand, by the accounts of displaced persons milling around in their millions, in a desperate state of misery, uncertainty and confusion. All of them, in one way or another, had been up-rooted by war. Grigor McClelland's letters tell the story of how he and his colleagues in the Friends Ambulance Unit, together with other voluntary agencies, the military authorities and the civilian population, coped with the problems.

It is a pattern with which we have become all too familiar in the half-century since. In Rwanda and Somalia, in Cambodia and Vietnam, and now in Bosnia and Albania, yet more millions of human beings have been uprooted. War has let loose passions that we thought we had outgrown. 'Ethnic cleansing' has raised its ugly head. It is not only in Nazi Germany that the veneer of civilisation has proved to be perilously thin. These man-made disasters have a horror all of their own which drives one to near despair about what human beings can do to one another.

Yet they also call forth a very human response. Quakers have for long involved themselves in relief operations and the part they played in Berlin after the 1914–18 war may well have eased the path for Grigor McClelland and his FAU colleagues. Oxfam and other non-governmental organisations have also played an honourable part in coping with these disasters, and their members and supporters will find this fascinating collection of letters from the chaos of 1945–46 Germany full of lessons for today's aid workers.

In Bosnia and Rwanda the agencies operated under the protection of UN forces. In the zone of Germany where the action of these letters took place, the British were in control, and like any country in control of another, we carried with us the administrative system with which we were familiar. We did it in our colonies—where on the whole it has survived—and we did it for our short period of control in Germany: military administration under ultimate civilian control, maximum possible use of the local population, and plenty of scope for voluntary organisations.

It worked reasonably well. The military—who on the whole were civilians dressed up in uniform—worked hard to discharge the responsibilities of the occupying power to the indigenous population, just as we had done in colonial days. Grigor McClelland concludes by expressing 'the mild surprise of a conscientious objector, at the end of a long war, finding that faced with manifest human need among the former enemy population, FAU members and army personnel saw very much eye to eye.'

Author's Note

In 1995 my wife and I were approached for the loan of any memorabilia that might feature in *Stille Helfer*, an exhibition on Quaker relief work in Germany between 1920 and 1950, which would open in Berlin and tour Germany in 1996–97. I therefore exhumed and read, for the first time since writing them, my regular letters home from Germany between May 1945 and June 1946. The background to my presence and work there is described in the Introduction.

The letters are a day-by-day account of our life and work, the people we met and what they said to us. A complete and exact transcript would have been a little more authentic but a lot more tedious. So the original has been cut by perhaps one-third, dates have been inserted and the material has been re-arranged into chronological order, as if in a diary. In places the text has been altered, but only for the sake of clarity and ease of reading—I have left unchanged such dated uses as 'crippled', 'girl' and 'English' to mean 'disabled', 'woman' and 'British', and any hindsight or later explanation is confined to notes inserted in square brackets or at the end of the book. At several points (for example, before home leave) the letters leave gaps, which it has been possible partially to fill from contemporary minutes, memoranda and other documents I retained. Such passages are duly signalled, and a different form of reference to dates is used in them.

The letters themselves, these other documents, and the report summarised in the Appendix, have been deposited in the

Library at Friends House, 173–177 Euston Road, London, NW1 2BJ, where they can be consulted by scholars.

I felt it desirable to compare my contemporary record with the subsequently established history of the period, and the works I consulted appear in the list of references. I found that there was a good fit between my own worm's eye view and the bird's eye view of the historian, and have added notes where I felt the confirmation striking or the complementarity illuminating. Translations from material published only in German are mine.

I am grateful above all of course to my late parents, who not only were the occasion of the letters and the first to read them, but who preserved them and handed them back to me later. I am also indebted to Lesley Yde, who transcribed with splendid accuracy many scruffy pages of faded typescript. Several kind friends commented on a draft or helped in other ways. A grant from the Joseph Rowntree Charitable Trust made publication possible.

Abbreviations

BRCS	British Red Cross Society
CCG	Control Commission for Germany
COBSRA	Council of British Societies for Relief Abroad
CO	Conscientious Objector / Commanding Officer
DP	Displaced Person
DPACS	Displaced Persons Assembly Centre Staff
DRK	Deutsches Rotes Kreuz, the German Red Cross
FAU	Friends Ambulance Unit
FoR, IFoR	(International) Fellowship of Reconciliation
FRS	Friends Relief Service
IVSP	Inernational Voluntary Service for Peace
LO	Liaison Officer
Mil Gov	Military Government
OR	Other Rank
PHO	Public Health Officer
PoW	Prisoner of War
RAMC	Royal Army Medical Corps
RASC	Royal Army Service Corps
REME	Royal Electrical and Mechanical Engineers
SPD	Sozialdemokratische Partei Deutschlands, the German Social Democrat Party.
UNRRA	United Nations Relief and Rehabilitation Administration

Glossary of German Words, Names and Titles

Arbeiterwohlfahrt	Worker Welfare, the welfare organisation associated with the SPD
Bürgermeister	Mayor or chief executive (see p. 216 n.8) of a town or community
Caritas Verband	The Catholic welfare organisation
Ernährungsamt	Food office
Innere Mission	Home Mission, the Protestant welfare organisation
Kreis(e)	District(s), local government area
Land	Countryside—hence *Landkreis*, a rural *Kreis*
Landjägerkaserne	'Yeomanry Barracks', the building used for the principal Polish DP camp in Einbeck, later re-named *Sikorski*.
Landrat	Mayor of a country area
Ober-	Senior-, a prefix attached to titles of officials at higher levels, e.g. *Oberbürgermeister*
Quäkerspeisung	Quaker feeding (originally, after the First World War)
Rathaus	Council building, county hall
Regierungsbezirk	County, an administrative area larger than a *Kreis*
Schulamt	Schools office, municipal education department
Stadt	Town (*Stadthaus*, town hall)
Stadtvikar	Title of a Catholic priest
Versöhnungsbund	Fellowship of Reconciliation
Wohlfahrtsamt	Welfare Office, Social Services Department

xiii

The Administrative Context for a Relief Team

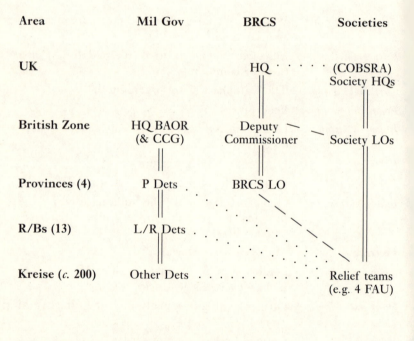

Area	Mil Gov	BRCS	Societies
UK		HQ · · · · ·	(COBSRA) Society HQs
British Zone	HQ BAOR (& CCG)	Deputy Commissioner	Society LOs
Provinces (4)	P Dets	BRCS LO	
R/Bs (13)	L/R Dets		
Kreise (c. 200)	Other Dets · · · · · · · · · · ·		Relief teams (e.g. 4 FAU)

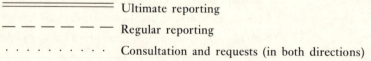

═══════════ Ultimate reporting

─ ─ ─ ─ ─ ─ Regular reporting

· · · · · · · · · Consultation and requests (in both directions)

Thus the Section Leader of 4 FAU at Dortmund sent fortnightly reports to the FAU LO (strictly 'Advisory Officer'—see
p. 130) at Vlotho (Michael Rowntree), who was ultimately
responsible to FAU HQ in London, but summarised and con-
solidated these reports from all FAU teams in the zone, for the
BRCS Deputy Commissioner (Col. Agnew). But we also kept
the BRCS LO for our Province (Penelope Torre Torr) fully
informed, and received guidance from her. When I did her job
for a fortnight I reported direct to Col. Agnew, allocated the
supply of Pacific packs between all teams, and visited other
teams, but did not give them instructions.

Dortmund fell into Arnsberg Regierungsbezirk (Mil Gov HQ
at Arnsberg), which in turn was part of Westphalia Province
(HQ at Münster). BAOR (the British Army of the Rhine) had
only three Corps for four provinces, so both Westphalia and
North Rhine (HQ Düsseldorf) came under 1 Corps (HQ
Iserlohn). Thus when we visited Arnsberg, Münster and
Iserlohn we were accessing the Detachments at three succes-
sively higher levels of Mil Gov. See the map on p. xxiii.

Members of
FAU Section 4[*]

(a) In Post in December 1945. (*See Plate 14*)

BRENDA BAILEY, 22. Quaker. Daughter of Leonhard and Mary Friedrich (q.v.). At Quaker boarding school in England on outbreak of war. In FAU in UK from 1941 except for two years studying social science. Married.

DIANA CLOSE, 29. Quaker. Physiotherapist. Admitted to FAU in October 1945 for immediate service in Germany, having medical and driving qualifications and fluency in German.

SHELLEY FAUSSET, 25. Letter-cutter and designer, formerly apprenticed to Henry Moore.

JOHN HAINES, 20. Previous FAU service with Free French.

BERNARD JACKSON, 21. Student of French.

BILL JUDD, 27. Formerly a clerk, Birmingham Gas Department.

KENNETH KING, 26. Ophthalmic optician. FAU ambulance work in Finland after the Soviet attack, stranded in Sweden after the fall of Norway, reached Middle East via USSR, taken prisoner in Greece. Freed and repatriated, May 1945.

MARJORIE KING, 28. SRN, SCM. Married to Ken.

BILL MCCLELLAND, 23. Quaker from Newcastle upon Tyne. FAU in mobile hospital work from 1942 with British, then Free French, in Middle East, North Africa, Italy and France.

---

[*] Ages at end 1945.

VALERIE ROBINSON, 21. Anglican. Secretary, with French.

CHRIS SMITH, 39. Congregationalist from Bristol. Schoolteacher (Latin and Greek), Boys Brigade officer and acting scoutmaster. Previous FAU hospital and relief work in UK.

JOHN TOVEY, 21. Methodist, West Country. College of Technology student.

TONY TREW, 20. Quaker from Gloucester, student of architecture.

(b) Left before December 1945 (*See Plate 1*)

ELLIS BENJAMIN, 25. Local government officer from Bristol. In FAU, helped organise emergency feeding in the Mulhouse area in February 1945.

GEORGE GREENWOOD, 29. In FAU since 1939. FAU career same as that of Kenneth King, except that (after attempts to escape from Stalag VB) he was freed and repatriated in September 1944. Leader of 4 FAU from April 1945 till return home in November.

JOHN HARRISON, 26. Anglican from Somerset. Oxford, fluent in French and German. Unconditional exemption from military service. Previous FAU service as a cook.

BILL PITTS, 38. Methodist. Correspondence clerk. FAU from October 1940, in London, Plymouth, Liverpool and Birmingham. Married.

RON WARNES, 27. Methodist. Law student. In FAU in Normandy from September 1944.

(c) Arrived in April 1946

MICHAEL TARRANT, 22. Baptist. Bank clerk from Surrey. FAU hospital and emergency feeding work in UK, then blood transfusion work in Italy. Became Section Leader in June 1946

LESLIE RICHARDS, university teacher from Wales.

Other Main Characters

(a) British

AGNEW, COLONEL BRCS Deputy Commissioner for Germany.

BATTERSBY, MAJOR Assistant PHO for Westphalia Province. See p. 125.

COATES, NEVILLE Leader of the FAU section in Berlin. Methodist. Civil engineer from Tyneside. Formerly in the FAU with the Free French.

COOMBS, FLIGHT-LIEUTENANT PHO for Dortmund. See p. 102.

ELLIS, DR. AUDREY Dietician, advising Mil Gov on supplementary feeding schemes for children

GARDINER, GERALD 45. Anglican. Educated Harrow and Oxford. Barrister (later Lord Chancellor). FAU member in charge of FAU relief work in NW Europe from January 1945, till return to UK in November 1945.

KENT, LIEUTENANT Intelligence Officer for occupation forces regiment in Einbeck, but acting i/c DPs until formation of DPACS in July 1945. See p. 39.

ROWNTREE, MICHAEL 26. Quaker from Yorkshire, student at Oxford. With FAU in Finland 1940 but got back to UK from Sweden via Iceland. From 1941, in Middle East, North Africa, Italy and France, with Free French. In charge of FAU sections in Germany from mid-September 1945, and of NW Europe relief work from November 1945.

TORRE TORR, PENELOPE BRCS LO for Hanover, then West-phalia till end of March 1946.

WAINWRIGHT, RICHARD 27. Methodist from Yorkshire. Cambridge (history), and CA articled clerk. FAU hospital work, and edited *FAU Chronicle*. Normandy, September 1944. Second in command for FAU relief work in NW Europe. Later Liberal MP.

(b) Others, in and near Einbeck

BOROWSKI, RICHARD Active social-democrat who suffered under the Nazis. Became Landrat of Einbeck Landkreis. Later, Minister for Home Affairs, Lower Saxony. See p. 48.

FRICKE, DR AUGUST German Quaker, Director of Education in Kassel. See p. 43. Daughter, Rohtraut.

KÖBBERLING, DR. JACOB Doctor for DPs in Landjägerkaserne, devout Baptist.

KÖBBERLING, MILKA Wife of Jacob.

KÜNKEL, MRS. Wife of naturalised US psychologist. Trapped in Germany on US entry into war.

MATYSIAK, CESARY Polish DP, interpreter and aide in the Landjägerkaserne (Sikorski) camp.

OHNESORGE, FRAU ELLY Teacher of English and German in Einbeck. Currently honorary interpreter and adviser for Einbeck's German committee for DP affairs. Husband a PoW in Russian hands, until September 1945.

ROPP, BARON VON DER Aristocratic Christian preacher and idealist. Son Christov had been at a Quaker school in England. See p. 66.

ROSIER, ERNA Elderly but leading Quaker at Göttingen. See p. 42.

URBANCZYK, GUNTHER AND LOTHAR   Two brothers, lawyers, half-Jewish, now leading Einbeck citizens.

VOGES, DR. HERBERT   Teacher of English, interpreter for Mil Gov. Doctoral thesis on the Tyneside dialects. See p. 40.

(c) Others, in Vechta, Dortmund and elsewhere

ALFREDO   Italian attached to Mil Gov 623 Detachment and remained with 4 FAU as a cook, steward, handyman.

FRIEDRICH, LEONHARD AND MARY   Quakers at Bad Pyrmont, parents of Brenda Bailey of 4 FAU. See p. 41. See Bailey 1994.

JACOB, DR WOLFGANG   Friend of Diana Close, member of the family with whom she had stayed in Germany in the thirties. See p. 143.

KATHMANN   The family who owned the farm and hotel at Calveslage, near Vechta, where 4 FAU were billetted.

KUBES, DR.   Czech medical doctor at Vechta, recently released from concentration camp.

LEVERMANN, STADTRAT GOTTLIEB   Director of the Dortmund Wohlfahrtsamt.

LÖTSCHER   Head of the *Don Suisse* team in Dortmund.

LUIG, STADVIKAR   Catholic priest, head of the Caritas Verband in Dortmund.

MENSCHING, PASTOR WILHELM   Lutheran pastor at Petzen, near Bückeborg, and a leading member of the *Versöhnungsbund*. See p. 62.

MERTZ, GEORGES   A Frenchman from Alsace, engaged in the education division of French military government at Mainz. See p. 143.

MERTZ, RUTH   Wife of Georges and relative of the Schauffelbergers (q.v.).

PALME, FRU ELISABETH   Member of the Swedish Red Cross team in Dortmund.

PEROZZI, CARMEN   Italian, friend of Dr. Kubes.

SCHAUFFELBERGER   A Swiss family living at Unna, relatives of Ruth Mertz. See p. 111.

SPENGEMANN, DR.   Dortmund paediatrician who worked closely with 4 FAU.

TATARINOV AND TITOV   Two of the three Russian LOs concerned with Russian DPs in Vechta.

ULLMANN, RICHARD   German Jewish refugee to UK, who became a Quaker and member of FAU. See p. 147.

List of Illustrations

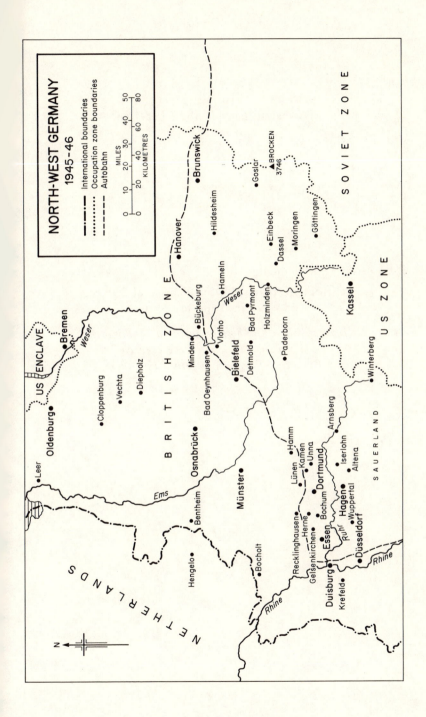

NORTH-WEST GERMANY
1945-46

International boundaries
Occupation zone boundaries
Autobahn

MILES
0   10   20   30   40   50
0   20   40   60   80
KILOMETRES

NETHERLANDS

SOVIET ZONE

BRITISH ZONE

US ZONE

US ENCLAVE

SAUERLAND

N

Leer
Oldenburg
Bremen
Weser
Cloppenburg
Vechta
Diepholz
Hengelo
Bentheim
Ems
Osnabrück
Münster
Bocholt
Recklinghausen
Gelsenkirchen
Herne
Bochum
Essen
Ruhr
Duisburg
Krefeld
Düsseldorf
Rhine
Rhine
Wuppertal
Hagen
Altena
Iserlohn
Dortmund
Unna
Kamen
Lünen
Hamm
Arnsberg
Winterberg
Minden
Bad Oeynhausen
Bielefeld
Detmold
Bückeburg
Vlotho
Hameln
Weser
Bad Pyrmont
Holzminden
Paderborn
Hildesheim
Hanover
Brunswick
Goslar
BROCKEN
3746
Einbeck
Dassel
Moringen
Göttingen
Kassel

To Diana
who shared many of these experiences
and many since

e'mber, n. (usu. pl.). Small piece of live coal
or wood in dying fire (& fig.)

Embers fall to the bottom during a conflagration.
When the fire is over, they remain.
But new life can be breathed into them.

Introduction

The Religious Society of Friends, or Quakers, began in England in the seventeenth century as a re-discovery of original Christianity. The new movement rejected formal statements of belief, ecclesiastical hierarchy, the sacraments and other ritual, and the division of people into clergy and laity. It found ultimate authority in the 'Inner Light', the truth directly perceived by each person looking within, tested corporately by waiting together in silence. Friends looked for 'that of God' in every human being.

From the earliest days the Quaker character was non-conformist, socially radical, and non-violent. Plain speech and plain dress led to ridicule. Non-payment of tithes led to widespread imprisonment. Quakers generally refused to bear arms: their founder, George Fox, declined a captaincy in Cromwell's army on the grounds that he 'lived in the virtue of that life and power which took away the occasion of all wars', and at the Restoration in 1660 the Society affirmed to Charles II: 'We utterly deny all outward wars and strife and fighting with outward weapons, for any end or under any pretence whatsoever.'

The positive counterpart of this refusal to fight has taken two forms, relief and reconciliation (Bailey 1993). At the time of the Franco-Prussian war of 1870–71, Quakers established a War Victims Relief Fund which distributed food and other

necessities to non-combatants in Alsace-Lorraine. During and
after the Boer War of 1899–1902 they provided help to those in
need 'of whatever race', including Boers. In 1914, a Friends
Ambulance Unit (FAU) was formed to undertake medical and
nursing work behind the lines in France. The feeding pro-
grammes in Germany after the 1914–18 war led to the term
'Quäkerspeisung' entering the German language.

Efforts at reconciliation, too, have been at many levels and in
many contexts. William Penn founded Pennsylvania on the basis
of peace with, and justice for, the Indians, and published
proposals for peace in Europe. In 1854 a mission visited Tsar
Nicholas in the hope of averting the Crimean War. In the 1930s
Friends maintained a presence in Berlin, and interceded with
Nazi officials for people in concentration camps, and for Jews
seeking to emigrate (see p. 63). On the formation of the United
Nations, the Society secured recognition by it as a Non-
Governmental Organisation, and has used this status for active
peace-making at the UN HQ in New York, and elsewhere.
Throughout the period of the East–West cold war (1946–89),
Friends brought together students, mothers, scientists or diplo-
mats from each side, and at its height sent missions to the
Soviet Union (1951) and China (1955). In the UK the Society
was instrumental in setting up the School of Peace Studies at
Bradford University, and has worked for understanding between
the communities in Northern Ireland. Individual Friends have
worked in the marriage guidance and community mediation
movements.

The introduction of conscription in 1916 posed a new
challenge to Britons who refused to fight. They became 'conscientious objectors', and many went to prison. Although members
of the FAU on active service in France were exempt, some
(including Corder Catchpool, see p. 63) chose to bear witness
by coming home and facing tribunals, courts martial and hard
labour. When in 1939 Britain again introduced conscription,
provision was made for exemption on grounds of conscience, as
determined by a tribunal.

This was the context in which, on the initiative of Paul

Cadbury of the Birmingham Quaker chocolate firm, the FAU was re-established in September 1939. In the following seven years it undertook a wide variety of humanitarian service in accordance with Quaker principles at home and abroad. At home we served in hospitals and air-raid shelters; in theatres of war we drove ambulances and staffed mobile hospitals; elsewhere—in places as far apart as Syria, Ethiopia, India and China—we provided civilian relief in the form of medical services, food supplies, and other welfare provision. In the official history (Davies 1947), the account of the Unit's work in Germany from February 1945 to June 1946 occupies only 11 pages out of 465.

The FAU (unlike the Friends Relief Service) was formally independent of the Society of Friends. Despite the name, its members came from all Christian denominations and from none. They totalled 1314, including some who died on active service, and a minority of women. All were pacifists, and almost all were conscientious objectors in the sense that they were subject to National Service under British legislation, had formally objected to serve on grounds of conscience, and had been through a tribunal and been given exemption, unconditionally or subject to conditions as to alternative service including 'ambulance work under civilian control'.

My own career in the FAU, since January 1941, had been not untypical. Six weeks at a training 'camp' in farm buildings at Northfield, Birmingham, with emphasis on first aid, nursing, drill, physical fitness, and working in a team. Three months training on the wards in Selly Oak Hospital, Birmingham. Air-raid relief work in Wapping, East London, followed by a motor mechanics course at Hackney Technical College and a spell in the FAU garage in Whitechapel. A 'refresher' six weeks at a casualty hospital in Dover, then in mid-1942, to the Middle East. With a British mobile hospital in the Western Desert, from Alamein to Tripoli. Transfer to an Anglo-French mobile hospital, the 'Hadfield Spears', serving the First Free French Division through Tunisia, Italy, and the invasion of France from the south, up the Rhone Valley to Alsace.

At this point, in early 1945, I applied for transfer to a relief section going into Germany. I felt it time for me to be back in a British context. I did not want to enter Germany in the company of a French army of occupation (see pp. 41–2), but I was interested to find out about Germans in real life and not just through the media. In this I was not alone. In Germany many FAU members 'saw for themselves as pacifists, though with great misgivings, a special challenge. There would be found the point of greatest tension, the scene of the greatest bitterness, the not unnatural severity of the conqueror and burning resentment of the conquered' (Davies 1947: 423).

But I felt particularly deeply engaged with this theme. At Leighton Park, the Quaker boarding school I had attended, some of my closest friends had been German Jewish refugees. In a speech competition in late 1939, I had chosen the title 'When we have won the war', to try to make the case for avoiding a repetition of the punitive measures of the Versailles settlement of 1919. I had taken a partisan interest in the controversy in which Lord Vansittart had alleged the age-old and irredeemably evil nature of all Germans, eloquently rebutted (in my view) by Victor Gollancz—of all people, a Jew. I had treasured throughout the war a copy of selected stanzas from a poem written on the outbreak of war by the then Poet Laureate, John Masefield, entitled *Some Verses to Some Germans*. In Alsace I was trying hard, with the help of the local Lutheran pastor, to improve my rudimentary knowledge of the German language.

As early as 1941 the allied governments had begun to plan for the civilian problems that would be met as Europe was liberated. There would be acute shortages of supplies, and everywhere there would be a hiatus in administration as German occupying forces withdrew and their collaborators were thrown from office. Above all, there were estimated to be over eleven million refugees in North West Europe. Most of these were 'Displaced Persons' (DPs) whom the Germans had deported from the lands they had occupied, to work in Germany in factories and on farms. It would be necessary to repatriate these victims of the Nazi occupation of Europe as soon as that could be done, and in the meantime it would be only just to provide for their welfare, regardless of the living conditions of the German population amongst whom they had been unwilling sojourners. There turned out to be nearly two-and-a-half million DPs in the British Occupation Zone of Germany alone, of whom nearly a million were 'westbound' and over a million were Russians, Poles and Czechs.

The allied armies, through their Civil Affairs Branch, had the initial responsibility for the government of liberated areas, including relief. The United Nations Relief and Rehabilitation Administration (UNRRA) was formed in 1943, and from 1942 British voluntary societies, including the FAU, began to coordinate their efforts and negotiate with the government through what became the Council of British Societies for Relief Abroad (COBSRA). In the event, UNRRA was unable to provide the contribution expected, and its intended role of control and co-ordination of civilian relief units working with the British forces was undertaken by the British Red Cross (Donnison 1961: 345).

Two FAU ambulance sections landed in Normandy in September 1944 and quickly found themselves involved with refugees and other civilian problems, in France, then Belgium, then the Netherlands. In November, 21st Army Group requested five more teams of eleven men each, so as to provide each Corps with such support.

One of these was Section 4, who were at Nijmegen in the Netherlands when I joined them on 9 April 1945, after home leave. They were attached to a Military Government (Mil Gov) Civil Affairs Detachment, No. 623, under the command of a major. As the front advanced, we moved on to Arnhem, and then Ede. There we dealt with part of the flood of westbound DPs—French, Belgian, Dutch—who had just been liberated by the advancing allied armies, and who were hot-footing it home. We saw to their registration, provided overnight accommodation and feeding in an empty school, ensured that they were deloused with DDT powder to prevent any spread of typhus, and arranged onward movement. We were at Ede on VE Day, 8 May, and it was from Ede that we drove to the German border on 25 May.

PART I

Work with Displaced Persons

Into Germany
25–28 May 1945

The non-fraternisation regime

25 MAY Friday. We started from Ede after lunch, in convoy following the Mil Gov Detachment. Bill Judd and I travelled in the Brummagem Belle [*a six-ton Leyland lorry*], driving turn and turn about. We have ten drivers in the Section and only five vehicles [*see Plate 2*]. We went through Arnhem, Zutfen and Hengelo, and stopped for the night a hundred yards this side of the frontier, thus avoiding the need to post a guard.

We parked in a field and some of us put our bedrolls in the byre of the farm, with cows looking through their bars curiously, and mooing, and swallows nesting in the rafters above. The field was rather soft, and three of the Detachment trucks got stuck, so we put chains on the back two pairs of wheels on the Belle and towed them out, cursing the Detachment drivers good and heartily.

After supper four of us walked into the prohibited zone 1100 yards wide which stretches all round the Reich 1937 frontiers. No civilians live here, and anyone found not on the main roads is liable to be shot without warning by British patrols. There was a notice 'This is Germany: do not Fraternise', but at this point no notice the other way (as elsewhere) saying 'This is Holland: you may Fraternise but must not Loot'.

After coming back we stroked the silky necks of the cows and then went to sleep.

26 MAY Saturday. Coming into Germany we went over a Bailey Bridge marked 'THE LAST BRIDGE OF THE WAR finished 0759 hrs, May 8'. We drove to Bentheim, then due north to Leer, then east to Oldenburg. After a long wait we moved into our billets. At the head of our street is a notice: 'Recreational Increment—Officers' Quarters'. The FAU occupies a very fine house on its own. As we were looking round the owner arrived to collect some things, having been given only two hours to clear out by the Canadians who first occupied the house.

So you see in what compromising situations Quakers attached to a conquering army can be put. However perhaps more good than harm is done—in the present instance the owner on leaving wished us happy times in his house.

27 MAY Sunday. Two of us and the Netherlands Liaison Officer (LO) drove to a Russian ex-PoW camp with a load of comforters (mattress–quilt–blanket affairs for DPs to sleep in) for another detachment. The road was excellent. We turned in at an aerodrome occupied by Russian ex-PoWs and oddments of the British army. A lieutenant showed us where to dump the comforters, gave me a receipt, told us they had four FAU men with them and took us along to the Mess to meet them.

We learnt that this area was a general assembly point for all DPs, who were being put into national groups—Russians around here, Poles on the left bank of the Ems, Italians and Yugoslavs elsewhere. This explained the many loads of Russians we had seen the previous day being driven up from Holland. The Russians were said to be very nationalistic, hadn't been too bad here at ravaging the countryside, got roaring drunk on petrol. Here there were 1800, expected to rise to 4000. The place was getting organised: they included four doctors and a good cook. The FAU men had been split off from the rest of

heir section, which was about 10 km away towards Wilhelms-
haven. Language with camp inmates was mostly pidgin German,
but we saw notices in Russian all over the place. Various red
flags and national symbols hung outside the hutments. The
inmates were dressed in a mixture of British battle-dress (with
which they were all eventually to be issued), Russian uniform,
and German PoW uniform, the last green and thick.

In the afternoon Shelley Fausset and I strolled round the
town, and in a very beautiful park in which people were taking
their Sunday afternoon stroll. Very few men of military age to
be seen; of those that were, a noticeable proportion were
crippled. So far I've only seen two dachshunds—and a pup—
but then I've only seen about ten dogs altogether. All the little
girls wore pig-tails. Silk stockings, and bicycles with tyres.[1]
Noticeable lack of little children asking for cigarettes and chocolate. Mil Gov can get a civilian for anything under 'Offences
punishable by sentence other than death', and for a great deal
under 'Offences punishable by death'. There is no way of
Germans getting to know about the non-fraternisation order.
Presumably they guess it, or assume we're made like that.

This order presents not insuperable difficulties. The Tommy
doesn't like it. Some officers don't think it will last. The larger
part of the Germans here look as if they would be friendly if
they were given a chance.

28 MAY Monday. Today I have been on orderly duty [*in every
FAU section, this was strictly rotated*], but washing-up is just a
treat with boiling water from a tap and two sinks. I had a hot
bath last night—a good job has been made of getting the boiler
going. We have electric light, too, and even goldfish in the
garden.

The prospects of work hover about us but never quite
emerge. But it is likely that we shall be moving south thirty
miles to a small town called Vechta, and from there supervising
several DP camps in the vicinity. But the Major has declared
his intention of not moving there until the electricity is on
again! You will gather that he is not the most conscientious of

men. He is still looking for billets there, having turned down
an offer of two hotels.

This house has an exceptionally heavily reinforced and pro-
tected air-raid shelter, with blast walls, concrete roofing, inside
propping, iron door, and all; gas masks inside and explicit instructions in the hall. Houses also have lists of inhabitants,
with dates of birth, on the doors.

Six months before I get leave. I should get a 48-hours in
three. But proposed measures to implement non-fraternisation
include the 'liberalisation' of leave policy, as soon as circumstances permit, as well as the sending to Germany of members
of the Women's Services 'and in relatively large numbers'.

I suppose your *Daily Sketch* headline refers to the man who
got three years for being in a boat on a lake with a German
girl, a story much quoted here. 'He didn't get punished for
fraternising', say the privates, 'he got punished for being
caught'. And again: 'These ruddy Poles can walk around and
do it quite openly. What's good enough for one man's good
enough for another.'

The latest news is that we are moving down to Vechta
tomorrow at 2.00 p.m., so work will probably be starting.

ONE

Vechta

29 May to 24 July 1945

*A mixture of nationalities in a variety of camps.
Negotiation with the Red Army Liaison Officers.
On/off evacuation plans. The 'Slavonic temperament'.
Anglo-Russian football. Some hard cases. The Mil Gov
Detachment leaves. International parties. Staff
Meeting at FAU HQ.*

[*The Detachment and the Section were to be responsible for all DPs
in the town of Vechta and the countryside around. Pending their
repatriation, the Allies were providing preferential treatment for
DPs in Germany, such as higher ration scales, whilst seeking to
maintain public order.*

*A civilian administration approved by Mil Gov was already in
place at local level. Allied occupation policy was for 'indirect rule',
through German officials appointed by Mil Gov (Donnison 1961:
192). Selection of such officials was rapid, though not always easy.
The first Bürgermeister of the Stadtkreis or town of Vechta, Georg
Gerhardi, is thought to have been appointed because he had been
the first to make contact with the British troops. The Vechta Landkreis consisted of the rural area around the town. It had been
occupied on 11/12 April 1945 and a new Landrat, the merchant
Dr H. Siemer, appointed on 14 April. Bürgermeisters in the Landkreis (at Gemeinde or what might be called parish level) were then*

13

*appointed predominantly on Dr Siemer's suggestions (Kuropka
1995: 34). The next stage was for Mil Gov to appoint local coun-
cils on a broadly representative basis, and the first in the zone was
in fact that of Vechta, which was to hold its inaugural meeting on
19 October 1945 (Landkreis Vechta 1995: 24, 28)*]

30 MAY   Wednesday. Most of the day was spent in setting up
the office [*in Vechta town*], taking what we wanted from the
office equipment of the Arbeitsfront [*home service*] organisation
which had been installed there before, buying things at a
stationer's on the German government (there's a nice problem
in economic consequences!) with an emissary from the Bürgermeister, and using the Brummagem Belle to move in furniture.

This little room [*at Calveslage, 5 km north of the town of
Vechta*] we use as a sort of sitting room in odd moments. It
occupies the sunniest corner of the house, has two large
windows, and is about ten feet square. One window looks over
the hotel garden to fields with pigs, calves, and a hen house,
and beyond, trees and indications of neighbouring farms. The
other looks over the main Oldenburg to Osnabrück road, to a
copse and barns on the other side [*Plate 3*]. The girls of the
village (which is really only one or two scattered buildings),
and the local lads (all crippled, or under military age), play
hide and seek among the trees of the copse, to the intense
mental agony of the poor sentry. With creased trousers, shining
boots and buckles, well blanco-ed webbing and a rifle, he strides
up or down, or stands at ease, and wishes he could fraternise
and didn't have to protect this damned unit.

The country is rich and green and the fields are full of cows
and calves and horses and foals, wild rose and honeysuckle are
in bloom, crops of rye, some rather sparse, are swelling, inter-
mingled with blue cornflowers; young frogs hop across the path,
juicy slugs and furry caterpillars wend their way among the
grass, there's cuckoo-spit and swallows and all the ripening and
growing young things of early summer. Lots of half-timbered
brick houses and barns, a remarkable number (in proportion to

the men) of girls and women at work in the fields, and one or
two large egg farms (next door to the hotel is a big hatchery).

31 MAY Thursday. A crucifix hangs on the wall near the head
of my bed. This district is extremely and fervently Catholic.
Crowds of people have been going to every tiny village church
today in the morning and the afternoon, all clad in Sunday best
and carrying prayer books. The feast of Corpus Christi was
celebrated today in grand style for the first time for many years.
Every village had its procession, passing from one wayside altar
to the next, and finally into the church, along streets lined with
flags and birch sprays, strewn with flowers and pine twigs,
spanned by arches and festoons of evergreen. In Vechta itself,
the entry of the procession into the church was very impressive, with lots of little white-clad children, the priests in
splendid vestments, and fat old men singing psalms heartily.

Shelley and I watched this in the middle of a hunt for representatives of various nationalities in order to find translations
of 'Displaced Persons', and 'Information', in all languages, and
'Poles', 'Russians', and 'Italians' in the corresponding ones. This
was for Shelley's notices in front of and inside the building
which we are using as DP offices. Poles and Russians already
have staffs of their own nationalities which have moved into
rooms in our building, and the Dutch and French LOs attached
to our Mil Gov unit are installed to deal with all others, while
in a big room, first left, all the information we collect is col-
lated and lots of other things happen too.

In the afternoon, after the Vechta Bürgermeister had got out
preliminary data for us, we undertook the first 'recce' of DP
camps. I rode pillion behind Shelley on the motor-bike. Everyone we saw was very helpful, and seemed delighted to see us,
and we soon got the technique of getting information[1] and seeing round a camp. But the side roads are very bad, and getting
from one place to another, finding places, and asking questions,
takes up far more time than one realises. But it brings you into
close contact both with the civilians and the DPs, exercises my
German, and is very necessary before we can send home those

that can be sent home, and do our best for those that can't, or
can't yet.

The most surprising thing is how many people don't want to
go home. Very few people I have met from eastern Europe
want to go and live under the Russians. Poles think it means
death and torture, I've met Latvians who are not forced labour
but families who have left their country rather than stay with
the Russians, Serbs who don't want to go back to a Tito- or
Communist-controlled Yugoslavia, and I'm quite sure that the
Balkan states everywhere feel the same. What is to be done?

From the other end of Europe, the only Frenchmen I have
met were staying here a few weeks to 'take it out of' the
Germans. They had been PoWs since 1940. Belgians and Dutch
are usually keen to get back, but out of less than a dozen I took
away this morning, two wanted to wait here till their parents
came to fetch them (from Hamburg), one of these being a girl
of eight who cried at leaving the village where she had been for
the past two years, where it had been 'very nice'. One more
wanted to stay and get married to a German girl; and two
others wanted to come back and work in Germany after visiting
their relations in Holland, because they like it better here. These
two paid very touching farewells to the farmer and wife and
family, and were sent on their journey by such words as 'Now,
are you sure you have enough money?' and 'Come back soon.'
One of these was very indignant against Russians who had
broken up the home of the farmer with whom they had been
working, a farmer who was 'definitely very good'. Italians also
as a general rule get on well with their hosts, and we left behind
one today who had no relations in Italy and wanted to work in
Germany for the rest of his life.

3 JUNE   Sunday. Today's job was the collecting of all DPs in
Vechta Kreis who were not Poles or Russians, to an assembly
point in front of our hotel, whence they were taken to two
camps in Oldenburg, one for Italians, the other for all the
others. In the afternoon I went with a convoy of four trucks (of
ten attached to us for this purpose, from the RASC) full of 86

Italians, to hand them in to the camp, where there are now 4000. It was curious to hear them singing 'Roll out the Barrel' before we started!

We have six Polish girls to do orderly now, for us and the officers, and to help in the kitchen and with room-cleaning, etc.

The recce work has also the advantage, that you come into contact with a variety of small communities, some of which are really delightful. The great snag is that so far we have had so much to do that we have had no time to accept such offers as a cup of coffee from one Russian camp, an invitation to a concert or classical piano recital at another, or any (or hardly any) discussion or talk with all these people on things outside their immediate living conditions. Ditto with Bürgermeisters and their staffs and other Germans—we have kept to business, not because of the non-frat order, but because of Time. Though I did accept a drink of 'sugar wine' at one Polish camp—a vile and powerful concoction. I turned down the offer of one of the Poles to show me where there were 50 gallons of it!

4 JUNE Monday. Today I have been for the rations. The Ration Point is miles from anywhere, and the journey takes you 1¾ hours hard going over atrocious roads. When there you hand in the indent and get a loading list, which is the same as the receipt, which you sign and leave with them. At 1.00 the Point opens and the queue of trucks moves through, one man driving, the other collecting various foodstuffs in tins and boxes at each stage and putting them in the back of the truck. Each truck has a number on the windscreen (ours was 108) and as the man dealing out, say meat, sees it coming, he refers to a list and has the right quantity of meat ready for you by the time you have reached him.

I have read several reviews of *In the Margins of Chaos* (fine title), but not the book. The majority of the FAU have done well to steer clear of the '*manie de grandeur*' she mentions. There is also a healthy awareness of the danger that relief work may become a matter of typed duplicated sheets of paper.

I had a letter from Hanna [*a Swiss girl whom I had met when stationed in Alsace*] describing VE Day celebrations in Strasbourg, where festivities went on in the streets all night long— 'Alte Männer und Frauen sangen mit Tränen in den Augen die Marseillaise und junge Leute fielen einander um den Hals.' ['Old men and women sang the Marseillaise with tears in their eyes and young people fell on one another's necks.'] Also one from Brenda [*Bailey—see p. xvi*], with photos of herself and her husband in case I should be able to meet her mother.

5–7 JUNE We divided the two Kreise into three areas, and two chaps were in charge of each. This left two at the Vechta office, one cooking, two on transport, and one sick. Interesting work, with unsatisfactory features, the main one being that when evacuation of DPs has to take place, we are all needed for that and cannot attend to our own areas.

With Russian Liaison Officers and British Mil Gov officers floating around, things do tend to happen. The Russians are supposed to be liaison between Russian DPs and British Mil Gov (that's us), but generally act on their own initiative, are very secretive and elusive, and are rather difficult to negotiate with. The conference between Tatarinov and Richards, for example, was a very slow and difficult business. The latter thought he had achieved something at the end of it all, but I was not so sure. I can imagine San Francisco [*the venue for the negotiations to establish the United Nations Organisation*] being exactly the same. The Russians are very stolid, very decided— will not budge an inch when their mind is made up, and have not heard of compromise—and all out for themselves. They have different aims—the British are out to keep order, the Russians don't care about that—and different methods. They are not demonstrative. They are childlike but clever, and not worried by any inhibitions about morality. They are extraordinarily likeable.

The work is made more difficult by the fact that nine-tenths of it is transacted in a language of which my knowledge is still extremely imperfect, and with people who sometimes know even less of that language than I do; by the interruptions arising from involvement in mass evacuations from other areas; by the difficulty of getting around—quite a lot of time is spent travelling—and finding places; by the lack of complete accord at the higher levels with Russian and Polish LOs; by the fact that we are new to this sort of work and don't quite know what is the scope and treatment, and are still feeling our way; by the lack of supplies for welfare and recreation and even decent living; and finally (when they touch us, which is fortunately rarely, since we have a large measure of independence) by the mass bungling inseparable from army administration.

After a conference on 7 June, I had 'tea' with the officers of the local battery, plus a Mil Gov officer, a Russian, and the German girl who had done the work of interpreting. Drinking tea while the others were drinking champagne, whisky, or a liqueur, I was treated to the unusual sight, across the tea-table, of this German girl receiving the rival attentions of the Russian Major and an English Captain, the Russian with the aid of an English–Russian dictionary, the Englishman in ways substantially at variance with the non-fraternisation order.

8 JUNE Friday. My commission for today was to tell the Bürgermeisters and camp commandants (appointed or elected from among the residents) that all Poles were to be ready to be evacuated from these regions at 9.00 a.m. on Sunday; to find out numbers as exactly as possible; to arrange meeting-points (generally at the Bürgermeister's office) for those living with farmers; to discover the best route for heavy trucks; to arrange that all bicycles in possession of Poles, which they had not bought, should be handed in to the Bürgermeister; to tell them not to take too much luggage—no furniture, only personal things; to give our ration scale for DPs to all Bürgermeisters who had or might have camps in their areas; and to tell Poles to wait at the collecting points till lorries arrived if they were not there at 9.00.[2]

I covered by motorbike 125 miles, and visited seven camps and five Bürgermeisters' offices. The job was complicated by

the uncertainty even of Bürgermeisters and Poles about what
other camps in the vicinity there were, and where.

Moreover, there was a lot of destruction in the parts I visited. Many canal bridges were blown, involving many detours.
But some of the side roads are atrocious. I passed many of the
old familiar notices 'SLOW: REPAIRED CRATER 100 yds AHEAD'
or 'ROAD AND VERGES CHECKED 8 ft'. Most of the Poles did
not seem unwilling to go when it was explained what good
conditions they would be going into. What irony now!

9 JUNE   Saturday. I went with TCTs (Troop-carrying Trans-
ports) to two camps in this Kreis to collect the Poles. The first
was a convoy of four trucks, the second of three. At the first
place it was a job to sort out the bicycles—I had been told that
none was to be taken, but it seemed as if this hadn't been told
to the Poles, and when I said they had all to be left behind
there was a chorus of protest from about half a dozen people
who said they had bought them. I then ruled that any owned
by Poles must still be left behind, but the Bürgermeister would
have to issue a receipt for them, and that the Polish NCO who
was with me would arrange for later transport of them; I
reasoned that otherwise anyone with a bike would say he had
paid money for it, and that having made a ruling you had to
stick to it and find a back door out for exceptions. Then, fifty
people had come in from farms that no-one knew about and I
told them to wait there until more trucks came for them or
someone came to tell them no more trucks were to spare.

In the afternoon I went by motorbike to Cloppenburg to get
a dozen maps of the Kreis. I took the Norton, which is a fine
bike and does not suffer from some of the faults of the Match-
less (a wonky speedometer, a clutch that never completely dis-
engages, a stalling engine, etc.). Coming back I had a longish
wait while a tank-transporter managed a Bailey Bridge that was
on a curve, and just too sharp for the giant vehicle.

A case in point of the bungling mentioned above. We have
already evacuated Poles to Leer, helped by the inducement of a
note in Polish from a Polish LO, by promises of good condi-

tions and so forth. Tonight news arrives that they are in fact living in rotten conditions. They have come, on orders from Corps, from farms and good camps where they were living comfortable happy lives. Their present accommodation is overflowing and a shambles and four good men from FAU 4 are requested to go up there and sort things out.

And I have to spend another long day on motorbike to revisit the nearly inaccessible areas I toured yesterday—to tell the Poles that though they had been told to be ready to move house and home at 9.00 a.m., they have to wait another week at any rate. It seems silly to move them at all until it is decided what is eventually going to happen to them, because here they are comfortably installed in a food-producing area, getting on well with the locals and often working in farms where they had been well treated; but I believe the idea is to evacuate a large area of all Germans and to settle them in that.

10 JUNE So on Sunday I was woken by alarm clock at 5.00 and was off by 5.15 to Saterland to cancel the evacuation indefinitely. I went via Oldenburg to miss a stretch of the 'Emerald' route which is a shocking surface. I wasted some time trying one short cut, but achieved another (only possible for motorbikes), and got to the first camp at 7.30 and the last at 9.00, so they prepared a lot in vain but had not been waiting. Coming back via Oldenburg I met the four on their way to Leer to right the shambles, and it was not till I got back here that I learnt they were coming straight back and that the evacuation was on after all for the following day. Such is the army!

The Protestant Church in Oldenburg has chalked on the doors 'Out of Bounds; by order, Mil Gov'. It is not right to worship in company with a war-guilty people, and anyway you might get a dose of Nazi propaganda.

Coming out of Oldenburg I stopped to ask the way. A little girl approached the bike and stared at me and so I gave her a rhododendron that a Polish woman had stuck in the handlebars. She took it and suddenly rushed out in front of me to the other side of the road where her mother was. In the middle of the road she was knocked down by a Dispatch Rider coming past at some speed, but luckily only suffered slight scratches though it was very frightening at the time. I went with her to a nearby Aid Post where a Scotsman dressed the grazes.

That afternoon I went down to the office to receive instructions and talk with Major Svensson about the route, etc. I persuaded him to let the main convoy go via Oldenburg and was later glad I did so because you have only to mention 'Emerald' to any of the RASC to hear 'I hope we're not going by that —— route'. I went round the camps again in a Bedford 15 cwt with a Polish officer who did the talking at the camps. In one camp they were dancing and he was off round the room in a flash, so I followed suit and then said I would do the last two camps and call for him on the way back, to which he readily agreed! At one camp there was a four-years medical student from Warsaw (who wanted to finish at Edinburgh) and her sister who was a lawyer. The encounter impressed upon me how greatly these people are wasting their time at the moment. This one had just started learning English.

11 JUNE Monday. By shortly after 7.00, six trucks from the local regiment[3] had turned up to supplement the ten Royal Army Service Corps ones attached to us, so we were off. We got to the largest camp and I sent three trucks farther on, then we started loading. Hutments around a square, and all trucks were able to enter and back down paths to the various buildings. About 25 people to a truck, baggage stacked under the seats and in the middle. There were 28 people I hadn't heard about living in a house nearby, and a truck had to be sent for them. Some lost trucks arrived and were dispatched to another nearby camp.

Germans crowded round wanting their property back. I told all the Poles they could take no furniture (most of the demands were for furniture), and got it all out of the trucks, but could do no more, so told the Germans that the Poles hadn't come here of their own accord: so that affair ended happily to the dissatisfaction of both sides.

The Poles for the second convoy were in a camp that I had visited on an 'angry gnat', or light motorcycle, borrowed from a policeman. But the trucks couldn't get to it as it was on the other side of an unbridged canal. They therefore had to bring their luggage to a footbridge opposite where we were. This was done by a midget railway engine on a factory line. After some delay, from behind a building came the little train of about six trucks piled high with baggage, gaily flying the red and white Polish flag on the engine! It stopped opposite and streams of people poured across the bridge with baggage to our waiting trucks. They had all worked in a factory for making peat coke (a lot of peat is cut in this region) for smelting and gasogenes, and the German owner was there, and other Germans, Poles and locals bade fond farewells.

There were some Lithuanians with a Lithuanian officer in the RAF who wanted to get himself fixed up as a Liaison Officer for Lithuanians, as many of them did not speak German and few other people spoke their language. He spoke good English, and had left Lithuania before the Russians came because his father had been a government official and therefore he expected the Russians would deport him. He said this group did not think of going back to Lithuania, they wanted to be allowed to live together in a self-contained community in some such country as France or even in South America.

This evening we hear that troops may now fraternise with children, although I haven't heard mentioned a maximum age. The position is laughable. You only learn how much fraternisation goes on when you speak to Germans! Or in occasional candid moments with the troops. But on the surface it is rare that you notice any. I imagine that in the many contacts that take place, the fact of it being forbidden drives the two law-breakers closer together. Non-fraternisation makes Mil Gov easier in the initial stages; it also safeguards Tommy's belief in the rightness of his cause. The first official intimation about it to Germans, I think I am right in saying, came about a week ago with a broadcast message from Montgomery to the German people, saying that he would relax it as soon as they realised their guilt. Their attitude is: 80 per cent realise the Nazis' guilt already, and non-fraternisation won't help the process of realisation at all; and how can Monty tell when they realise it? I don't think they are ever likely to be repentant at having fought the Russians.

I could not have stuck the army, not least because of the caste system. You should hear what the men here say about the officers' fads and fancies. Five years of fighting have made extraordinarily decent chaps, among the garrison officers, consider only the *power* side of a situation—in the case of the Russians, only (1) the disposition of patrols; (2) what they may legally do, e.g. shoot without warning after curfew;[4] (3) the effect (as a deterrent), of one being killed. They work for a system based on fear rather than agreement.

15 JUNE   Friday. After all other nationalities had been evacuated from this area, it was official policy to concentrate Russians in fewer and larger camps. But it seems that the Russians didn't want this, and things might have brewed up to a storm. I heard that the Osnabrück Lieutenant was around (straight from the Red Army as LO, not an ex-PoW) and urged that he be contacted. George as Section Leader said: 'It's your area where all the moves have to be; go and see him yourself.' So I went. After a grim beginning, an excellent entente cordiale was established.[5] It convinced me more than ever that Russians are inherently distrustful but very co-operative once they are convinced you are trying to help them. But in dealing with the Russians in the camps, I find that to get something done, one has to be prepared to repeat the same instructions in the same words three days running, for people to say 'Yes' and do nothing about it.

The concentration into fewer camps makes it easier for us to organise 'bread and circuses' and for the Garrison troops to watch the environs during the hours of darkness. Some disorderly camps have moved out of the areas they were terrorising, on the other hand some peaceful ones have been disturbed out of a tranquil home—but all schools are now empty, which is necessary for re-starting education.

At last we may be able to settle down to a little welfare work of one sort or another. I plan to have a football match, FAU v. Russians, to get the variety show round to other camps, maybe even to start teaching Highland dancing, since the Highland Fling performed by me at a camp wedding feast to the rhythm of many Russian hands clapping far too fast and even speeding up in the middle, seemed to have such a tremendous reception. But I bet something else will come along to give one no time for all this.

Russian hospitality knows no bounds. It is difficult to avoid drinking the most filthy schnapps. Apart from that, though, you get served meals at extraordinary times of day, and invited to every sort of occasion. The Slavonic temperament was well expressed in a recent variety show—wild, vigorous, crude, healthy, hugely enjoyed. The Russians seem to have more a sense of fun than of humour.

We are indeed fortunate, in this Section, to see the Russians in small groups [*Plates 5 and 6*], and not in their thousands; but even in this Section I think Shelley Fausset and I are the only ones who can really say we like the Russians and enjoy their company. I have been using my few Russian words quite a bit and they are always greatly appreciated. There are some charming characters in our camps. And yet I can quite see how fatally easy it can be, through not knowing them in their better moments, to hate the Russians. The Germans hate them. It's very doubtful whether the British avoid the same mistake, as they begin to have dealings with them.

My chief impression over the last few days is of charming people of all nationalities—Germans, Russians, Poles, Hungarians, Italians, and so many others; and English of course!

24 JUNE   Sunday. A Russian Concert at Vardel Camp, to which I took the Commandant of Visbek and some others, plus four or five FAU.

Then a football match between the Visbek Russians and a team composed of six FAU, one Mil Gov officer and three Other Ranks, and Alfredo, our Italian orderly. Two Scammels (heavy lorries) had turned up from 6 Battalion, bringing Russians from Goldenstedt to watch the match. It began at 8.00 p.m. and pressure had been brought on me to make the Russians agree to only 25 minutes each way, which was all we poor out-of-training scratch side could take—the Russians were very disappointed, wanted 50 minutes each way, and asked if I meant 25 minutes four times! They had the pitch beautifully ready for us, and turned out of their 'pavilion' themselves, trotting in single file, very smart, to the middle of the field. The crown was large, and very good spirited, laughing heartily whenever anyone came to grief, and thrilled at every extra fast or tricky encounter.

The Russians supplied a referee, and we soon got to know which rules they knew and which they didn't, and to play accordingly. For example there were no offsides; but he was pretty smart onto handling. At half time we were one goal up, but they scored four in the second half, warming up towards the end, when we were played out. They had an excellent forward line, energetic, fast, tricky. I called for three cheers for the Russians at the end, and they responded. We promised to play 40 minutes each way, next time.

30 JUNE Saturday. Another evacuation cancelled at the last minute. We have three Russian camps near Vechta with a total of about 1000 people and today we thought they were all going to be moved. Trucks come from Osnabrück and take them to Minden where they entrain for Russia. The stated time for evacuation was 1.00 p.m., and cancellation came through at 12.30.

1 JULY Sunday. R.H.S. Crossman's article in a recent *New Statesman* entitled 'A Voice from Berlin' has struck a chord with local officers. I have now given it to the Vechta Bürgermeister, a man who lived in America before the war.

4 JULY Wednesday. To Oldenburg. We had several assignments:
   (1) To see if three Russian patients in the DP hospital were

ready to be discharged. We found two had already gone, and one was still ill, but needed baggage bringing up.

(2) To find out how to get tobacco for DPs. At Mil Gov a major in the Trade and Industry department gave us authority for tobacco for 4000 people. In the same office was a 'Civilian Mil Gov Officer'—the first sign of the Control Commission taking over.

(3) To pick up one of the Detachment drivers, stranded the previous day. We took him to the park where his vehicle had been dumped after its crash. This was to get a '108' form, evidently a necessary preliminary to having the vehicle 'BLRd' ('Beyond Local Repair').

After last weekend, we have only just got over the feeling that the Russians are going any minute, which is rather a stop to planning. However, we can get on with distributing more clothes. Today I have been working with figures a bit—numbers of women and children in different camps, numbers of dresses and shoes of different sizes, reconciling the one with the other, etc. For statistical returns demanded I now go the fountain-heads—half-an-hour with the Russian LOs can elucidate all the camp population figures, in ex-PoW, women, children, etc.; and for DPs still living on farms, I get someone in the Vechta Bürgermeister's office to ring up all the outlying Bürgermeisters for me.

Work for individuals is of course not to be deputed so easily. A frequent request is from Russians who do not want to go back to Russia for fear of the consequences. The sort of Scarlet Pimpernel activity that we have once or twice undertaken can hardly be applied to many cases, however, if good relations with the Russian LOs are to be maintained. Though when people say imploringly that they would rather be dead in Germany than alive in Russia, or that too many throats are cut back there, it is hard to say it is not for us to decide whether they go or stay.[6] And there is no doubt that the orthodox Russian thinks fanatically that justice is the ruthless securing of the state's interests.

Other individual cases. A Bessarabian lady, gone to Memel-land, had to go into hospital somewhere near the Weichsel as the whole village was on a refugee trek from Memelland to Germany early this year. She got cut off from her four children, and though I have sent off Red Cross letters for her with a covering note, their whereabouts is so completely unknown that goodness knows whether they will ever get in touch again. In the farmhouse where she is living, I mentioned the sad case of a British family, who lost two sons, and had one badly wounded and taken prisoner, all in a fortnight. But the farmer's wife knew of a family of four sons, all killed in the same five weeks. The mother was 'ganz kaput', shattered.

A Sudeten German wanted a permit to go home. Home was in the American zone, on the frontier between Czechoslovakia and Bavaria. I rang up 803 Detachment of Mil Gov. Impossible, unless a special case, such as mother dying. I question him again, and find he had been in concentration camps since 1938, including Buchenwald. 803: 'That makes all the difference. Send him down.'

The other day I met a Portuguese lady, a Frau Krause, married to a German, with a small son whose nationality was Brazilian. Her husband had been a trade union official in Berlin and Hamburg, until they left Germany and began farming in Brazil. Two years ago a message had come through the German Consul telling them they had to return to Germany, that if they did they would be unharmed, but that if they did not his parents would be put in a concentration camp and they themselves would be hunted down by the SS in Brazil. They came. Now they want to go back. But then we learn that the husband has been arrested by the British for interrogation. No communication, no knowledge of for how long, etc., and she has had a bad shock.

Hanna [see p. 18] sent me an article on England from a Swiss journal. Main points: 'A miracle that the total war effort has left freedom undiminished. After brief celebrations England is turning to the problems of peace. The domestic problems are felt to be simple compared with the new Weltpolitik ones. The greatest danger is that Englishmen will turn their attention away from these (e.g. the most progressive Englishmen are not prepared to take up posts in Germany's civil administration).

Englishmen feel peace is not yet, not because Japan is un-
conquered, but because USA and USSR are building up their
continent-wide, self-contained systems, and at the same time
treading outside their areas, as young, strong and expansionist
powers. Even if England does not contribute by foreign policy,
to the world's problems, she contributes, as an example of how
to reconcile freedom and order, individual rights and industrial
development, tradition and progress, authority and criticism.'

The FAU is private enterprise in a highly and centrally organised state. It cherishes the right to select and post its own
personnel, and to withdraw from any job if conditions become
unsuitable. It feels a large part of its value is in filling in the
gaps of officialdom, and in being independent. On the other
hand, it is the state that has given it the right to employ men
and women 'conditionally' registered as COs, and complete
discretion in how it uses them. It does not need to account for
any one of them; but all its overseas work is done by permission of the state, and in most theatres the needs that it fills are
decided by the state, though it can suggest what it should do.

I notice that many people living East of the Rhine have an
anti-Russian complex, and many people living West of it have
an anti-German complex, but that does not give me an anti-
them complex. The 'twirp of an officer' [*referred to in an earlier
letter*] was an exception. The British officers at Goldenstedt,
with whom I had tea yesterday, the officers in Vechta whom I
see from time to time, the officers of the detachment which has
just left us, are nearly all friendly, hearty, genial, sensible, practical, sober, amusing, responsible, dependable, intelligent, and
good company. The Germans have a sense of humour at least
as great as that of the English. And at the same time that we
begin to see how great the lie is, that the Germans have no
sense of humour, they too begin to see how great the lie is, that
the English have no sense of humour.

9 *JULY* Monday. Dreadful! No-one here received voting
papers [*for the British general election*], we don't know why. I
trust my proxy voted!

11 JULY Wednesday. I toured my camps with a Hygiene
Captain from Oldenburg. With hot weather coming on, the
Captain wanted extensive anti-fly measures taken, which has
meant quite a lot of blitzing of Bürgermeisters and camp
commandants on my part. We have recovered from the
apocalypticism caused by thinking the Russians might go any
day, and now think they may be here even for months. The
story goes that the last lot of 4000 was refused admittance
over the Elbe since the Russians couldn't cope with what had
been sent already; so transport is all held up till everything is
ready.

12, 13 JULY We have been short of transport, and Thursday
and Friday mornings I spent in the office, having the truck in
the afternoon. We have been distributing clothing for women
and children [*Plate 9*], the latter involving getting all the children
in the camp into a room; then separating boys and girls; then
fitting them from a rather limited range of sizes, with frocks,
trousers, and shoes. Today we got a complaint that the commandant of one camp had been giving out some of the clothing I had
given him for distribution, in exchange for schnapps. Clearly
this was a matter for the Russian LOs to deal with, and I
explained it to them and they will take a pretty strong line if I
know them.

Titov looked at the Bürgermeister's car today and said in sad
incomprehension: 'the Germans have lost the war and yet they
can still go around in a car like that.' Which led me to explain
that only Germans working for the British were allowed cars
and only if essential to their work. They might possibly be
surprised in their compatriots' Zone; at any rate in one camp
Tatarinov issued a non-fraternisation order, which we think an
un-Russian idea. In another Russian camp, consequent on the
visit of a senior officer, there has recently been a renewal of
military training, and a culture drive. The gentler spirits say
sadly they can't go out walking any longer, they are so busy
marching and exercising.

14 JULY   Saturday. We are in a real heatwave at the moment.
Yesterday the Mil Gov Detachment left, and we are now living
on our own, and gradually handing over the work to a DPACS
(Displaced Persons Assembly Centre Staff)[7] team consisting of
one British Lieutenant and about ten others including two
Warrant Officers. The Italians refused to go with the Detachment and are staying with us. There is a much more free-and-
easy atmosphere about Calveslage now that we are on our own
here. Even the guard has gone.

A Pole last night held up a nearby farmer at the point of a
pistol, and a three-man pacifist manhunt set out, but we failed
to trace him. This morning we heard he had slept at another
farm. He was from the Polish Division, said he'd been to
Osnabrück on three-day leave, but had no pass. We took his
paybook down to 803 Mil Gov. They sent out a patrol but he
had gone; but with his book they have him taped.

We have moved into the front dining- and sitting-room where
the Detachment had their mess, and the Kathmann family have
moved back into the parts of the house we are no longer occupying [*Plate 4*]. Frau Kathmann and her merry maidens, with
the active co-operation of our two Italian cooks, look after our
cuisine, and do us proud, treating us to every variety of the
produce of the countryside in exchange for the tinned and other
conservable food of our rations.

I met today one of the men who produce the Oldenburg
German-language newspaper—a staff sergeant. The main
trouble, he says, is shortage of staff—both on the English side,
and in getting non-Nazi German journalists. Even men of good
will have a Nazi style of writing—it was so drummed into them
in their job—quite unconsciously. He has to train new men in
journalism. Policy is: (1) to give only the facts, without much
propaganda; (2) to withdraw as soon as possible, as has been
done in Aachen. The Bürgermeister, who lived pre-war in
America, was advising him against this: (1) because people have
been taught not to think, and need a lead; (2) because British
control will be necessary for a matter of years, to make sure.

We have come to know Dr Kubes, a Czech, and an Italian

girl, Carmen Perozzi, who was in a concentration camp with him. He comes from Brno, which is really quite pronounceable. He is a cultivated and sensitive man. Yesterday afternoon I took him to Vardel Camp to visit an ill woman. The Medical Orderly there is a very nice fellow, a schoolmaster in civil life, teaching literature in Siberia; but medical service being his military occupation, and he used to practise it for two or three months every summer, in military camps. Afterwards I had tea with Kubes and Carmen, and a girl who played the accordion while he played the guitar—'My Bonny is over the Ocean', 'Lily Marlene', 'Roslein in der Heide', etc.

Further bathing, in this gorgeous weather.

We had a Section meeting in preparation for NW Europe Staff Meeting, to be held shortly at Bad Pyrmont Quäkerhaus, if the town is not out of bounds owing to a recent outbreak of infantile paralysis. John Harrison and I were elected representatives. We agreed minutes for inclusion in the pre-circulated agenda, including one on a 'concern' of mine about East–West relations. The main problem concerning the FAU as a whole at this time is how to carry on when all older and more responsible members have been demobbed.

15 JULY Sunday. To Church again this morning, with two others of the Section. Near the end of the service, the Pastor repeated the Lord's Prayer in English.

In the evening an impromptu party arose, since Hannalore, a refugee girl from down the road, dropped in with her parents to take a glass of apple juice at the Kathmanns' reopened wayside inn, and was persuaded to play the piano. Alfredo, our Italian general-purpose manservant, rigged himself out with two knives, a plate, jug, glass, cup, teapot, bell and gong, and went haywire as drummer. (He is a man who can do anything from conjuring to cooking, but excels in mimicry.) An FAU violin, and Dr. Kubes' guitar, led on to an impromptu Sir Roger de Coverley. With curfew at ten, activities closed down early, but when all others were gone, the strawberry punch appeared (the same recipe as that which two of us had tasted in the days

when the Kathmanns were cooped up in their own egg-
incubating house and conversation with them was conducted
behind closed doors).

Once the idea had occurred, plans were set on foot for having
a proper party. The percentage of DP guests necessary to throw
dust in the eyes of possible unexpected visitors, the distance
over which it would be safe to transport people after curfew,
plausible reasons for driving round the countryside with an
assorted ambulance-load in the small hours; entertainment,
music, and refreshments; guests, date and time—were all discussed and decided.

18 JULY Wednesday. A very international gathering was the
result, including Czech, Italian, German, Dutch, Belgian,
Latvian, Swedish, and Hungarian. The Lieutenant from 2
DPACS, the Bürgermeister's secretary and the Calveslage schoolmaster's daughter; and two from 6 FAU with partners of whose
nationality I am not sure. Alfredo acted as conjuror: he broke an
egg into a copy of *Punch* and nearly made it disappear, but just
as we were convinced it dropped out. 'Auld Lang Syne' was
followed by vociferous cheers.

19 JULY Thursday. At my invitation the three Russian officers
paid a visit in the evening. Titov and Ellis Benjamin played the
violin, Bill Judd sang 'The Red Flag'. Tatarinov picked up a
British Socialist newspaper in mid-election campaign with a
cartoon of 'Profiteers, Capitalists, etc.' sitting on the bound
body of the common man while Churchill with his cigar grinned
benignly from the background. This had to be explained in
great detail to Tatarinov, so foreign to his experience was
criticism of one's country's leader; but when he understood it,
he roared with laughter and explained it to the others with
great glee.

The Russian LOs think that at Potsdam Churchill and
Truman begged Stalin's help against Japan, and that Stalin will
come in kindheartedly, shortening the war from six months to
two weeks! They haven't had enough fighting and want to go

East. It was evident that much publicity had been given in Russia to the question of an early second front; but equally, that much had been given to RAF bombers flying between bases in England and Russia and dropping bombs as they flew each way. Tatarinov had been a partisan leader behind German lines for a long time, capturing trains etc., and had been dropped supplies by English planes (though whether English pilots I am not clear).

The DPACS team which has joined us is a queer unit, formed of odd people who had got separated from their units through being in hospital or for similar reasons. The Lieutenant in charge is a very weak character, and the unit is run by one of the two Warrant Officers, both of whom definitely intimate to the Lieutenant that he should keep his nose out of the work—which he seems quite happy to do. One WO is a very active character but comes to the work with ideas preconceived from 'the book', and every day has had some new wild scheme, in accordance with 'the book', but just not applicable to the situation as it is. We have had a fine time dissuading him from these, apparently with such tact that he is very friendly. The rest of the unit has been fully occupied running itself—that is, with a vast amount of paper work—returns and forms and what not.

20 JULY Friday. Four of us drove to Hanover. The centre of the city is completely obliterated. We went for a long way without being able to see a single building not a ruin. This is the first large city I have seen that is completely destroyed. It is a terrible sight. The most surprising thing is the large number of civilians, apparently interested in going places among the ruins [*see Plate 19*]. Already some trucks are being loaded up with bits of metal salvaged from the debris and loads of stones scooped up by an automatic grab. It is said that, if the citizens of Essen could move a thousand tons of rubble a day for twenty years, they could clear up the mess. If so, it seems silly to begin operations on anything less than a giant scale. Of course there are short term considerations such as getting the pavements clear. It is a great relief when, coming out into the suburbs, you see for example the first house with nothing but the windows smashed.

Having left our two companions in a gigantic barracks, *en route* for leave in England, John Harrison and I went on to Staff Meeting at our HQ at Vlotho, just south of Bad Oeynhausen.

From Hanover to Vlotho most of the way is along the auto-bahn, and to get on and off it we used four-leaf clover cross-ings. Great fun. The army, curiously enough, enforce a speed limit on autobahns, which seems funny unless it is to avoid wear and tear on engines, which in most army vehicles are in any case subject to a governor. Several bridges blown involved a long detour along atrocious roads. 'One sees why they *needed* autobahns.' But notwithstanding the fact that for peacetime purposes Germany would have done better to make her side roads as good as England's, autobahns do solve the problem of long distance road travel, in that you can go fast with a maxi-mum of safety and a minimum of trouble and discomfort.

At Vlotho we met Gerald Gardiner [*Plate 8*] and Richard Wainwright. Among the other representatives were several I knew from earlier FAU work. I had been together with one at the Dover Hospital Section in 1942. Since then he had been in Ethiopia, and like other FAU men there had been working with one other Englishman, a thousand miles from anywhere, talking Italian and Amharic, cutting off legs and performing lapar-otomies when people would obviously die if he didn't do it, getting mail six months late and other amenities never, and yet seeming to enjoy himself. The latest teams to come out are mixed teams, and two women FAU members were present. Vechta being in very flat countryside, it was a pleasure before supper to walk along the Weser and then to climb a hill and walk down again enjoying a beautiful view. After supper there was much chatting until ten, when we climbed a hill and held a meeting for worship on top.

JULY 21 Saturday. Staff Meeting occupied the whole day. We decided we should refuse to be put on any list of voluntary societies eligible for civilian decorations to be awarded for work in this theatre.

One section was dissatisfied with the work available.[8] This section has been out since Normandy, and always doing very high powered emergency coping, so finds it difficult to adapt to changing conditions. However, most other sections were busy, and felt themselves to be doing a good job, and that there would be plenty of work here for a long time yet. It was thought that the change from meeting emergency needs to providing welfare facilities was one which increasingly demanded linguistic ability and the power to get on with foreigners and be sympathetic to individuals, rather than general practical or organising ability, and that members should remember this when considering whether to stay in NW Europe.

The FAU and COBSRA were not in favour of members leaving to join UNRRA, unless their financial position had changed, and they thought they would be missing an opportunity. Gerald Gardiner thought the army would have no objection to our working for the German civilian population, if we were able to point to a specific job which needed doing and which we were qualified to do.

We had never agreed to non-fraternisation and had agreed at the last Staff Meeting that if Gerald were asked whether we agreed or not the reply must be No. Gerald recounted our having been asked about our attitude by a brigadier at 21 Army Group, who was much taken aback at the answer, but then said that honour would be satisfied if Gerald would read out the order at each section, which he has conscientiously but non-committally done.

Richard Wainwright made an excellent Clerk and the business was conducted in a thoroughly Quakerly manner.

Afterwards, representatives of 30 Corps sections [see map, p. xxiii] met Miss Torre Torr, Red Cross LO between us and Corps, a very capable woman. For us especially she had interesting things to say, all about the job we are going to on Tuesday, south of Brunswick. There were 19,000 odd Poles in a three-Kreis area to be collected into several large camps, two of which were still occupied by the British Army. There was a Friends Relief Service team already in the area, and we would be attached to a Mil Gov Detachment, with a good Commanding Officer. But hardly anything had yet been done about these Poles. We will be on the edge of the Harz Mountains, in beautiful countryside, and quite near the American and Russian zones. The nearest FAU sections will be No. 1, north east of Brunswick, engaged in swapping French and Russian DPs out of the Russian zone and into it; and No. 7, at Celle, finishing off the repatriation of Czechs and turning their attention to several large camps of Poles.

22 JULY Sunday. We drove back to Vechta. Coming over the last range of hills we had a tremendous view northward over the great north German plain. We passed through the village where the Control Commission was setting up its HQ.

23 JULY Monday. A day of tying up loose ends. I introduced the two Section 6 chaps, coming down to take over the skeleton of our work, to the Lieutenant and WO of DPACS. I took Richard Wainwright to Diepholzstrasse Camp, and we also visited the Russian LOs to say goodbye. They were in the middle of a dinner party with an officer from the Red Army, who spoke French. They gave me a photo of themselves with three of the 623 Detachment officers [*Plate 7*]. Then Richard and the FAU Personnel Officer from London and I went round the Visbek and Goldenstedt camps, I saying farewell and explaining everything to them at one and the same time. At both camps I left snapshots, well appreciated.

In the evening, our farewell party. Herr Kathmann showed us films of his family, including 'Dieter', the little boy of 3 who was such a character, and of the chicken-producing—eggs being collected, marked, put into incubators, cooked, hatched, young chicks taken out, registered, sorted, etc.

Following the Detachment's departure, and the ensuing domestic rearrangement, it has been very pleasant at Calveslage, and we were sorry to leave.

TWO

Einbeck, First Period

24 July to 25 September 1945

Geordie spoken. Visit to Bad Pyrmont. Quakers at Göttingen and Kassel. Individual problems of Serbs, Croats, Belgians, French—to go back or not to go back? Problems with the largest Polish camp—I go in with two armoured cars. Food, fuel and the winter. Wilhelm Mensching's church near Bückeburg.

24 JULY Tuesday. We drove via Hanover to Goslar, where we contacted the Mil Gov Detachment in charge of the whole area and learnt that we had the Kreis of Einbeck to look after, along with a DPACS which had just arrived, and an Intelligence Officer (Lt. Kent) of the local troops, who had been doing the job so far as he could up till now. Goslar is a wonderful old town, full of beautiful old houses with wooden carvings.

On to Einbeck town, and we installed ourselves in one of several empty houses the Town Major showed us. Two Americans came in to supper, they were 'staging' here, as this used to be an American area, and is near their MSR (Main Supply Route?) to Bremen which with Bremerhaven is an American port [*see p. 165 n.2*]. I went out with Shelley to put up a couple of signs to guide in John Harrison who would be late as he was collecting rations before following on. Then he and I and some others went for a stroll in the town and were

38

directed to an old house absolutely covered with very beautiful carvings in wood.

Einbeck is 40 miles due south of Hanover, and is a lovely old town in a basin surrounded by hills; not so near the Harz, but within easy distance, and lovely country. We live on our own, in a house in the town, with our three Italians. We have a small Kreis and only 1800 DPs, but there is a lot to be done and it will be interesting. All nationalities, chiefly Poles. My largest camp contains 600.

25 JULY Wednesday. In the evening, a section meeting, about work, mess fund, payment of the Italïans, etc. Then four of us got out a revised questionnaire as a guide to the visiting of camps.

26 JULY Thursday. Two of us surveyed the Immensen camp. In the afternoon we visited the two Einbeck camps and in the evening had a bathe at a really lovely open-air swimming-pool. Later we had a conference with other people involved with DPs in the Kreis, whom George had asked round. Lt. Kent, the Intelligence Officer of the Sherwoods, has lived for many years in Berlin and speaks perfect German. Up till now he has been in charge of DPs in the Kreis, but has not had enough time to give to it. Mr Urbanczyk, a German Jew of Polish extraction, is head of a German 'DP Committee' which has done wonders in organising DPs in the Kreis and supplying them with rations, clothing, etc. Lt. Pye is in charge of the DPACS, which has just been formed, and he is new to the job.

Lt. Kent, a most interesting talker and good raconteur, was able to give us quite a lot of dope about what had been happening up till now. We in turn told him what we proposed to do, and in general we planned our work together. We have learned a lot from our experience in Kreis Vechta. It will eventually work out, I think, that we will hand over to the DPACS questions of supply from army sources and the distribution of it; they are at a great disadvantage, in dealing with the camps, of not having anybody who speaks German. Kent and Urbanzcyk are delighted

with the fact that we will be able to get things moving as regards
improvement of conditions, evacuation of certain nationalities,
further supplies, and so on.

27 JULY   Friday. In our office Bernard introduced me to a
visitor, as having a common connection with Tyneside. This
German, Dr Herbert Voges, had called because he had a Finnish
friend who wanted repatriation. He speaks Swedish, German,
French and English perfectly and has studied phonetics. The
first time he came to England he disembarked in Newcastle and
he asked his way, to be met with the reply: 'Aa divvent knaa,
hinny'. He thought he must have been studying the wrong language! Such was the shock, that he studied the Tyneside dialects and has written a thesis on them. He can speak perfect
Geordie, and you can imagine how strange it was for me to
hear Tyneside phrases coming from a German in the heart of
Germany!

For part of the war he was an interpreter in Bordeaux, and
told me that the Germans used to send ships all over the world,
though when I mentioned Argentine he said no, it was too
difficult to land. But of one lot of ten ships sent to Japan for
rubber, only six got there and back. Of the six, one was rounded
up into an English convoy by destroyers, but gave no sign and
was not identified as German; it continued with the convoy to
India and there left it at night.

27 JULY   Friday. Miss Torre Torr, BRCS LO at 30 Corps,
came to supper. We thanked her for having got us again an area
job, and asked many questions about what to do with odd
nationalities, having several types of neutrals, ex-enemies, Balts,
and so on, in the area (a Swede, four Swiss, lots of Rumanians,
etc.). She is efficient but also jolly, with a fund of news and
stories from other sections of the FAU.

Three chaps from Section 7 have looked in, including a
former professor of German in Newcastle. He said that he
found Germans very changed from pre-war days.

29 JULY   Sunday. Six of us drove to the Quaker centre at Bad Pyrmont and saw Leonhard and Mary Friedrich.[1] Leonhard has been three years in Buchenwald but had taken it pretty well [*Plate 10*]. It was perhaps just as bad for his wife who, having worked so much with Jews before the war, knew exactly what it meant. Three members of an FRS team from near Brunswick arrived a little later. They had been working in Belsen, and in discussion comparisons emerged between Belsen and Buchenwald.

So our lunch party (the Friedrichs wouldn't hear of us leaving any sooner) was quite large. We had brought our own rations, and they were supplemented by potatoes and beans from the garden. The Friedrichs were of course very pleased to have first hand news of their daughter, whom I had seen on my last home leave, although now they have regular communication through FAU HQ at Vlotho.

We were shown round the Quäkerhaus, with room for meetings, and also the remains of Leonhard's book business. The Nazis had confiscated and destroyed 120 cwt of his books. *Der Quäker* appeared up till March 1942, and he told me his printer had given him paper for it till a later date than for any other. At the moment in Bad Pyrmont no meetings or church services are allowed owing to the outbreak of infantile paralysis.

Coming back via Vlotho we went over a ferry. Each end of the raft was connected by a rope and pulley to a transverse rope reaching across the river. One of these two ropes was shortened, and the other lengthened, so that the craft lay diagonally to the current, and so the current pushed it across the river. At the other side the lengths of the ropes were reversed, and back it came. As the Weser is very fast, you fairly shot across in the middle.

Richard Wainwright is here at the moment, with a member transferring to relief work from Ham's unit.[2] They had been in at the end of Berchtesgaden, where they found five grand pianos, all wrecked, also a library of gramophone records, likewise broken. They stayed three weeks in the area and the troops looted and raped and burnt down houses. The FAU got themselves

billeted each one separately in a house to save it from the
French, and thus earned some unpopularity. The French did
not allow civilians access to the nearest Mil Gov Detachment
an American one. The family with whom this FAU member was
living, who had spent many years in America, compiled statements from all those who had been looted, raped, etc., and the
FAU got it through to the Americans, which hastened the
departure of the French.

Richard said he had been commissioned by FAU HQ at
Gordon Square to write a 'chatty' article about DPs for the
Royal Institute of International Affairs, and that he wrote it
also making clear that it was only the experience of a small
section of those dealing with DPs, namely the FAU. A version
had then appeared in *The Times*, with all these qualifications
cut out. Very annoying for a precise thinker.

31 JULY   Tuesday. I had to go to Göttingen with a TB patient
from the large camp, and visited two Quakers there—Dr Hans
Wieding, a young man from Hanover who just finished his
studies during the war, an extraordinarily nice chap, thoughtful
and with humour; and Erna Rosier, an elderly lady with many
connections among English Friends and keen to begin again on
some sort of Quaker educational work, in particular hoping
that Friends will be able to start a Quaker school in Germany.
She said of the Occupation: 'It is not so bad to be hated—but
to know that one is despised...'

1 AUGUST   Wednesday. Two of us made a long trip to Giessen
to get a spare part for the central heating system in the large
Polish camp. If we can get the central heating going in that
camp for the winter, it will save a lot. Giessen is in the
American sector and to get a permit for the release of the
replacement I had to go to the American Mil Gov Detachment
there. I asked a Yank policemen where Mil Gov was, and he
said 'What's that? Is that near Giessen?' thinking it was a place
name, so evidently some of our abbreviations aren't the same as
theirs.

At the factory there was also a release point for demobbed Wehrmacht [*the German army*]. A lot on parade were said to have come back from being prisoners in France; quite a few of them were extraordinarily old and decrepit, with long beards, and I suppose they must have had some sort of job with the occupation forces.

On the way back we spent an hour or so in Kassel with Dr August Fricke, the Quaker and Director of Education [*Plate 1*]. His daughter Rohtraut described how she used to get things for Jews in Vienna, who otherwise never got served so long as there was an Aryan in the queue. Kassel is another badly damaged city, but not quite flat.

2 AUGUST Thursday. In the evening I visited Herbert Voges, and we talked solidly from 8.00 till 12.30, about everything under the sun. He showed me his thesis on Tyneside literature. He has some old Tyneside 'broadsheets', *The Pitman's Pay*, etc. Towards the end of the war he was employed listening in to English wireless communications—in the field, and in bombing planes, etc. It took them a long time to discover that 'the cab rank' meant the fighter-bombers held ready to attack specific targets as directed by forward units on the ground.

3 AUGUST Friday. Two of us went to Bad Harzburg to try to arrange for the dispatch to a camp there of all our minor nationalities. The arrangements came to nothing but the trip was most enjoyable. We passed first through Goslar, where we called on a Quakeress called Eva Herrmann. In Strasbourg I had met a nephew of Albert Schweitzer, who had last visited her in a Zuchthaus or convict prison. Whereas Herbert Voges held that if Germany had won the war Nazism would have died a natural death, no longer having the support of those who had thought it to be a terrible but necessary means to a desirable end, i.e. the saving of Europe from Bolshevism, she thought it would have been able to perpetuate itself by terrorist methods and that the only hope had been the defeat of Germany in the war.

Bad Harzburg is a typical watering place, lying on the north side of the Harz, with wooded slopes rising steeply from behind it. It is a 30 Corps leave centre with all sorts of facilities laid on. We returned home over the Harz and via Nordheim. There is lovely country on the top of the Harz and beautiful views, and though they are not sharp rearing mountains, this means there are vast expanses of wooded or open upland of great beauty.

On the way back we gave lifts to several people. One was a lawyer just out of the Russian zone, with one more story of the wholesale deportation of cattle, etc., to the east. Another was a girl whose home was in Tilsit, who was making her way from Mainz, where her sister and brother-in-law lived, to a place near here where she hoped to get a job as a book-keeper, and settle down—alone in the world. The table of rations she gave us for Mainz, which is in the French occupation zone, works out at 900–1000 calories. Many of the occupation troops are Arabs, she said, and implied that they were completely lawless. She stayed with us overnight and after a three-hour wait this morning got another lift.

One of the camps is infested with bedbugs and this morning I had to chase up its disinfestation. Some bedbugicidal liquid has been found and a specialist is coming from Göttingen to do it. I also visited the Ostarbeiterlager (Eastern workers' camp), an empty camp in Einbeck which had been requisitioned for British troops but never used. We are to try to get it for DPs; it would provide good accommodation for about 250 and is suitable for winter use.

During the last three days the great post dam has been released and the flood came pouring over, so I now have seven letters awaiting reply.

As regards Dr K.'s relatives in camps, Red Cross Enquiry Forms are the only way of sending a message, but they may not be accepted for Latvia, Lithuania, or Estonia [*Dr K. was a doctor in my home town of Newcastle upon Tyne, originally from one of the Baltic states*]. We are allowed to accept them for other parts of the Russian area (this I suppose includes Danzig), but the machinery for dealing with them is not yet set up. UNRRA are at present establishing a Central Bureau for all enquiries in British and American zones, and will send out to us and all other Red Cross teams the enquiries for people living near us. When this organisation is complete, UNRRA will then say to the Russians, 'We are able to deal with any enquiries from your side for people on our side; and we have a lot of enquiries from our side for people on your side; will you set up the organisation to deal with them.' This will take months, but I think it is the only way of getting a message to Camp Schitthof. He has presumably already sent off such Red Cross forms, but I enclose one just to be sure that it is the same. If Danzig is considered Poland, and not USSR zone of Germany, then BRCS London deals with the enquiry, not UNRRA.

You quote Mr F. on fraternisation: 'as a married man he had no use for it'. It was well said by one magazine that it was a pity the relaxation had been for reasons of sex rather than of principle. It is also a pity that the word has become debased in the English language. In fact, fraternisation is definitely not confined to members of the opposite sex; although there are some curious attitudes, for example the 623 Detachment people could have understood us fratting with girls but could not understand us fratting with Mr and Mrs Kathmann. Once or twice German lads have walked across the path of my truck rather slowly so that I had to slow down, less 'veiled insolence' than the attitude 'why should I hurry up to get out of *your* way'. Perhaps that is insolence; it seems to me very *British*. These people are in a definite minority, although of course one doesn't meet them so much as those who are willing to be friendly. But even now the vast majority are just happy not to be in the Russian zone.

The doctor for the large camp, Jacob Köbberling, is an interesting man, who has lived in Kassel and knows Dr Fricke, who was mentioned in a recent issue of *The Friend*. Since he is going down to Kassel this weekend I was able to give him a copy to deliver to Dr Fricke. He (Köbberling) has been at conferences in England as a representative of the German Student

Christian Movement. He is doing his present work on FAU principles—'serving where the need is greatest'.

Frau Köbberling had been in London from 1933 to 1936 as governess to the daughters of a family for which her mother had been a governess, and to the third generation of which she had always hoped to send her daughter as governess. Now, she is afraid that feeling against Germany in England runs too high for that to be possible. Dr Köbberling nearly went to a concentration camp in 1944. She persuaded him to keep his mouth shut, saying, 'If all good men in Germany go and die in concentration camps, who will there be to build the new Germany?' She is surprised we talk so much about the camps in Germany when we say nothing about them in Russia.

6 AUGUST Monday. The rehabilitation of the Ostarbeiterlager (which we reckon can take 200 comfortably) is a major preoccupation. It will ease the overcrowding in the Einbeck camps, and empty some of the scattered barracks unsuitable for winter. With Lt. Kent I visited the Town Major to get it de-requisitioned, Mil Gov for permission to use German labour on it, and Mr Urbanczyk to see to the alterations and supplies needed. In the afternoon I made out a list of everything that needed to be done and gave it to Mr Urbanczyk, who had it translated.

7 AUGUST Tuesday. Took the list to the Stadtbaumeister (municipal building officer), and he and I went round the camp, deciding in further detail on the necessary jobs.

My area includes many people of different nationalities who live privately. I had to go round and inform all Serbs and Croats who wished to go back to Yugoslavia that they should be ready to be taken to Celle on Friday. It was one of those occasions when a cancelling signal is sure to come through at the last moment, but still… I met two Serb families and one Czech one who had lived the last sixteen years in Belgium and wanted to go back there. Whether they could be admitted is something that can only to be decided by a Belgian LO. Where can we find a Belgian LO? No-one can tell us, we will have to tour

Germany and find one. Another Serb family wished to return home, but had more luggage than army transport could possibly cope with; what chance have they of ever getting it again, if they leave it here in store? Another Serb, a political refugee from the Communists, does not want to return so long as Tito is there. He has lived in Vienna and would like to go there, provided the Russians are not there.

Or take the French. All who do not return by a certain date next week will be branded as deserters from military service. We have one with a German wife who has already tried to get her home with him, but failed, and does not want to leave her. Which is his worse fate? Then there is an Austrian lady who lived in Lorraine and has property there. We have no French LO on the spot, but I think her chances are nil of being able to return there to live, or of getting her property.

8 AUGUST Wednesday. The Commandant of the Herberge, one of the Polish camps from which we hope to move people into the Ostarbeiterlager, came round it with me and promised to supply ten men the following day for work on the preparation; and we discussed the ways and means of living in and running the camp. The following morning he told me his people refused to work there, because they did not want to live there, because it was not good enough. After long discussion with them I promised to look into other possibilities of accommodation, but George thinks we would not be able to take any other building anyway, so I referred them to him and in the meantime we continue to prepare it—without Polish labour!

Most of the Poles here want to go back to their own country and I can't think why they shouldn't be able to within the next few months. However, we have to reckon with winter conditions, and so must see to the provision of stoves, fuel, etc. We hope to start a scheme whereby the DPs collect wood in our transport and cut it up with a band saw at one of the camps. With the boiler wall we got from Giessen, the Landjägerkaserne central heating is in working order, and we are supposed to get a winter ration of coal or coke for every DP.

We are turning our attention to recreational facilities and we
have received a lot of Polish books from the Polish Red Cross.
I am arranging for English lessons in the large camp, and I
hope Shelley will be able to start some woodcarving with them.
However, with people who can't even trust themselves to
organise their own kitchen in a large camp for fear of theft, and
to whom work which *could* be done by Germans must be very
tactfully mentioned—things are not all plain sailing.

9 AUGUST   Thursday. Spent the evening (again, until the small
hours!) in a three-cornered discussion with Herbert Voges and
Herr Borowski, the Deputy Landrat, an old Social Democrat, a
very deep thinker and, it seems to me, acute diagnostician of
society.

Herbert Voges is one of many who see European civilisation
threatened by the encroaching materialistic ideology from the
East. He looks for light to Borowski, whom he greatly admires
and who sees hope for the future. This man, because of having
been Party Secretary for the Social Democrats, was put in a
concentration camp during the summer of 1933, and when
released was treated as a Staatsfeind (an enemy of the state),
that is to say, had to report every few days to the police, was
not allowed to travel nor to take any job, was not entitled to
receive unemployment benefit or any such help, and was closely
watched by the Gestapo. He used up his capital, withdrew his
two sons from a private school, sold his life insurance policy,
sold all his books.

In 1936 his wife died, having been ill for two years. In that
year, too, he was allowed to take a job in a quarry, and later to
be in charge of the works, though still forbidden to travel, and
under police supervision. In 1944, after the attempt to assassi-
nate Hitler, he was again thrown into a concentration camp, as
part of a general security round-up of Staatsfeinde, and was
kept there for a month. His status as Staatsfeind continued till
the end of the war. There were few people he could speak to,
because his friends found it too dangerous to greet him in the

street. If ever a man has suffered from the Nazis, this man has. Yet he is willing to sit up till all hours discussing things with Herbert Voges, who is not easily to be convinced. Surely this is a commendable way to treat people who have different ideas from yourself.

Though we censor them no longer, letters must now bear our name and address on the back.

Suddenly secret directives come, *encouraging* fraternisation. If we, i.e. the English in general, are not careful, we shall find ourselves fraternising too much with the women and children to the detriment of the men. There have even been murmurs here of the old hair-cutting business; three suspects were pacifically kicked downstairs by the officer before whom they were brought. On the other hand, the Sherwoods threw a dance last night at which officers and men, Poles, English and Germans, girls, male civilians, and Wehrmacht demobbees, mixed with perfect equality and cameraderie. It is to be a weekly event, but was overcrowded by 200 per cent.

All the signs are that the winter will be hard. They want us to start a food dump for DPs, under our control, to ensure their food supply in case ordinary supplies become too bad. And this in a food-producing area! I can't think that the English are so hard-hearted as they claim to be. On the other hand 'policy' which sounds all right in theory has already caused a frightful lot of unnecessary suffering and is very difficult to change by those in contact with the real state of things.

To answer your question, I have seen no hatred about the bombing of German homes. I *have* seen a sort of numbed despair, that so many beautiful cities, that one has known once, are now no more—one can hardly yet realise the extent of irreparable loss. I have also seen a wondering incomprehension of how the English, who are recognised as a normally humane people, could descend to 'terror bombing'—for time and again examples will be quoted where the homes were hit and the factories left untouched, cases where no questions of inability to distinguish between the two could arise. Most people think that war with England was avoidable. They quote the beginning of the war with Russia as 'the first war that seemed to have any sense in it'.

Watched a football match between Poles and English. Nearly an international incident. The Polish goalie refused to stand in goal for a penalty he thought unfair. So the English team walked off the field and were only brought back by the authority of a Major.

10 AUGUST   Friday. The atomic bomb, the Russian declaration of war against Japan, and the Japanese offer of capitulation conditional upon the Emperor's position being safeguarded, are the main news items of the last few days.

13 AUGUST   Monday. I drove down to Stockheim to fetch a Pole who had lived in France pre-war and wanted to return. The place was a small aluminium factory where the DPs had been working. One of them kept rabbits, piglets, geese, hens, and a tame sheep. On the way back we picked up the mothers of the families at Immensen—two Yugoslav and one Czech— who had lived in Belgium before the war and wanted to return.

Then to Diepholz with Ellis Benjamin to take west-bounders and would-be west-bounders there. Through Hanover, with a stop by the roadside for a picnic lunch. At Diepholz I saw the French LO, and gained some curious but necessary information. There is no upper age limit to the decree that all Frenchmen who had not returned to France by 15th August would be treated as deserters from military service. Frenchmen who had married German wives could not take them back with them to France since the French government did not recognise any marriage before German authorities; all they could do was to return to Germany later to marry them. If, however, they had children, or if the woman was pregnant, then she could enter France: 'avec des enfants, tout s'arrange—du point de vue démographique, n'est ce pas?...' Anyone, including Austrians but not Germans, residing in France before the war, could return. A French woman married to a German before 1927 (when she could not retain her own nationality) but applying for French nationality after 1927 (when she could), could return, and so could her husband, even though of German nationality. All these rules touch cases in our Kreis which we have not been able to answer ourselves. Some Frenchmen, nicely settled down here, are faced with a very grim choice by the 'treated as deserters' rule; one of them is trying to get German nationality.

At Diepholz all our passengers got out. The French family would stay; the others, who wanted to see national LOs, were to stay the night and be picked up by us the following morning.

On to Vechta, where Ellis had tea with the DPACS and I visited my friends in the Bürgermeister's office. Then to Calveslage to stay the night with the Kathmanns. The last visit there, for a similar purpose, brought back stories of a terrific welcome—and also of two of our camps of Russians not behaving themselves—this we put down to the absence of our Quakerly influence!

We gave them all our news and various messages, and heard theirs, and saw some photos which Chris had left behind there to be developed. I went over the road and had a chat with my former teacher of German.[3] All the Russian DPs had gone, the previous day, en route for Russia, and only the officers were remaining for the moment. They greeted us like long lost comrades, embraced us, slapped us on the back and of course FORCED us to drink vodka. Then we visited Carmen Perozzi, who gave us news of our friend Dr. Kubes, still in hospital with TB but now on the road to recovery.

14 AUGUST Tuesday. We left Calveslage overshowered with presents of black bread, eggs, etc., and supplied with sandwiches and hard boiled eggs and fresh apples for the journey. We stopped in Vechta to see the DPACS, but before we got in the door, all our acquaintances seemed to come along the street at the same time. There was the Captain from the battery at Goldenstedt, a former geography teacher now in charge of the Regiment's education. There was Hannalore, the girl who played the piano at our parties, with her father. And there was

Frau Krause, the lady of Portuguese birth from South America, whose husband had been arrested well before we left Vechta and of whom she has still had no news (it seems unnecessarily unkind that all very minor Nazi Party functionaries such as Ortgruppenleiters, who have been arrested and are undergoing 're-education', are not allowed any communications with their families whatsoever).

According to Ellis the DPACS were at their wits' end, one Sergeant-Major having just come back from leave, and the other having gone on leave, and the Lieutenant having disappeared, and 'rockets' coming in 'right, left and centre' from Corps, etc., about winter accommodation; so they wanted to know what we were doing about winter accommodation. We found the Sergeant-Major away, but the Lieutenant re-appeared; however he, not taking a great interest in the work, didn't want to ask us questions, although I had tactfully to decline a proposal that I should decide the case of a Latvian who was bothering him.

15 AUGUST Wednesday. I went round the Ostarbeiterlager with Ellis and the Stadtbaumeister, seeing what had been done, and subsequently typed out a long list of the things still to be done, which Herr Urbanczyk's secretary translated into German for me, and on which the Stadtbaumeister will mark the dates when each job will be finished.

In the afternoon to Immensen, where we can get the use of the local school in the afternoon and one of the camp inmates will take classes for both children and adults.

16 AUGUST Thursday. I made arrangements for a stage show to be put on in the town cinema for the benefit of the Poles, by an Italian who has a company scattered around these parts. This involved going with him to see his ballet troupe, the cinema director, and the mess officer of the Wiltshires who disposed of the services of some of his musicians. In the afternoon I went to the Landjägerkaserne to get information about DPs who had been in concentration camps, about unaccompanied children (now acceptable by England and Switzer-land), and about skilled builders (wanted in Hanover).

17 AUGUST Friday. In the morning I was present at a collection, through the whole camp, of the bowls in which the meals are handed out. Only 400 were found, of 900 which must be in the camp, and since there are 600 people it was not pos-sible to start a system of making each person responsible for having one.

In the evening I visited the Frenchman who wants to remain here, to explain the situation, and spent a pleasant evening with him and his wife, and another couple with whom they live, of whom the husband, a chimney sweep by profession but really a jack-of-all-trades, speaks French and English, and showed me a leaflet dropped by the RAF over Berlin in August 1940, which he had carried with him, as a German soldier, throughout the war—a very risky thing.

18 AUGUST Saturday. A group of Poles in the camp, being dissatisfied with the food, blamed it on the German kitchen staff, and held a protest meeting. I went down with Urbanczyk and saw the leaders. When they started quarrelling among them-selves I told them they ought to decide among themselves first, and then write down what they wanted, and then bring it to me for consideration, but until then not behave in a disorderly manner. Later in the morning there appeared a deputation in our office, the leaders, the now 'elected' camp commandant, etc.

During the afternoon Urbanzcyk and I went to Nordheim to try to get a commandant for the camp from the Poles there, a step we have been considering from some time. While we were there, the old commandant returned from holiday, restored the previous administration, and disappeared again. When we returned to the camp, wondering very much which government would be in office, we found that the new Premier, 'elected' that morning, had completely disappeared, that one of his henchmen was the representative of the old commandant, again on holiday, that the old commandant's secretary, who had resigned that morning, was back at his post, and that another of the leaders of the mob was absorbed into the new administration! [*Plate 13*].

In the evening, another dance, not so overcrowded as the previous week. The attractions of Boomps-a-Daisy, the Lambeth Walk, Chestnut Tree, and the Palais Glide are being taught to the local population!

19 AUGUST   Sunday. I went to church (this is a Protestant region). The sermon chiefly rendered thanks for the end of the war with Japan and therefore for peace throughout the world.

20 AUGUST   Monday. The 2 DPACS officers, Lt. Kent, Mr Urbanczyk and the head of the Wirtschaftsamt had a conference with three of us on the question of supplies. It lasted from 9.00 till 12.00 and we discussed several other aspects of the work as well, for example the question of fuel storage for the winter (anywhere inside the large camp is lootable, anywhere outside means more carrying); and the question of a central food dump for DPs during the winter, which Goslar order, on the grounds that the food situation will be so bad that we cannot leave the supply of the camps to be done by Germans as at present. The latest news is that Poles in camps are to go onto DID (British) supplies.

A drive to get the large camp in good order. It is very difficult since whatever commandant you have, has no authority over the rest and cannot get any work out of them. Trying therefore to support his authority with my own, which has worked before, I myself asked one of the Poles to do a job of cleaning up. The man slunk away, and so having no real status vis-à-vis him, but not feeling able to let him have the last word like that, I took his name and room number. Later, chatting over the phone to Captain Shewell of the DPACS over the matter in general, I mentioned this case and also that the commandant said that if it were possible for us to back him up by throwing one or two chaps who disobeyed him into prison for a while, things would go much better.

The next thing I knew, five minutes later, was that the phone rang to say a patrol was coming down to arrest the person who had disobeyed me and would I stand by to lead it to the camp! Once having recovered from the shock of such rapid action, one was able to appreciate the picturesqueness of the situation. We swept through the town on top of two armoured cars, entered the camp courtyard in fine style and halted impressively in the middle. Lt. Kent, the two DPACS officers, myself, a couple of corporals and several privates, entered the Polish office and accompanied the commandant to the room of the poor culprit, who was arrested, for having disobeyed a command of 'this officer', and stuck in an armoured car.

While we were having a pow-wow with the commandant subsequently, the wife and child entered and demanded to be arrested as well, so they too sat on the armoured car as it drove away to the prison, getting out through a vast crowd at the gate, a crowd so vast that the Commandant, a nervous individual, whispered anxiously to me 'Haben Sie nicht Angst?' ('Aren't you afraid?'), since I left the grounds in a private car driven by the Pole in charge of the Kreis, well behind the two armoured vehicles. However the coup has had an excellent effect in that the commandant has gained great confidence and the place presents a far better appearance than before. And judging from the merriness of my English lessons, there's no ill will. However, as the Quaker who called in the Armed Forces of the Crown to get people to pick up pieces of paper for him, I get merciless teasing from my comrades, the more so when I make arrangements to affirm and not to swear at the trial on Monday. That was all right by the judge ('I'm an atheist myself, old man').

21 AUGUST Tuesday. I had a long talk with two schoolmasters from the large camp, trying to get them to sponsor adult classes, lectures, gym, singing, etc.; but they say the material is too intractable and the equipment non-existent.

In the evening after supper, two of us with two German guests went out and had a glass of beer in a small inn on the top of the hill where the old coach road to Hanover used to go. I have met many Hanoverian Guelphs, a party who want at least the separation of Hanover from Prussia, if not union with England. I don't think there is much love lost between those two parts of Germany.

22 AUGUST Wednesday. In the evening I went with Mr Urbanczyk's secretary,[4] Frau Ohnesorge, to a concert, a piano recital of pieces by Bach, Beethoven, Debussy and Chopin. I have had to explain the difference between 'Careless' and 'Carefree', because a British officer here before us used always to call her Mrs Careless, which is not quite accurate.

25 AUGUST Saturday. Two of us drove to a two-day conference near Salzgitter, south of Brunswick. The Friends Relief Service team there live in a palatial farmhouse, in a large and progressive farm. Present at the conference were representatives from three Red Cross teams, and from teams of the Guides International Service, Jewish Committee for Relief Abroad, International Voluntary Service for Peace, FRS (two) and FAU (two). The female element was very noticeable, most of these teams being mixed, and each sending the leader or leaderess and a representative of the opposite sex. The leader of one of the Red Cross teams was Rupert Compton-Ford, an old pal of mine from 1942–43, when we had been together in the No. 1 Mobile [*a mobile hospital serving the Eighth Army in the Western Desert*]. I had last seen him in Blood Transfusion in Naples. He had recently come home, got married, and switched to the Red Cross for financial reasons. He was having a rather hectic time, and most of these teams seem to talk in thousands of DPs where we talk in hundreds.

In spite of the immense variety of the tasks with which the different teams had been faced—ranging from the first days at Belsen, to trying to trace Jewish families—I was struck by the extent of experience we had had in common, or rather by the fact that different experiences had taught the same lessons. I think the FRS teams had been doing the best work, with the FAU close behind. This is because we have been able to have far better training, and have been out here longer, than the average COBSRA team. The lead of the FRS (which it goes against the grain to admit) is due partly to FRS having special-ised in welfare work, largely to the fact that they have women, which lends variety of abilities and interests, and also possibly to the fact that the flower of the FAU is largely in other theatres. For example, the best men in the FAU in England when other fields were closed went to China, and the first batch of trained relief workers went to the Dodecanese.

27 AUGUST Monday. The trial of the Pole duly took place. He was acquitted on grounds of insufficient evidence, largely, thought Herbert Voges (present as official interpreter), on account of the careful and conscientious way in which I gave my evidence. [*In fact I could not be really sure that the defendant had understood my instruction, spoken in German.*] I was oppressed by a sense of the tediousness of the examination of such a trifle. Ask anyone who has experienced a trial to imagine what it would be like if everything was said in either German, English or Polish, and had to be translated into the other two languages. Voges and Matysiak were kept busy jabbering to each other in German and to others in English and Polish respectively. Mr Urbanczyk, brother of the DP Committee one, was Counsel for the Defence, and a Captain Shanks the Prosecutor.

28 AUGUST Tuesday. Today has been a mixed bag. I need to assess the extent of overcrowding in the largest block of the Landjägerkaserne. We are trying to get the Regimental Medical Officer to release the swimming bath for DPs. We need notices for the Ostarbeiterlager translated into German and Rumanian. I tell a Pole that he can marry a German but we have to enquire at Goslar about how that would affect his repatriation. Lt. Kent and Capt. Shewell tell me of their plans for smashing a distillery in a camp. I find that a couple of Polish officers, who had turned up at a camp to register the ex-PoWs, had authorised the removal of people from one camp to another, though this requires the permission of British authorities. Finally, much to do in connection with the Italian variety show which is to take place on Friday evening.

There is a shortage of food everywhere, but it is not being shared out evenly. British troops still get over 3000 calories a day, DPs 2000, and Germans 1300.[5] Here with the rain in the middle of harvesting the grains have started growing till whole stooks are tinged with green; yet I am reliably informed that for horses kept for the amusement of British officers in this town, 20 lb of oats each are required to be delivered daily, whereas the normal ration for a working farm horse is 8 lb. Germans are going to great lengths to save electricity, yet no mention of its scarcity and of the need to save it, has ever been made to British troops.

The most natural thing in the world would be for Danish food supplies to go to Western Germany, now cut off from her normal source of supply by the 'iron curtain' of Russian occupation. It is only a question of time before the British will have to have food imported into their zone of Germany. I see the *News Chronicle* is already preparing the British public for the idea that thousands will die in Germany this winter, by telling them that Mil Gov is telling Bürgermeisters to prepare graves while they still have healthy labour.

There is also a terrible fuel shortage, and we must wrestle with the problem of getting enough fuel in to DP camps for the winter, and letting the Germans shift for themselves. Millions of people are being turned out of house and home, without any provision for them having been made, to face the worst winter Europe will have seen this century.

It has not been possible so far to get Poles back for the winter because the Russians have insisted that all Russians be evacuated first, and that did not happen until recently because the Russians found themselves unable to deal with the numbers we were sending over, and a halt occurred. Then I thought that the Polish Government would say: 'It's going to be difficult enough this winter without resettling all the DPs; let them stay in Germany where they live on the fat of the land compared with the population and are the worry of the British.' However I was wrong and last weekend we had very short notice to find out: (1) how many Poles in our camps had lived east of the Curzon line; (2) how many, living west of it, wanted to go straight back now to Poland as they knew it; (3) how many, living west of it, did not yet want to go back. [*The Curzon line had been adopted at the Yalta conference as the new frontier between Poland and the USSR.*] About 75 per cent of the total were living west of it and wanted to go back. What percentage of them will be repatriated before the winter makes transport impossible, is anybody's guess. Those living east of the line will not be repatriated yet.

No German is a DP, technically [*the definition required a person to be outside his own country*]. They may be evacuees from wiped-out cities, or refugees from the Russian zone. Some of the millions from the new Poland have passed by here, but in general they are all held up at the Soviet–British frontier, and cannot pass. According to Gerald Gardiner, they arrive in thousands in Berlin, which has the greatest difficulty in feeding its own population, and are given a slice of bread and a bowl of soup and told to go on. Here, we are just south of the beaten track, which is the autobahn, running between the Ruhr and Berlin through Hanover.

After Nazism it comes as a shock even to intelligent Germans to realise the implications, for the state, of our position [*as conscientious objectors and civilians*]—particularly under the 'rule of Churchill'.

From a letter from one of my friends at Vechta:

And what about the pamphlet 'What Buchenwald *really* means' [*by Victor Gollancz—see Introduction*]. I am glad that there are at least a few men who have the right opinion about the concentration camps. At first I supposed that the book was written against all Germans, that it was to say 'Every German is guilty.' I hear this every day, and it is very hard for us. Yes, I feel ashamed for those cruelties which happened in our concentration camps;

and so sometimes I myself cannot understand, how it is possible that nearly no German knew about it. But the power of the Nazis and the Gestapo must have been too great. But is it correct how the Nazis are treated now? One cannot wipe off a debt by taking the same debt upon oneself. Then this debt will never leave the world. The Nazis, above all the SS leaders and the responsible men of the concentration camps, have to get a punishment, a severe punishment. Yes; but the way they are punished is not correct. For I am told that many Nazis are treated the same way, [as] the inmates of concentration camps have been treated before. It is terrible. Where is charity? We never get real peace if we have no charity. For how can there be peace, where there is hate in the hearts and souls of people? It is impossible. And so I don't know what the future brings. Every man should try to lead a good life, to show his charity to his neighbours. That's the only way to get a better world. And as we know this, we have to act accordingly.

Many Germans are still in their thinking against the English. And as soon as I tell them that I don't look upon the English as enemies, they are surprised and disappointed and do not agree with me. Last week I lost two [former] school-mates of mine, because of my thinking about the English. They are real good comrades, one of them is a girl, the other a boy. But when I told them that I don't look upon the English as enemies and foreigners with whom we don't speak, when I told them that I even speak privately with them in our office, they left me and don't speak with me any more. They reproached me that I have no national pride. I tried to explain to them that it is nonsense that Germans shall only talk and associate with Germans, that that has nothing to do with national pride, etc. But all was in vain. I am sorry that people think in such a way, but I have nothing to reproach myself with in this case.

Today we got a newspaper. And now I know about the Potsdam communiqué.... What shall the future be like, if on one side there is such a communiqué and on the other side such a thinking? Every understanding is impossible. Why cannot there be true friendship among the different countries? Why do so many people see nationality first and only then the men? I cannot help it, I see the men first; and if they are good and noble-minded, their nationality does not matter.

4 SEPTEMBER Tuesday. Richard Wainwright was here, and told us of the two million refugees from the east to come into the British zone, and of the disastrous misunderstandings over the Neisse at Potsdam [*when Poland was authorised to administer German territory as far as the Oder and Western Neisse rivers 'until the peace treaty'*].

5 SEPTEMBER Wednesday. Christian Smith and I, with Dr Köbberling, went to Frau Paquin's circle of theological students at Göttingen, and heard passages from her diary, kept in English throughout the war, partly for the benefit of her two daughters in England. Very moving in particular was her description of the days just before and just after the outbreak of war.

7 SEPTEMBER Friday. We move to a new and better, though slightly smaller, house. I had been talking to the Town Major and asked him how his housing position was, and he replied that it was dreadful. I said that the house we were living in was very large and we could easily take in other people. He suggested that we look over another smaller house which he was about to 'de-requisition', and if we took it he could de-requisition the larger house in which we were then living, which would be better for the town.

We all had breakfast in the old house, supper in the new, and lunch at the house of our cook's mother, a very pleasant occasion. In the morning I was again at the court, this time in connection with a Pole who had been arrested for making schnapps at the large camp [*see p. 57*]. I had acted as interpreter to Captain Shewell at the time of the arrest and was therefore called as a witness. The still consisted of a large can over a wood fire with a sealed top from which a pipe led to a can of water, through which it coiled, and the liquor was caught dropping out at the far end. All very home-made but effective. The man got six months. Captain Cummings' blurb, attached to the sentence, went something like this:

The distillation of schnapps is a pernicious practice, not only because it is illegal, and defrauds the revenue, and consumes foodstuff, but because it may result in serious illness and even death to the consumer. The man who makes schnapps is a menace to life.

8 SEPTEMBER Saturday. I was a guest of honour at a communion [*sic*] breakfast at the large Polish camp, and sat with the Padre, the Commandant and the two schoolmasters, at the end of a long table lined with boys, very smart, and girls in white, tucking in and watched proudly by a crowd of mothers in the background [*Plate 12*].

I sleep out regularly on the balcony when it is fine as it has been most of this week, and have had a cold bath every morning except today. Yesterday I followed the example of two other members by running round the cinder track encircling the football field opposite, before breakfast. This nearly killed me, which shows that I ought to do it more frequently.

9 SEPTEMBER Sunday. In the afternoon some of us went to a village near Bückeburg where Pastor Wilhelm Mensching has his church. He is head of the German Versöhnungsbund or Fellowship of Reconciliation [*an international Christian pacifist body, begun as a result of an Anglo–German handshake on Cologne railway station on the eve of the First World War*]. We took with us several Germans from Einbeck including the Köbberlings, who already knew Pastor Mensching. Mike Rowntree was there from Vlotho, and the Friedrichs and others from Bad Pyrmont.

First we had 'tea' in Pastor Mensching's house, with coffee and plum tart, and then proceeded to his charming church nearby. It actually turned out that *we* were expected to address his congregation, and answer questions about pacifism, religion and education in England during the war. Mike gave a résumé of conscientious objectors' position and treatment and of the work of the FAU, and Chris Smith passed on some messages from people in England including the Secretary of the FoR in England, Mensching's opposite number.

I got out of making a speech by getting the Pastor to translate and read out two paragraphs from a letter I had just received from Corder Catchpool [*Quaker representative in Berlin in the 1930s—a figure indispensable to any study of British Quaker action vis-à-vis Germany and especially the Nazis. See Hughes 1956*]. Another paragraph of the same letter reads:

> With regard to the suggestion that SS men had become creatures beyond reach of redemption, this has never been my view. I knew them at the height of their pride and power in the months before the war, as I constantly had occasion to be at the Gestapo head-quarters on behalf of Jews and political prisoners, and when we ourselves of the Society of Friends, both German and English people, were in difficulties, as was often the case—even then I still found human elements to which appeal could be made.

The speeches were given in English and translated sentence by sentence by Pastor Mensching and heard with the greatest of attention. Messages from English and French Friends were read out. Then many questions were asked about British life in wartime, chiefly on the educational and religious sides, and some discussion took place about the tasks facing Friends and others of good will in Germany.[6]

11–14 SEPTEMBER Tuesday, Wednesday and Thursday mornings I have spent on the tremendous job of registering all the DPs in the Landjägerkaserne, on DP2 cards, which record everything from a person's mother's maiden name to how many languages he speaks.[7]

Three girls fill in most of the stuff and then the people come through to me and I have an interpreter for those who can't speak German and I ask them their profession and note if there are any unusual points about them such as wanting to go else-where than Poland and so forth. Then I sign the cards. 'Peasant' occurs so often that I have learnt the Polish for it, *rolnik*. But I have also had such occupations as what I could only put down as 'Maid of All Work in a Railway Station'! The best girl can do about 60 cards in a morning, so it might have been possible for me to have to sign my initials 360 times. But this mass production is much quicker than what some others of the Section have been doing at smaller camps, namely, doing it all themselves, and I hope to get the same team on to the Herberge.

On Tuesday evening we went to the opera at Göttingen, taking our cook and four other Germans. 'God Save the King' was played at the beginning. The British at the front rose to their feet, followed by the rest of the audience, although not very many British were there. To play it, though in accord with the spirit of the times, struck me as rather a gratuitous insult.[8]

I try these days to get in two German lessons a week with Frau Ohnesorge, two English ones for the Poles, and at least one for two other Germans. The father of one of these is a painter, and wants to paint my portrait as a return gift. I am afraid I do not get the time I would like to work on my German. When I get the opportunity of addressing groups of Germans as at Göttingen I become increasingly impatient at not being able to speak it better.

14 SEPTEMBER   Friday. Mike Rowntree and Gerald Gardiner were here, the one greeting all FAU sections, the other saying goodbye. They say Poles start going in a week's time, 40,000 a week by sea to Danzig, from the Ruhr first, then from this Corps area. So they should be all gone in a couple of months, those who want to go. Then we get the German refugees, or alternatively we go earlier to the Ruhr for work with a Public Health detachment.

The Government realise that we have to help the food situation, for today we have started distributing British rations to all Polish DPs in camps. How much simpler it would be administratively, if the rations released for 500,000 Poles in the British zone could be sent direct to the Ruhr instead of being distributed to hundreds of camps all over food-producing areas which can easily live on the surrounding country.

In the evening the brothers Urbanczyk came in, and we had a very interesting discussion with our four visitors, partly on 'shop'—the Poles—and partly on the general German situation, including the forthcoming war criminal trials, Allied propaganda, and the extermination of Nazism. Gerald gave very interesting details about Belsen [*where FRS and FAU teams were working from a few days after its liberation. For his attempts to secure immediate medical help for Belsen, see Box 1983: 64–5*].

A Polish Liaison Officer came down from Goslar today and spoke to the Poles in the large camp; he said they had to look after themselves and dispense with the German administration. It was arranged that the change-over should take place gradually.

15 SEPTEMBER Saturday. However the next morning the Polish commandant walked into the kitchen and insulted everybody right and left; and the Poles also made a demonstration, when wood was being taken away to be sawn up, because they thought the Germans were taking it away for themselves. As a result the Germans were withdrawn forthwith and we left the Poles to shift for themselves. Today they get British rations, though on the same 2000 calorie scale. We will see what sort of a job they will make of it. I think Mike and Gerald quite enjoyed seeing the camp in a very revolutionary atmosphere.

Then off to meet some Rumanians to decide which of them should move into the Ostarbeiterlager; or rather, really to say to them, 'your political squabbles do not alter the fact that men should move into a camp suitable for men, and families into camps suitable for families; we will move these and these, and the situation will then be such and such; then you can decide how to divide yourselves up subsequently.'

We are moving office shortly as the school where we are will be required. We will move in with the German DP committee to the Landratsamt [*County Hall*].

The variety show for DPs, put on by Signor Enrico Corini at my instigation, has come and gone. Ticket selling went well and the crowded house was practically entirely filled with Poles and Rumanians. Shelley had done two good posters, Alfredo did a comic turn which went down well, I did a lot of transport work for both players and audience. The charming group of ballet dancers, who looked so graceful on the stage, an hour or two previously had been hauling on a rope to get my ambulance off a slope of slippery grass.

16 SEPTEMBER Sunday. Today I took ninety blankets to the Polish camp at Dassel, and at the same time transported the Baron von der Ropp, from Luthorst, where he had been 'getting the Church going', to Friedrichshausen, where I had lunch with the whole family, and an interesting discussion. Before the war he had done a lot of work trying to foster Anglo-German friendship. He got Lord Lothian to speak to Hitler in 1937, and had met Lloyd George, Lord Halifax, and others. His son Christov had been at school in England with me before the war, and has been in touch with us over the last four weeks. I think he was the only German at the school at the time who was not a refugee; he came because his father knew some English Quakers. And he is probably the only Old Leightonian to have served most of the war in the German army.

20 SEPTEMBER Thursday. Baron and Baroness von der Ropp came to supper. The Baroness said what a pity it was Christov had not been able to be in some such organisation as the FAU, instead of in the Wehrmacht, which was not a suitable finishing school for an Old Leightonian. '...and all you young men, with a sense of responsibility, and keen on interesting things'.

21 SEPTEMBER Friday. We moved fifty Rumanians out of the Landjägerkaserne into the Ostarbeiterlager (ready at last), where they will be able to found a specifically Rumanian camp. We had to get them to dismantle the beds (which take to pieces) and take them along, so that they shouldn't be used afterwards by the Poles for firewood.

After lunch, to Mil Gov to ask about the position as regards giving copies of pamphlets, essays, talks, etc., to Germans, and putting them in the Reading Room for Germans, which has now been installed in the town. They could give no ruling themselves, but said they would write to a higher level to find out the position. They said they thought anything to be placed in the reading room would have to be vetted at a higher level in Mil Gov first, and that as it was, newspapers could be put in only which did not contain criticism of one Ally by another. I then saw the head of the Translations and Writing Office in the town, who is very keen on duplicating some papers I have, to tell him the position as I had just heard it.

Back at home there arrived two young interpreters from the German Military Hospital in Einbeck, to ask if we could procure for them a Bible in English. I lent them mine and said I'd try and bring one back from leave. One was from Vienna, one from Hamburg.

To supper came Frau Ohnesorge and a friend of hers (a girl who used to work in the DP Committee office) with a QMS (Quarter Master Sergeant) of the Wiltshires with whom she is very friendly. She had bemoaned the fact that being a refugee and only having one room she had no place to take this QMS to sit down and chat of an evening, so Frau O had arranged to throw a small party for them at her flat. The arrival of Frau O's brother from the Ruhr had made this impossible, and I had offered that they could come and spend an evening with us. This was the result, and the QMS was cross-examined with great interest by the FAU over the supper table about his travels and what life in the army now was like. He told us about the forthcoming presentation of their colours to the regiment and how he blanco-ed his stripes. I am thankful I am not in the army now. The most incredible amount of spit and polish is done; it is unbelievable, to anyone who has seen them under wartime conditions, that they would ever go back to that.

At 8.00 was a gathering at the home of Dr. and Frau Köbberling. There were four of us from the Section, and eight local guests of various professions. After biscuits and coffee Dr. K. passed round hymn books and we sang a hymn to the accompaniment of Frau K. on a recorder. Then Dr. K. read a passage from a book entitled *Der Dichter und die Jugend*, on the importance of quietness, and suggested we might like to tell the company something of the pacifist movement in England, rather as had been done at Petzen with Pastor Mensching. After some hesitation I repeated the gist of what Michael Rowntree had said then, and this was followed by a discussion, which ended with another hymn. A most charming, simple and natural evening. Dr. K. gave me yesterday a pre-war pamphlet by the Nazi philosopher Rosenberg, which quotes at length a Dr. Dibelius, now Bishop of Berlin and an acquaintance of Dr. K., and criticises him for having supported the cause of conscientious objectors and their right to protection by the Church.

There will be many more Germans to come in than Poles go out. There are under 500,000 Poles in the British zone, of whom under 400,000 will want to return before next spring.[9] But 2,000,000 Germans are to come in. In this Kreis we never had more than 2,000 DPs, but are likely to have 11,000 Germans, in other words more than the peacetime population of the principal town.

It is easier to understand the position of those people who refuse to collaborate with the British in Germany, after having had the behaviour of patriots in occupied countries praised to you; and it is easier to understand the motives of quislings, after having talked to German 'quislings' at the moment.

For the last three nights I have attended the Baron's addresses in the Marktkirche, the church being fairly full.

On Monday he went to Hanover with Tony and saw a General there, who said he would move 250 Poles out of this area so that von der Ropp could have the Erholungsheim [*convalescent home*] for his school. He told me he had been asked to help in the formation of a Christian political party, for which Mil Gov had asked.

22 SEPTEMBER   Saturday. The Quaker circle at Göttingen has grown and is improving very encouragingly. Yesterday I took the Baron von der Ropp there and he gave a talk.

25 SEPTEMBER   Tuesday. Yesterday evening Frau Ohnesorge's husband came back from Russian PoW-ship. Very weak, and ulcers in the mouth, and has to stay in bed and drink soup, but the main thing is that he is back, and can be nursed by her.

Today to Göttingen, taking patients there from the Land-jägerkaserne, a very full ambulance-load. I also asked, on behalf of the Baron, about the method of getting printing permission. The answer was that now none is given. It seems fantastic that not even the printing of Bibles is allowed, when and where paper is available; there is some justification for the Baron's point that we are hindering exactly our allies inside Germany most, and helping our enemies.

To the Landratsamt, to attend an imposing conference, Captain Shewell in the chair, Lt. Kent as interpreter, two of us, Lt. Pye of DPACS, and Urbanczyk. Round the rest of the table, all the Camp Commandants from among the Poles, including about six people from Landjägerkaserne—Commandant, Deputy Commandant, his secretary, new Lagerführer (camp leader), Quartermaster, and Padre. Many questions about the new food rations from British Army stocks, but only to the 2100 calorie scale. Then more questions about other things—clothing, stoves, Red Cross parcels, the Polish car, etc. Solid talk from 3.00 till 5.30.

[*On 6 OCTOBER, though not mentioned in a letter, I attended a meeting at Vlotho, and kept notes, summarised below.*]

The meeting consisted of representatives of the sections in Germany of FAU, FRS and the International Voluntary Service for Peace (IVSP), a body with close affinities to Quakers. Several matters were discussed:

(1) Poland was 'no place to send anyone this winter'. The Russian and Polish authorities were putting every obstacle they could in the way of repatriation, for example refusing to feed repatriees passing through the Russian zone—resulting in the need to establish a transit camp, to which one team was on its way. Some repatriated Poles had disliked the political conditions they found in Poland and had managed to get back to the British Zone under an assumed nationality.

(2) Teams faced opposition from DPs over splitting up Red Cross parcels but it was important to hold the line.[10] Colonel

Agnew had spoken to the authorities about using them for starvation relief but had been told that to supply them to the German civilian population would be a breach of faith with the donors.

(3) New international machinery was now available to deal with unrepatriable DPs, and information was sought about persons who claimed to have or have had 'Nansen' passports. It was not certain whether it would deal with Volksdeutsch [*members of German communities settled for generations in eastern Europe*] or Russians; the test was whether they had been oppressed or had grounds for believing that they would be oppressed if they returned to their country of origin.

(4) A British consul-general had come out to see to those who claimed British nationality, British-born wives of Germans, and DPs who married British soldiers, and we should seek questionnaires for such people.

(5) It was reported from Berlin that the influx of Germans evacuated from the borderlands into the British Zone would soon begin.

(6) Demands for BRCS teams to work on the problems of the civilian population were urgent and widespread. There was no objection up to Corps level, but 21 Army Group HQ said it must await a Cabinet decision. Gerald Gardiner had seen Philip Noel Baker [*commandant of the FAU in France in the 1914–18 war, at this time Minister of State at the Foreign Office*] about this in London.

(7) Some sections had surpluses from their own rations and wished to give these to Germans in need. FAU HQ would stand behind us in any proceedings resulting from such action. It was agreed that such surpluses should be transferred to Berlin via the Vlotho monthly meetings.

THREE

Einbeck, Second Period

24 October to 30 November 1945

*Changes in the Section. Discussions with the Einbeck
intelligentsia. The Section's work. Polish repatriation.
Visit of FAU 'top brass'. Handing over to the Guides.*

[*I had home leave until 24 October. I had been designated Section
Leader, to succeed George Greenwood when he left the Section at
the end of the month. It had been agreed that two women members
should join the Section from the UK. Personally, I had been opposed
to this on the grounds that it would 'take our minds off the job'—
a judgement proved correct in at least one particular, as later events
were to show. One of the two was Brenda Bailey, daughter of
Leonhard and Mary Friedrich. I had known her in the FAU in
London in 1941–42. The other was a physiotherapist, Diana Close,
whom I met briefly at FAU headquarters in Gordon Square during
this leave. They left London on 21 October, but before joining the
Section, Brenda spent five days at Bad Pyrmont with her parents.*]

25 OCTOBER   Thursday. We arrived at Ostend in the morning,
and the train that evening was cancelled so we had to wait 36
hours there. On one shop window were posted newspaper
pictures of fraternisation and also of concentration camps, and
a comment about being unable to censure our liberators, but
equally unable to congratulate them.

27 OCTOBER   Saturday. The train journey was not half so bad
as I had expected. There were six in the compartment, which
was a first class and quite comfortable. We had breakfast at a
halt at Wesel just as dawn was breaking. We passed through
Münster and Osnabrück, and the others, who had not been in
Germany before, were aghast at the destruction wrought. It
would be fair to say that Münster is 99.5 per cent destroyed,
and I can well understand how everybody says it is the worst
place of any size that they have seen.

Two of the officers were back from Burma and described
fighting against the Japanese; two were employed by army
broadcasting and were going to visit the station at Hamburg.
And one was an old regular, a PT instructor, who had spent
the war training in England and was really as keen as mustard
to get overseas, quite excited, and a little bit of a joke amongst
the rest of us.

Bad Oeynhausen, where I got out, is a spa and looks it. It is
21 Army Group headquarters and they occupy all the hotels
and so on; their crossed swords emblem was all over the place.
The Rail Transport Officer (RTO) rang up Vlotho and within
half an hour a truck arrived to take me there. Staff Meeting
discussed future work with German civilians, liaison with HQ,
information policy, selection of new recruits, and helping
German Friends and other churches.

Even with Brenda and Diana, Section 4 will be down two
when George also goes, but Richard Wainwright offered me the
choice of a married couple (the man having been captured in
Greece and having spent five years as a PoW in Germany), or
two young members, fresh from training in England. I plumped
for the former. We shall be going to the Ruhr in about a month;
there will be five FAU teams there altogether, doing public
health work or something like it. We have to wait for UNRRA
to form a team to relieve a Scouts team which will come to take
our place in Einbeck.

28 OCTOBER   Sunday. Next morning some of us went to Bad
Pyrmont for meeting for worship. We took our own food and

had lunch with Leonhard and Mary Friedrich, very happy to be reunited with Brenda, but sorry to be losing her after only five days, although she will be able to visit them frequently until we go to the Ruhr. Brenda had all her old dolls out! In her shoes I think I would have spent five *weeks* at home! The BRCS Rest Hostel here is an excellent place for a short leave, a lovely house in a lovely town in lovely country.

29 OCTOBER Monday. The whole day at the office with George, taking over the ropes.

30 OCTOBER Tuesday. He and I went to see our Mil Gov Detachment at Goslar, to whom we are responsible. Captain Dickson, the man who really runs the show, is a competent and very nice man; besides ourselves, they are in charge of an UNRRA team (containing two Quakers) at Gandersheim, and an FRS Quaker Relief team at Goslar.

Apart from that I have spent every day this week arranging things so that I know what is going on, and at the same time will have enough time to get round and see what other people are doing, and also 'sit back and decide on policy'. It would be nice to be able to leave the Scouts with a clean cut-and-dried set-up with policy for this, that and the other laid down on the basis of our experience, and started off. John Haines helps me in the office work; he is good and I shall be able shortly to let him deal with most things, except for correspondence and reports. Bernard Jackson is in the office every morning to deal with visitors and shield me from the crowd.

The others more or less have their set jobs, but there are always things they wish to refer to me. With only five trucks I have had also to arrange what they shall do each day. Diana and Brenda have been going round seeing the set up and deciding their line. I have had to help them in that. They are starting to look after the children under six in the large camp, for whom there is no school. Brenda is also in charge of the large camp, and of our house and food, while Diana does medical work and will eventually expand their children's work to other camps, since she can drive pretty well. They held a clinic in the Ostarbeiterlager the other day and lots of people came who had not bothered, or dared, to see the doctor—people with all sorts of quite serious complaints. They are both proving very valuable and settling down well, so I am glad I chose the married couple and hope we get them.

31 OCTOBER Wednesday. A Kreis meeting—members being: CO troops, CO Mil Gov, Wiltshires DP Officer, Wiltshires Adjutant, Town Major, Bürgermeister, Landrat, Chief of Police, and myself as FAU representative. The idea is each fortnight to get an idea of what has been going on in the Kreis and what the present position is, with regard to food, fuel, accommodation, transport, refugees, DPs, health, entertainment, education, sport, political activity, crime, etc. Very interesting and also useful. Impressed again by British sense of responsibility for doing a job well.

We have now no-one (such as DPACS) to shield us from the papers that pour out at us from higher army levels, and the multitudinous returns they demand. However, I am getting on top of this, and in the end I do not think it should take up more than 25 per cent of my time.

Decentralisation is the keynote for a Section Leader, and I am fortunate that the FAU is accustomed to that and likes having small provinces the responsibility of one person. Thus, Bernard is i/c our NAAFI stores and supplies, Tony our transport, Chris our equipment, Bill Judd our cash, Brenda our mess arrangements, Shelley the DP rations and ration store, John Tovey all other supplies, including clothing, for DPs. In addition, Brenda, Bernard, Bill and Chris are responsible for the various groups of camps.

Thus theoretically I should be dispensable.

Following home leave, it has been grand renewing old acquaintances (within the Section of course as well as without). Last night we went to Göttingen and heard Dr. August Fricke of Kassel speak on 'The Meaning of Quakerism' to Erna Rosier's Quaker circle. We took five German guests, and the

Polish girl from Landjägerkaserne (heartily welcomed by Erna). Dr Fricke's address was excellent. He speaks with great sincerity and urgency, and depth. Also present was one of the UNRRA team at Gandersheim.

30 OCTOBER Tuesday. In the evening there was a Bach and Handel concert arranged by the elder Urbanczyk, with the Hanover orchestra plus a pianist living in Einbeck, and other soloists. The cinema is used by troops except on Fridays and Sundays, so it was in the Münsterkirche, which was full, but there was no clapping since it was a church.

The autumn is very far advanced here, the good foliage has come and gone while I have been away, and now the trees are practically bare, though there were some lovely colours around Bad Pyrmont last Sunday and the trip to Goslar on Tuesday was a delight.

A committee is to be set up to decide the nationality of doubtful cases. It must consist of representative Garrison troops, Mil Gov, etc. We actually have all the dope about all the doubtful cases in this Kreis, and all the rulings which apply, and I think it will be simply a case of putting details and recommendations before the committee. It is to deal in particular with Soviet and near Soviet nationals, since the Russians say they are not getting all the people back they should. But it is a job for us to extract from our files all the relevant matter; this has been started by Bernard.

31 OCTOBER Wednesday evening at about 8.30 the telephone rang and the two girls and I were invited round to the Köbberlings. The surprise party was most enjoyable, and Diana and Brenda were very interested in talk of the German churches, etc., and could bring to the comparison of war-time life in the two countries much more recent and more thorough knowledge of conditions in England than I have [*I had left England in June 1942 for the Middle East*]. Dr. K. was very interesting on the subject of poets and writers who were able to write books during the Nazi regime with meanings that escaped

the eye of the censor, and quoted with relish an article in the
Hannoversche Kurier, by one of them, strongly critical of
Thomas Mann, who after living comfortably in America
throughout the war now speaks to the Germans in a tactless
manner without any appreciation of what has been happening
in Germany since the war and earlier.

NOVEMBER   There is bags of transport here doing nothing,
bags of petrol being wasted on parades. We distribute these
super-excellent Red Cross parcels to Poles with an already adequate diet. From 1st November our rations are reduced to
3400 calories, those of troops at home being 3288 calories (and
average civilian consumption 2300), owing to 'serious world
shortage of meat, bacon, sugar, fats and dairy produce'; 'it is
only through some sacrifice ... that the present civilian ration
in UK can be assured, and that starvation can be prevented in
the countries of NW Europe which have been recently liberated from German domination.' The last two lines are of course
nonsense, since neither France, Belgium nor Holland receives
food from UNRRA. I enclose an extract from a letter from
Fritz Künkel to me for his wife in this connection.[1] He by the
way writes very interesting letters, about his friends Gerald
Heard, Aldous Huxley, and Co.

2 NOVEMBER   Friday. The elder Urbanczyk was one of five
lawyers in Hanover province asked to take part in the defence
at the Nuremberg trials. He refused, partly on the grounds that
his health would not be able to stand the great strain of five
months or so daily appearances and nightly conferences with
the accused and with other lawyers, and partly because it was
not possible to decide whom one would defend, and some of
the accused he was not prepared to defend by any means.
Speaking as a lawyer, he thought they could have a strong
defence, though he had not yet had an opportunity to read the
indictment *in toto*.

   I told him of Richard Wainwright at Lüneburg having lunch
with Colonel Backhouse, the Prosecutor. He had said that they

couldn't make out Kramer, who seemed to be genuinely of the opinion that these atrocities were terrible, and that he wouldn't like to be the man at the top who was responsible for them. Backhouse had also said that if he had been on the defence, he could have got Kramer off, but all the good army lawyers had been used to prepare the indictment, and the present defence were mugs and doing it all wrong, for example treating the witnesses as if they were scoundrels and liars, instead of with sympathy for their sufferings.

Urbanczyk said he asked many Germans: 'If you were ordered to shoot a child, would you do so?' and the vast majority said Yes; a great difference, there (and he is right), between Germans and Englishmen. We also discussed a mutual acquaintance who had been a Nazi; according to Urbanczyk, he was just beginning to change his mind. I asked him whether he felt no constraint in discussing these things with people who had supported people who had persecuted him, and he said no, not with this individual, who took no offence, since for his part he [Urbanczyk] felt absolutely no desire of revenge at all, no rancour. I believe that the very finest of anti-Nazis, who have suffered most, are in this position; Borowski is another, and so is Leonhard Friedrich.

4 NOVEMBER Sunday. This morning five of the Section went horse-riding at the Polish stud farm at Erichsburg at the invitation of the captain, who keeps paying courtly compliments to Diana. John Haines' horse went under two interlocking trees and left him hanging in mid-air. Meanwhile I sent off the leader of a Polish football team to Mil Gov to get a permit for a vehicle to take them here. Civilian vehicles are not allowed to travel on Sundays; but Major S. over the phone said it would be all right.

We hope to have a section meeting tonight and also to present George with an engraving of Einbeck as a memento and farewell present.

6 NOVEMBER Tuesday. We held a section meeting after lunch, at which Chris was elected Deputy Section Leader; he is 39 so

I have plenty of experience at my right hand. We made decisions about transport, work, Red Cross parcels policy, and handing over to our successors.

7 NOVEMBER Wednesday. Chris and I went round to the Köbberlings to meet three friends of theirs, journalist, lawyer, and schoolmaster respectively. The journalist I knew; he is now in charge of the refugees' welfare bureau. They meet together with the Köbberlings from time to time for an evening, and after a cup of (ersatz) coffee have a discussion, introduced by one of them with something prepared. This time the schoolmaster opened up, on a book which an English officer had given him, called *The Lost Peace*, by a man called Butler, mostly it seemed an account of his travels in Europe between the wars, and of conditions and affairs in various countries, but also full of pungent comments on national characteristics, such as: 'The Frenchman looks on a badly cooked dish with the same horror with which an American regards a car that won't start on a cold morning.'

The discussion opened out on diverse lines. Details of industry, business, and economics in Germany under the stress of war and particularly of large-scale bombing. The schoolmaster gave a remarkable 'confession' or autobiography. Starting off, in his student days, with strong leanings towards pacifism, internationalism, and so on, he had been strongly influenced by Nazi doctrine about 1935–37, and then revolted from it, but not strongly enough not to feel his patriotic duty during the war. Now he felt that the wheel had come full circle and he was back where he started, having to work things out afresh from the viewpoint of his student days. Dr. Köbberling (himself a keen Baptist and a pure and consistent anti-Nazi) found it very interesting that it was so easy to go from such pacifistic idealism into Nazism, and told me afterwards he thought being closely bound up with essentially *Christian* ideas was the only way for people of that generation to have avoided it.

9 NOVEMBER Friday. To Goslar in a jeep with Capt. Colsey, Wiltshires Officer for DPs insofar as they are a problem concerning the garrison troops. A good chap, Lt. Kent's successor, and co-operates well, but has too many other jobs to give much time to it. At Goslar is the Mil Gov Detachment under which we come, along with an FRS and an UNRRA team for the other two Kreise in the area. Capt. Dickson there is a first class man, and very helpful, and we sat for two hours talking with him, since I had reports and returns to hand over and many questions to ask.[2]

Next week is going to be busy, but all the more interesting for that. I think this Section (a) does a very full job, in which its manpower is employed to capacity, 90 per cent in jobs worthy of them and in which there is infinite scope; (b) lives well together, has an excellent spirit, and is as capable of playing hard as working hard. I also think that it is on the upgrade and that some members in it are gaining greatly from the experience. The section meeting on Tuesday confirmed my decision to ask for the King couple to bring up our strength.

10 NOVEMBER Saturday. Took Frau Ohnesorge's husband from hospital to home, he having been there with typhus ever since coming out of Russian hands near the end of September; he is still weak.

At a lecture by a professor on 'The Evil in the World, and English Religious Trends'. He spoke very sincerely and well, although from a comic system of notes: a man with remarkable knowledge of England and its religious history, which he seems to have been studying for the last fifty years. A good discussion ensued.

11 NOVEMBER Sunday. We bought our poppies from the troops, but went out riding at the Polish stud farm in the morning so did not have any hand in any ceremony. It was a typical November day, dull and wet though not raining, with some low cloud about and the landscape bare; but very invigorating, and a grand antidote to office work.

With Herbert Voges a few miles away to have tea with a Baroness—he thought I would like to see a different part of

German society for a change, and we enjoyed arguing gently with a true-blue conservative outlook over such things as the arts. Evidently an old Hanoverian family.

Evenings have been pleasantly occupied, either at home (what a difference it does make to have a couple of women around the house, concerned that one should change one's socks, or have a cup of tea before going to bed, or suchlike trivia!) or visiting.

WEEK ENDING 18 NOVEMBER The Section's work. We are all very hard at it and the only solution has been to send people away on three-day leaves to Bad Harzburg. Diana and Brenda are going full steam ahead on Child Welfare, Mothers' Help, and Medical Care. They have got schools and kindergartens and play centres and clinics going right left and centre. Diana visits the outlying camps once or twice a week, and Brenda is in charge of the largest Einbeck camp. Their advice on questions of clothing, food, and so on has been invaluable. The only trouble has been lack of equipment for Play Centres, but they are remedying this by making toys, etc. Diana drives anything except the six-tonner, and Brenda is learning. We have been so short-staffed in other departments that we have had to use them for some other jobs, e.g. ambulance work; perhaps this will be easier next week, with reinforcements.

Tony has been very busy on transport, and now has John Tovey to help him, and also to learn to drive the six-tonner. The stores have been taken over by Chris, as well as his round. Tony and John are going next week to Brussels to fetch our Ford V8 for which the retention certificate has at last come through and which was taken out of REME by George. Bill Judd has had a day or two in bed but is now up and on his round again. Bernard Jackson, in the office and on visits, has interviewed most people of possibly Soviet nationality, and most of the west- and south-bound nationals who have refused repatriation. John Haines, in the office, has kept the paper war going, and dealt with applicants for Red Cross parcels. Shelley is still busy at his store, and has organised the processing of Red Cross parcels on mass-production lines.

All Czechs, Greeks, Italians, French, Dutch, Belgians, Luxemburgers, Spaniards, Latin Americans and Swiss still here have at last, with two special exceptions, been struck off all DP rights and status, and their DP2 cards are now on the way to National LOs. All Balts will shortly be either struck off or evacuated to camps near Goslar, and Estonians and Latvians have already been interviewed by accredited representatives of their Democratic republics. Next Sunday about 320 Poles will be repatriated from this Kreis, and this will enable us to bring all others into camps at last. This will mean a lot less work, both for the office and for the store, in the distribution of parcels and clothing to people living privately.

It looks as if this time the Red Cross parcels distribution really may succeed the way we want it to. The system has been explained by the Polish LO from Goslar to the administration of the largest camp, who have promised their co-operation if we take responsibility. So the stage is set, for distribution next week. Those being repatriated will get theirs whole, with 48-hour rations and if needed an overcoat, at the station on Sunday.

Twenty tons of coal is waiting to be picked up at Northeim as soon as the Wilts have trucks available, and the allocation has already been planned. A wood policy, to supplement the coal ration, has still to be worked out and put into practice.

12 NOVEMBER   Monday. A dinner-party to celebrate (two days late) Diana's birthday. We were joined by the Ohnesorges, the Köbberlings, the Sohns, Frau Matteus (the dentist). Many of the guests appreciated an evening completely divorced from normal life (which normal talk never is divorced from)—'like peace-time', in other words. On the continent, in France as well as Germany, there was this feeling, quite foreign to Englishmen, that one should not dance, etc., while there are people at the front being killed. A party where grown-ups behave like children (round-the-table pingpong and clumps were on the menu), is therefore of tremendous value when people must wrestle with daily life after a war strain far greater than we have known.

Mr Ohnesorge, still weak from his typhus, is nevertheless well on the way to recovery, though this must have been the most 'un-invalid' evening he had had since his captivity. He is spending his time quietly doing a lot of reading, and was interested to hear English viewpoints on economic questions: a charming though quiet man. The Sohns, Shelley's friends, an artist and his Norwegian wife, are also a charming and colourful couple. He was three years in Norway during the war and loved the country.

14 NOVEMBER   Wednesday. Polish repatriation. We got the first news about it by phone from the Polish LO in Goslar just before lunch; no definite date was given, but we had to find out how many Poles were willing to go straight home, and return figures by that evening. I saw the Landrat straight away, and got him to phone all forty Bürgermeisters in the Kreis, to get them to tell camp commandants to bring the figures in, and to interview themselves all Poles living privately in their Gemeinde or parish and phone figures back.

The circle in the evening contained anecdotes from the Russian zone. A Russian riding a brand-new bicycle up a hill saw a German boy riding an old bicycle down the hill with arms folded. Stopped the boy, changed bikes, and did it himself. The boy buzzed off on the new bike.

A lady coming across the frontier was stopped by a Russian officer. He said he had waited three years to stand there and watch Germans starving to death. She offered him schnapps to let her across (the usual method), but he refused. She said she was glad to see he didn't drink, real Christians didn't. He said yes, he was a Christian. She said real Christians didn't like to see other people starving to death. He let her across.

Russians have to live on the land but individuals seem to realise Germans are short too; at any rate, a soldier after asking someone for food would only take half the number of rolls he had, and several stories confirm the idea of Russians wanting to 'go 50–50'.

15 NOVEMBER Thursday. The Polish LO came down and gave us more details—evacuation by train on Sunday from Einbeck station, all those going to be medically inspected, 'dusted' (with anti-louse powder) and 'screened' (asked in our presence if they *really* want to go). Then I went with him to the Sikorski Camp (as the Landjägerkaserne is called now), and he tried to get them to get more people to go (only 300 in the Kreis had volunteered, and he had room for 500), but agreed with them that they would be better looked after by staying here through the winter and that in their shoes he would do the same. He also put over to them our scheme for dealing with Red Cross parcels.

16 NOVEMBER Friday. The next day was rather busy for the Section, since all the Poles had to be told, and Medical Inspection and screening had to take place, as well as various arrangements for their welfare on the journey. Captain Colsey and I had to go all the way to Goslar in a Jeep in the afternoon (bitterly cold journey), at very short notice, for a conference about the repatriation, called by the Major commanding 817 Detachment—quite useless, since he could have said it all over the phone.

Capt. Colsey (now to be called Marcus) and I came in frozen from the Jeep at about 5.00 and had some tea and chatted till supper at 6.00. The Polish captain from the stud farm at Erichsburg, with all his old-world charm and courtesy, was there, and after supper we had a very interesting chat, Capt. Colsey being an exceptionally enlightened man, with the right ideas about Russia, etc. (e.g. that she is frightened). Later Chris played very finely on the piano (now tuned).

At about 10.00 p.m. two officers of the Swedish Red Cross arrived to be put up for the night, being on convoy between Prague and Stockholm, and caught in the fog. One had a paper signed by Bernadotte, the other had been to Belsen before its liberation to arrange (by permission of the German Government) evacuation of Danish, Swedish, and Norwegian inmates, and had spoken to Kramer [*Nazi commandant at Belsen concentration camp*], who he said did not seem unduly worried by the starvation there. Both were working incredibly hard for the Red Cross from pure idealistic motives as emergency temporary service. They said Sweden was 90 per cent anti-German, but it seemed to be even more anti-Russian (having had strong contacts with Finland). Proud of having had no war for so long, and said that being fortunate they had the chance to help others less fortunate; therefore the Swedish Red Cross was a very big organisation with a lot of work in Germany, Czechoslovakia, Poland, etc.

17 NOVEMBER   Saturday. While DDT dusting took place in the morning, Captain Colsey and I arranged things at the station and laid on various necessaries, such as straw for the cattle-trucks in which the Poles would be travelling, cleaning of the trucks by German staff at the station, bottles for those without them, to have something to drink on the way, and bottles of milk for the babies. In the afternoon, there being a shortage of FAU personnel, I went round several villages with an RASC truck collecting people, since we had arranged to get all those living privately into the Landjägerkaserne that evening, so as to make things simpler for the transport in the morning. Tony went to Gandersheim to collect some clothing, which had just arrived there, for the children being repatriated.

When I arrived back at the Sikorski there was Diana and the doctor trying to register and examine all the people who had been brought in, in a large disorganised badly lit room with people milling around, which reminded one of more chaotic conditions as at Ede, Holland, or with the Free French. I took some tins to the station, where rations, Red Cross parcels and clothing had been stored ready for distribution the following morning. The tins were to serve a special purpose on the journey in the cattle-trucks (an idea passed on to us from the Goslar section), and since Diana had found a source of supply they became known as 'Dianas'.

Matysiak said that so many people were changing their minds so often that you would never know who was going till they got on the platform. So I arranged that he and Theresa, the Polish secretary there, should make a nominal roll of all those going, the following morning on the platform as they entered our 'Sausage Machine'.

In the evening at about 9.00 when all were together, we planned the following morning. Trucks would roll up at our door at 7.00 a.m. with Captain Colsey in a Jeep. The Poles were to be collected from four camps, and truck convoys to these camps would be led by Bill, Diana, Brenda, and Bernard respectively; they would be in charge of loading and come to the station themselves with the last truck from each camp. Colsey and I would pick up Matysiak, Theresa and a type-writer from the Sikorski, and take them to the station. Tony would take Shelley and John Haines to the station, stopping at the Landratsamt for the other typewriter and some spare DP 1 and 2 cards in case any of the repatriees had not been regis-tered; then he would pick up milk from the *Zentral-Melkerei* (Central Dairy) and deliver it to the station. After that he would be i/c of getting our Sawyer boiler to the station and making coffee for the repatriees, in which he would be helped by Bill as soon as he returned from his camp. Chris and John Tovey were to go straight to the station and prepare the issue of over-coats for those in need.

The 'Sausage Machine' would consist of the following:

(1) DP 1 cards checked by Diana for Medical Inspection and Screening. This due not to any need for these processes but to weed out any trying to pass through the Sausage Machine (and collect the goodies) without the real intention of going to Poland. Any with blank cards or no cards to be retained for questioning to see what evidence we had that they had put their names in earlier for repatriation.

(2) Matysiak and Theresa to enter on nominal roll, with two typewriters going full blast full time.

(3) John Tovey to examine for needing overcoat, and mark result on back of DP1 card.

(4) Issue of Red Cross parcels by Shelley, and overcoats by Chris.

(5) Issue of milk to children under six by Brenda, and cross in red pencil on back of card.

This was to be done through a passage to which there was only one entrance and one exit, a covered hall at the entrance side and the platform at the exit side, and plenty of rooms opening off, for stores and processes, etc. Three of Captain Colsey's twelve men to do policing inside the Sausage Machine and see that the procession went the right way and didn't miss anything. Until Brenda and Diana arrived, John Haines and I would stand in for them. Issue of children's clothing, 'Dianas', and rations would be done afterwards when all were in their trucks. Issue of blankets for those who had been living privately (and using big eiderdowns belonging to those on whom they were billeted) was to be done with the overcoats by Chris and John Tovey. Colsey's men would guide the crowds, and let them enter wagons at 35 a time.

18 NOVEMBER Sunday. The morning started with many things not going according to plan. Colsey had a fourth contradictory signal about time and route of train (for a time we had thought DPs from other Kreise were to be brought to Einbeck by road for entraining) which nearly made us decide to postpone operations an hour; we didn't, however, and that was a right decision. On arrival at the station we found the station staff were against the geography of the Sausage Machine as we had planned it, as it meant going through a luggage room, etc. They wanted us to use the main hall, with benches to direct the crowd. This caused some delay for thought, but shortly I decided that our original plan would have to be adhered to, and this too was a right decision, since the stream came through fast and well policed and the station staff ended up pleased at the way it was handled.

Then, the railway wagons were not ready, having only just arrived, and we had to let the crowd onto the station and pass it through the Sausage Machine before they entered the wagons, which was the contrary of what was planned: however this did not cause chaos, due to good geographical control of it, and

information efficiently spread under our instructions by responsible Poles. Stacks of straw had arrived and I had to ask the
Station-master to take some out of the wagons, one half of each
being piled high with it! The expected 300 dwindled, in the
event, to 200, which meant that everybody could be accommodated in nine wagons, and get 30 rations for each 25 people
[*Plate 16*].

These things did not disturb the main functioning of our
plan, and the Sausage Machine passed through 2–3 heads a
minute and got finished in nice time. Matysiak and the Sikorski
Quartermaster chose two responsible men from each wagon to
collect the rations, Brenda and Diana distributed children's
clothing and surplus milk to the greatest needs after the Sausage
Machine process was over; the coffee boiled at the right moment
and we handed it round the wagons; and 15 minutes afterwards, that is at 11.00 a.m., the train rolled out of the station
to join the main train at Salzderhelden junction.

So all went smoothly. The distribution of various 'extras',
and the making of coffee just before they went, had a very
great effect on those responsible Poles whom we had asked to
assist us, and they came and thanked us afterwards for having
so busied ourselves to give their compatriots a good send off.
The Poles who went were singing national songs just before the
train went out of the station, and asked if we were not coming
too—whereas it might have been a soulless operation. Captain
Colsey I think was struck that a voluntary organisation could
put some polish on an organisational job, and the soldiers who
guided the crowds seemed to enjoy the whole affair and be
interested in the general activity which was going on. Once the
station staff saw the Sausage Machine procession not producing a pandemonium in their precincts they too seemed to be
pleased at being treated benevolently, and we left them smiling
after they had shared in the coffee and been thanked for their
co-operation. In fact, Germans, Poles and English had shared
in the job, as had conscientious objectors and soldiers.

A ride in the afternoon provided rhythmic open-air exercise,
a complete contrast with the last two or three days.

19 NOVEMBER   Monday. I took the Brummagem Belle to the
Dassel backwoods for a load of wood [*Plate 17*]. The morning
was crisp and fine, I was well wrapped up, driving this huge
monster without a cab, taking in fresh air by the gallon. Beyond
Dassel the scenery was beautiful, almost fairylike and slightly
unreal since you seem to be sitting so high up. Into the woods
we went, guided by the wood merchant we picked up at Dassel,
a gentle old man, along lonely tracks hedged in by the forest.
Two deer crossed about a hundred yards in front, and stood
looking at us as we approached, for several seconds that seemed
like years. At the wood pile I helped load, some solid exercise
being warming and congenial. Then I remembered what Tony
had said about greasing the steering mechanism to make the
turning easier when fully loaded, and got out the grease-gun
and whipped round the joints. It was grand coming back, too,
with the winter sun shining, noisily down hills in third with five
tons of wood and five men in the back; backfiring through villages,
everybody looking at this strange apparition, and even the geese
cackling at it.

Leaving the Belle at the Ostarbeiterlager to be unloaded, I
arrived home for lunch. We had a visit from our VIPs, known
in FAU circles as 'cheeses' [*Plate 18*]. Richard Wainwright was
bringing Tegla Davies, current head of the FAU world-wide,
and Paul Cadbury, patron of the FAU in this war and head of
the chocolate firm.

After lunch they came round four camps with Brenda and
myself. No doubt this tour will have repercussions somewhere,
if only to add local colour to some hot air at home. After supper
the two visiting cheeses 'said a few words' to the section. This
developed into a discussion on the work, meaning, and future
of the FAU, and connected points. Paul Cadbury is very bucked
about a recent House of Commons debate on the demobilisation of conscientious objectors,[3] in which the FAU seemed to
carry on its shoulders all other COs to an embarrassing extent,
and no MP had anything but praise for COs generally. To him,
after experiences in 1914–18, and having defended COs against
great prejudice in the early stages of this war (for example on

the Birmingham City Council), such a state of affairs was almost unbelievable.

Tegla Davies proposes that the FAU as such should wind up on 30 June 1946; there are a lot of technical and practical reasons in favour. There would be a successor body with entirely different structure, scope and work: an organisation with 80 per cent of its members between 18 and 23 could not be expected to carry on the present work without a paid administrative staff.

At 8.00 some of our local friends arrived. After conversation with the Köbberlings, Paul said he would try to get some Baptist Church in Birmingham to 'adopt' the one in Einbeck. He is full of enthusiasm, though his stories of the FAU in the First World War would begin to pall on a constant companion. He has evidently bagged Tegla, a schoolmaster who has blossomed out during his Unit career into a first-rate administrator and leader, for 'Industrial Education' for Bournville. Voges booked Richard to talk on Quakerism to a conference of schoolmasters in Hanover.

20 NOVEMBER Tuesday. Ken and Marjorie King arrive, bringing our numbers up to 13 (*absit omen*). Ken had been captured in Greece at the same time as George Greenwood, but not freed till the arrival of allied forces in May this year; he drives and speaks German, and is also interested in dietetics, medicine, and sanitation; he is 28 and a Friend. Marjorie is a State Registered Nurse and midwife, a Friend, and a cheerful and energetic person. They will make a very useful contribution.

21 NOVEMBER Wednesday. Some stories from the artist from Berlin. The Yanks for their behaviour are called 'Russians with creases in their trousers'. The Russians, wanting watches, used to call out 'Uhri, Uhri'; at a news-theatre, when Attlee and Stalin were shown shaking hands after Potsdam, Stalin seemed to be doing a round-the-wrist handshake—and the cry went up in the audience: 'Uhri, uhri'.

22 NOVEMBER Thursday. We are to go to Dortmund next week. Reports of work possibilities have been received, and the

scope is unlimited. An FAU team will be in each of the five
largest towns of the Ruhr proper, so we will have a monopoly
of voluntary societies in that area for work with Germans.

23 NOVEMBER   Friday. Visit of Lt. Carpf, the Polish LO from
Goslar, in the afternoon. At the Sikorski (alias Landjägerkaserne) he discussed among other things the vexed question of
Red Cross parcels [*Plate 15*]. Brenda and I sat there while he
argued with them, and at one time he wanted us to give in and
change our policy; we thought this would be weakness and that
we held the whip hand and were glad we took that attitude
since it called their bluff. Now the whole thing is decided by
higher authority, since henceforth the parcels MUST be split up
and distributed with the rations [*see p. 69 n.10*].

We entertained Captain Cummings of Mil Gov, a fine middle-
aged man doing a very good job after starting from scratch, an
idealistic atheist who fought, and would fight again, for Europe,
Europe being the only thing worth living for. Says one is always worse off at the end of a war than at the beginning, but
that wars are fought to save one from being worse off still.

25 NOVEMBER   Sunday. Rohtraut Fricke and her mother are
here from Kassel, and came with me and Herbert Voges to
Barsinghausen near Hanover to see a Professor Munch, in
charge of preparing schoolbooks for use in Hanover Province.
He gave many details of the methods of making up schoolbooks
for the future, and the difficulties to be encountered, spoke
enthusiastically of the co-operation and encouragement given
by Mil Gov, and talked at large of the general educational
position. All this very interesting for Rohtraut, as a teacher
herself and daughter of the Director of Education for Kassel.

Back in the evening in time to greet the Girl Guides team
which had arrived to take over from us.

26 NOVEMBER   Monday. Showing the Guides' leader, a Miss
Bailey, around. There were four in their advance party; the rest
arrived today, two or three men and nine women in all. Poor

men, they look subdued. But they are keen on welfare work and should do well when settled in, though they suffer from a lack of German speakers. The previous evening I had written out a lot of notes for her, and we talked them over in the morning, visited umpteen military and German contacts, and saw a little of the office.

By the evening some FAU reports about work in the Ruhr had arrived and were devoured. Chris and Bill had late suppers after nearly completing Operation Round-up with two army three-tonners.

A short section meeting was held to plan the change-over and this week's work. I made the point that we should plan to hand over the work to the Guides as completely as possible as soon as possible, since we needed a break, for rest and for overhauling vehicles and equipment. This policy was agreed, and has been carried out moderately well, although some members of the section find it very difficult to let other people take over their responsibilities, and to stop getting let in for details. It has given the section time to wind up all extraneous odds and ends, and to have a good blitz on transport, and to have some days of relaxation, I hope, as well.

The Guides, though with a very different approach from ours, consequent upon their previous experience, which has been working inside only two camps, not dealing with a Kreis-full, will probably settle down all right, although there have been many expressions of regret from Poles, Rumanians, and Germans, at our departure [see p. 93]. Two Mil Gov officers were heard to remark that 'they are rather WVS'. The two male members, one a Quaker and the other a Communist, suffer a bit from feminine preponderance I think; but we have started them off well and with several good German contacts.

28 NOVEMBER Wednesday. Another Köbberling evening, when the two male Guides accompanied Chris and me there. I had shown Dr. K. a short article I had written a year ago in Alsace, called 'When Barriers Fall', and was asked to read it out. In it I had attempted to classify Germans by their stance vis-à-vis the Nazi regime. Though based on no first-hand knowledge of the country or the people, it appeared to meet with a large measure of agreement.

29 NOVEMBER   Thursday. Diana, Brenda, Shelley and I went to dinner at the Wiltshire officers mess. It was in the Thyssen mansion, but we were equal to the occasion, rolling up in our Ford V8 like any pair of dukes and duchesses in the land. It was a so-called 'informal' night, but any period of such 'informality' would quickly stifle me; however, it was an excellent evening, and we all enjoyed it immensely. Capt. Colsey is really a first class man, probably a good deal more enlightened than the others.

30 NOVEMBER   Friday. Our farewell party, with thirty or more guests, from all classes in Einbeck. It was a huge success, largely due to Brenda's efficient organisation. Conversation and eating were interspersed with a game of musical chairs, and with a performance by Alfredo 'der Weltbekannte' ('world-renowned'), including imitations of most of the members of the FAU section and of many of our visitors, the tap dancing railway engine and 'the man getting into a bath'. At the end we all sang 'Auld Lang Syne', and I said how sorry we were to leave Einbeck and how much we thanked all those who had made our stay so pleasant.

Oboz Polski im.

GEN. SIKORSKIEGO

Einbeck, dnia 1. 12. 1945
Landjägerschule

W imieniu spoleczenstwa Polskiego miasta i po-
wiatu Einbeck skladamy Panu, Panie McClelland
oraz wszystkim czlonkom tutejszej placowki Bry-
tyjskiego Czerwonego Krzyza nasze najserdeczniej-
sze podziekowanie za prace dokonana nad polepsze-
niem bytu Polakow.
Z zalem zegnamy Panow i zyczymy dalszej, owocnej
pracy dla dobra ludzkosci.

. . .

Im Namen aller polnischen Staatsangehörigen der
Stadt und des Kreises Einbeck, sprechen wir Ihnen,
Herr McClelland, sowie allen anderen Mitgliedern
der hiesigen Abteilung des Britischen Roten Kreu-
zes, unseren herzlichsten Dank für die durch Sie
alle getane Arbeit auf dem Gebiete unserer Betreung
Es tut uns herzlich leid, Sie von uns scheiden zu
sehen und wir wünschen Ihnen für die Zukunft weite-
re, fruchtbare Arbeit zum Wohle der Menschheit.

. . .

In the name of all Polish subjects of the district
and town of Einbeck we should like to express to
you, Mr. McClelland, and to all other members of
the British Red Cross here our sincerest gratitude
for everything you did for us. We are very sorry,
that you leave Einbeck and wish you for your
future further useful work for the benefit of
mankind.

Thanks from the Poles, in three languages.

PART II

Welfare Work in the Ruhr

Reports at Vlotho HQ

2–3 December 1945

2 DECEMBER Sunday. I packed and handed over all outstanding matters to Chris, and in the afternoon got away with
Brenda in the Fordson en route for Dortmund via Bad Pyrmont
and Vlotho. Kenneth and Marjorie King had left the previous
day in an ambulance, to spend the weekend with a relative
before joining the Section Representatives' meeting at Vlotho.
The rest of the section will stay at Einbeck till Thursday, and
I hope take things easy.

   Arrived at Brenda's parents at Bad Pyrmont, we parked the
Fordson (difficult to back with trailer!) in the Schloss, now
occupied by Regimental HQ—over a moat bridge and through
a veritable tunnel in the walls. A meal and chat, and bed, all in
the most homely and comfortable atmosphere.

3 DECEMBER Monday. We paid a brief visit to the Youth
Movement rooms run by Brenda's mother, and were off. At
Vlotho, after supper, the meeting was addressed by William
Hughes, British Friends' representative in Germany, and Hans
Albrecht from Berlin, clerk of Germany Yearly Meeting.
William Hughes said how much FAU contacts had meant to
German Quakers, and how good it was that the way should be
re-opened by forward looking youngsters instead of old fogeys.
Some material from two meetings now follows.

Section Representatives' Meeting, Vlotho, 3 December 1945

Reports on the work for Germans were given by three sections already engaged in it.

Cologne 35 per cent destroyed is the most accurate estimate. Transport needs are a bottomless pit. Private cars, or motorbikes, for our own personnel would help enormously in making the best use of trucks and ambulances. The shortage is due firstly to petrol (1200 vehicles reported idle in the Regierungsbezirk, for lack of it), secondly to spares.

Task of surveying Welfare Services, and 're-activating' them. With supplies, they would do their own reactivating. But there is a good job to be done, walking the tightrope between them and Mil Gov.

Essen There were 700 major breaks in the sewage system and 200 remain. One hospital has 40–50 cases of typhoid. No potatoes for 3–4 weeks, swedes instead. A definite job to give the welfare organisations drive and enthusiasm, and a little supplies would go a long way to help.

Duisburg With only a small team, one must work through Germans; therefore a need in our teams for people who can organise. The DRK (German Red Cross—Deutsches Rotes Kreuz) is divided into Welfare and Medical, of which only the latter is efficient. The Catholics are the most energetic, but were pushed into the background under the Nazis, and there is therefore friction now with other bodies. A task, to co-ordinate all these bodies and get them working together. Large incidence of typhoid, and 3–4 per cent deaths from diphtheria cases. The RTO (Rail Transport Office) issues passes at the station, strictly against orders, for Duisburg citizens to get home after curfew. Need for MI (Medical Inspection) room and more overnight accommodation for refugees passing through and waiting for trains; sometimes 4000 people at a time. Story of Jewish refugee in the RTO, who came back to Germany to 'get his own back'; but now helps.

IVSP (International Voluntary Service for Peace) gave some

details of the camp for westbound refugees near Göttingen, coming from the Russian zone. 6000 people came through each day. So far, 25,000 returning evacuees, chiefly for Rhineland; 4500 refugees from the East, and they are a growing proportion.

Operation 'Income'—50,000 evacuees returning from the US zone.

William Hughes said that in his report to Friends at home on the situation in Germany, he was saying that relief, on a scale to make any difference, could only come through Government action, and Friends should concentrate on pushing public opinion. Personal effort should be concentrated on particular places and purposes, through the personal service our teams were able to give. *Save Europe Now*, he told us, was still very active, and Attlee had told a deputation that he would advise the voluntary societies to concentrate on relief for children. But pushing public opinion was best done not by headline stories but by accurate, selected information.

Richard Wainwright stressed this point, mentioning Gerald Gardiner broadcasting to America with some material we had sent him, which had been instrumental in his replacing on the broadcast someone who had a bee in his bonnet about 'Germany's needs' being exaggerated. He said Robin Whitworth, another senior FAU member, was broadcasting next Friday at 7.30 on the Home Service on 'What next for Germany?'

Meeting of Section Representatives with Colonel Agnew, BRCS Deputy Commissioner

Of the most recently received Red Cross supplies, a goodly proportion are to be allotted to the German work. Medical and surgical parcels, bandages, swabs, and 26 cases of toys. But he wants to be able to say, in case of a row, that it is all for the infants and the sick. Tomorrow Agnew would be seeing Count Bernadotte, who had offered to help in German relief under BRCS aegis. The meeting suggested the following things be asked for: artificial limbs, bandages and dressings, children's footwear, milk foods, vitamin tablets, Swedish pre-fabs, cotton and mending materials, school equipment, children's games. Possibly glass.

Dr Audrey Ellis, dietician, was to tour Hamburg, Berlin and the Ruhr, to develop a scheme for supplementary child feeding for the British authorities. BRCS teams are expected to be needed in order to make the best use of concentrated rations being released by the War Office, to be given to special groups; these are thought to be one million 7 lb Arctic packs and some Pacific packs. Head of Food and Agriculture Branch, Allied Control Commission, thought there was a danger of the Cabinet not allowing enough wheat to Germany, and shops running out of bread for days at a time.

Altogether the impression gained was of a variety of important people trying to do their utmost to get Germany fed and generally helped, and that supplies—from International Red X, Swedish Red X, and FAU—would grow. Most encouraging.

Dassau section gave a short report on Operation Eagle— 3000 per day passed through, now over 100,000 had gone, and there were no more who wanted to go.

Berlin section said Operation Stork finished a fortnight ago, after evacuating 25,000. Report of reception at Oldenburg was encouraging. Similar operation from French sector to French zone was planned. Supplies from the International Red Cross would be coming through. A team for refugee camps in Berlin was badly needed. Mil Gov were determined to see these people comfortable, but needed someone trustworthy within the camps. Nutritional survey of school children, to compare Berlin's need for COBSRA supplies with those of others, was starting tomorrow.

FOUR

Early Work in Dortmund

4 December 1945 to 31 January 1946

Section members' work. Christmas occasions. The
Swiss and the Swedes. Maltavena, a new baby food from
the Union Brewery. German welfare organisations.
Problems with our transport fleet.

4 DECEMBER Tuesday. Brenda and I had a good run down, along the autobahn, eating lunch while driving, and arrived at the Dortmund Town Major's at 2.00 p.m., the appointed time. There we met Graham Wood, our Liaison Officer in the Ruhr, and went with him to look over two houses, which will be ours tomorrow afternoon. Meanwhile we are practically the guests of the Assistant Town Major, Captain Murphy, at his residence. Ken and Marjorie King had been to Hanover to pick up Miss Torre Torr, BRCS Liaison Officer for the German work in Westphalia, and arrived about 7.00. [*It seems clear that Torr was transferring from Hanover Province to Westphalia, and Wood withdrawing to concentrate on North Rhine Province.*]

Dortmund is very bad—estimate 70 per cent destroyed [*Plate 19*]. Our arrival seems to have been awaited with great expectations; I hope we shall meet them. They are waiting till we arrive, for example, before winding up the present German Red Cross as being Nazi and/or inefficient, so that we can nurse the future one into being.

5 DECEMBER   Wednesday. Miss Torr (now Penelope) and I saw Fl-Lt. Coombs, Mil Gov Public Health Officer. He is a doctor with experience of public health administration in England and in the five weeks before we came had done an extremely good job in surveying the Dortmund situation and presenting reports with recommendations in no uncertain terms, some of which have had their effect already. These reports, which he lent us, put us very well 'in the picture' straight away. He has met the FAU before and is ready to give us anything we can tackle and is indeed keen to prevent us wasting time on smaller matters; he had put in one of his reports that our 'presence is urgently required'. This attitude is excellent since we derive our status and much of our instructions from him though he leaves us a pretty free hand and says 'so long as you come and see me when you think you ought, that's good enough'.

We moved into our new house or rather houses in the afternoon. They are two adjacent semi-detached houses and a door between them has now been made. Although Plettenbergstrasse is in the 'Gartenstadt', the best remaining residential district of Dortmund, much plaster is down, one wall is very shaky, and the pointing is shaken off the tiles; also several windows are out. This is being put right. We had to turn the inhabitants out, and they moved to other places, either with friends or found for them by the Wohnungsamt, or Housing Office [cf. Bailey 1994: 236–7]. This required some strength of will, and conviction of our usefulness here. However, we are living, at a pinch, fourteen people in what held eight—because we live communally—which is not to be said of most military billets. We were useful to the people in moving some of their furniture, and giving them more time to gather things together than is usually given; we also wrote a chit to help them through the queue at the Housing Office and for this all were grateful.

There is a piano and we have started carol part singing for Christmas under Chris Smith's tuition. We have got a good cook and her daughter helps in the kitchen and house work.

The next day Penelope moved to live with Mil Gov since there would not be room for her when the section came; and the section arrived in the evening. It was good to join up again, even though the separation had only been for four days: to hear the news of the last few days at Einbeck, and of the adventures of the journey.

7 DECEMBER Friday. We settled in, unloading vehicles and so forth (there is good cellar accommodation for all our stores). I took Tony to 55 Anti-Tank Regiment and got the questions of garage accommodation, petrol supplies and so on all tied up. In the afternoon I took Chris to Mil Gov to see the major in charge of education. He was just going off for six weeks to England on leave and a course, and was sorry to leave his job, which he enjoyed; but he assured Chris of all co-operation from his (German) secretary (who was remaining in sole charge during the next six weeks!) and put us on to the German in charge of education in Dortmund. Then we saw the Stadtrat about office accommodation, preferably in the Stadthaus or Town Hall; this question has now been shelved for lack of something suitable (the middle of the city is so badly destroyed that even the most vital organisations exist in the most shaky buildings). However, we may have an office with the German Red Cross (DRK) in a shelter which we are to use as a reception centre for refugees.

In the evening Brenda and I went to see the leader of the DRK at his house; we talked over his organisation's work and the refugee situation, and then went on to see some friends of his, also members of the Red Cross. There we talked over their plans for Christmas for various needy sections of the community, and the general structure of the DRK as it had been. All very pleasant but they are all innocently Nazi in outlook. This is combined with good humanitarianism—typical nationalistic WVS-ism.[1]

9 DECEMBER Sunday. After an early lunch, most of us went off in search of some pleasant country. Altena was our destination, being among the range of wooded hills to the south of the Ruhr. It was a perfect day—cold and crisp, the atmosphere intensely clear and crystalline, the sky cloudless, a delicate frosty shade of blue, fading away into very pale blue at the horizon. People were full of beans, and our walk, up and over a steep wooded hill with some bare fields at the top, was merry and energetic. We took a football up, and played with it at the top; then split up into several parties to try several ways back to the ambulance. At the end we ate apple tart and then drove back as night fell. 'Just what the doctor ordered', we all felt. There was a thin layer of snow on the ground, hardly thick enough to cover it where rough; the district is in handy distance for skiing when that weather comes.

10 DECEMBER   Monday. The question of a store for our Red Cross supplies was settled and now John Haines is sorting our stuff and preparing to receive a further six tons in two days time. I saw Coombs with Ken and Marjorie in the morning—they had been poking around in Public Health and had several points to raise. This is something he has very well taped and we will need a good deal of solid spade work in the field before we can make much valuable contribution in an advisory capacity; as regards refugees, however, he is willing to accept practically all our recommendations.

11 AND 12 DECEMBER   Tuesday and Wednesday. Our social contacts with the army are growing. A troop captain turned up and whisked Brenda and me away to the officers' club, which is just round the corner. He came to supper on Tuesday and we went to his mess on Wednesday. This morning five of us had noonday drinks with the Lieutenant Colonel of the West Riding Regiment in his officers' mess. There are some good chaps in both messes, and we hope to return the hospitality some time. Each mess was in a palatial house, and the dinner was pheasant, with wine, followed later by champagne. I was closely cross-examined about our work, which seems to have great interest to officers here. They said they didn't generally ever have any serious discussion among themselves until after midnight!

13 DECEMBER Thursday. In the evening:

Section get together, 13 December 1945, for people to talk about their work

KEN described the plans for scabies clinics and dusting teams. The idea had been Coombs', but our function was to get it moving, and this was being done. We would also have to see whether enough clients could be organised together to make use of the power-duster worthwhile. Germans would drive the vehicles and give the treatment, but instruction would have to be given to them initially in the use of the English equipment.

There was useful work to be done in investigating whether and why milk turned sour before consumption, and in getting faults righted, which no-one else seemed able to do. The Mil Gov Food and Agriculture officer had asked us to visit two farms outside his area whence it might be possible to get an extra 15,000 litres per day for Dortmund; his own hands were tied. (Present supply is 40,000.) He also wanted information about the condition of school children, and refugees, to prepare a case for giving them extra meals. This we can easily give him.

Finally, we were to survey hospital needs for building materials and labour which might increase bed-space and facilities, and present the results to Coombs.

MARJORIE added a description of hospitals and clinics visited, and mentioned the great need of glucose for undernourished unwanted orphan babies received at one place. The schools health officer was keen to do a heights and weights survey to show how much children were out-growing their strength, and we will contact Berlin for information about procedure. Another need we might help to get fulfilled is for citric acid to put in milk as a rickets prophylactic. Various signs such as infantile mortality rate, and increase of weight in children when in hospital, showed how serious the position was.

CHRIS gave an account of schools visited and the general position. Major Wilson had been correcting text books and since he was now away in England we could speed up their badly needed publication by carrying on the work. We could do something about badly needed school supplies, and possibly on the Information and Youth Movement sides.

DIANA on Miners said their food, soap and coal position was satisfactory, although the families certainly got some of the extra rations intended for the men. Men from the Wehrmacht whose homes were in the Russian zone would be housed in camps, in which there might be work on the lines of DP camps, though the collieries would probably be looking after them fairly well. A second lot of clothes for these men was a crying need, and better transport facilities would increase production.

BERNARD spoke about the work of the Wohlfahrtsamt (municipal Social Services Department) and their need for some reserve of transport and supplies, which we might supply, to meet the most crying needs. We might encourage them to arrange communal cooking in some areas to save food and fuel. A survey of refugees is about to be carried out by DRK at our instigation, and will give us an exact idea of the nature of the influx.

BRENDA said that we would have a lot to do with the building up of the new DRK when the new organiser was appointed. At the moment work was developing in improving the refugee hostels; instituting Warmehallen (warm places) for the local population or the mostly needy strata of it, and a new Übernachtungstelle (overnight shelter) for incoming refugees, in the air-raid shelters; and arranging an initial large and subsequent regular small evacuations.

14 DECEMBER   Friday. The section seems to be very happy getting its teeth into the new work. We are meeting excellent co-operation from both sides of the fence we straddle. At the moment any actual jobs we decide to do or which are handed to us by Mil Gov or BRCS, have the important secondary value of giving us a clearer picture of the situation; after barely a week our knowledge and contacts are extraordinarily large.

15 DECEMBER   Saturday. A meeting in the Stadthaus, about the distribution, cooking, etc., of milk to school children, now to be available at the rate of ⅛ litre per head per day. The meeting was attended by representatives of the Catholic, Protestant and Socialist welfare organisations, of the welfare, food, and education departments of the municipality, the town Medical Officer for children, and others. Transport, fuel, utensils, finance, had all to be considered. The discussion of the difficulties involved was most interesting; several good ideas were remembered from the Quäkerspeisung (Quaker feeding) of the early 1920s. The meeting later discussed broader issues. I do hope we shall have enough time to do the 'information' side of this work well: we are in as unique a position in Dortmund, as we were in Einbeck, for having our 'ear to the ground'.

In the afternoon those of us who will be affected by the FAU's decision to wind itself up on 30 June 1946 went to a conference at Essen to discuss the position, and in particular the question of a 'successor body'.

[*A week is here missing from the account in the letters, but something can be reconstructed from other documents.*]

On *20 DECEMBER*, Thursday, a visit to some of the living accommodation in central Dortmund. Less than 30 per cent of pre-war Dortmund accommodates two-thirds the pre-war population, as well as large numbers of DPs and Allied troops. Nearly every visitor to the ruined cities of Germany, seeing the population going about its business among apparently uninhabitable ruins, asks: 'Where on earth do they live?' Today we saw [*Plate 19*].

Our first visit was to what had been a fine large house. It was now a mere shell, but the cellars were strong enough to hold the bricks and rubble piled above them, and in four cellars lived sixteen people, of whom ten were children. None had a window more than nine inches high, and in some cases these were boarded up, or covered with a blanket, and the only light came from a feeble electric bulb projecting from a holder in the wall. A woman was slicing swedes (the only food we saw all morning) into a pot; the stove in the corner (not a range) was said to take two hours to boil anything. They burned sticks gathered from old window frames and furniture in bombed houses, but said they were very hard to find. None of the children went to school, for lack of footwear.

These families had been evacuated to Czechoslovakia, whence they had been turned out last May. They had walked back to Dortmund in nine weeks, carrying everything on their backs. The man had an amputated arm. He showed us with pride where he had reinstated the lavatory on the ground floor above. 'It flushed and everything.' Then the roof had fallen in and it was all in vain. I looked up and saw the high narrow wall, up four storeys, with four cisterns still clinging to it, and the sky beyond. Now he 'had to take everything away by hand'. Another piece of wall, separated off by a gaping crack going down two storeys, a matter of a ton or two of bricks, was supported on only six bricks. It seemed as if the first frost or the first wind would bring it crashing down on these cellars and their inhabitants.

Our second visit was in a completely desolate area behind the railway station. Behind what had been a row of terrace houses but was now a pile of masonry was a wash-house about seven feet by eight, but with a dry roof. An old couple had moved in here from their cellar when the rain came through. He had an amputated leg but hoped to be re-employed on the railway when he got an artificial one (I think he will wait a long time). Again, swedes and a stove. Again, apparently home-made bedsteads and the most amazing spirit—'it can't be worse, it must get better', they seem to say.

On *21 DECEMBER*, Friday, we held the first meeting of the Working Committee of Voluntary Organisations in Dortmund, the Welfare Committee for short [*Plate 20*]. This had been established under a Zone Policy Instruction of 22 November, and brought together the senior representatives of the four main voluntary bodies, plus a representative of the municipal welfare department. These included Pastor Heinz Schmidt from the Innere Mission (Protestant), Stadvikar Luig from the Caritas

Verband (Catholic), Fräulein Minna Sattler from the Arbeiter-wohlfahrt (SPD), and Stadtrat Gottlieb Levermann from the Wohlfahrtsamt (municipal). There was also a representative from the German Red Cross (DRK), but from the following meeting (11 January) the DRK was represented by Herr Ullrich. A circular from Mil Gov had explained that the Nazi welfare organisations had been suppressed, that the Protestant and Catholic organisations had more or less resisted the influence of Nazism, and that the Arbeiterwohlfahrt had been suppressed in 1933 and revived since the war. The DRK (German Red Cross) had become a para-military organisation under the Nazis, and de-nazification now had 'so far retarded its activities'.

The meeting was held in our house, I took the chair, and Brenda Bailey and Chris Smith also attended. It was first 'ascertained that all German members had completed the Frage-bogen' [*the detailed questionnaire which was the principal initial instrument in denazification*]. The main business was to decide the ultimate recipients and the distributing agencies of supplies we held of bedding, clothing, crockery, food, soap, and medical items. This was done amicably and expeditiously, the exercise laying the foundations for mutual trust and practical cooperation.

[*Extracts from letters resume.*]

22 DECEMBER   Saturday. The school ceremony was most touch-ing. The headmaster (member of a pacifist movement during the Weimar Republic) gave a talk on the meaning of Christmas, and used it to introduce all sorts of songs, recitations, and tableaux around the Christmas tree which stood at the top of the hall, with the stable of Bethlehem, the shepherds, and so on, mod-elled beneath it. Some of the recitations were very well done. The community singing—'Stille Nacht', 'O du Fröhliche'—was also impressive. The Mil Gov Education Officer, a major, gave a rather stodgy speech, well responded to by the headmaster. Then we sang one or two of the carols we had been practising.

At the youth gathering, there were songs again, and speeches and recitations. Halfway through, in came John Tovey and

Diana, just back from Brussels after fetching a Mobile Kitchen which has been turned over to us. This meant that our second two carols sounded much better than our first, when we had only had one alto and one bass. At the end we sang the club's own song, standing round rather as for 'Auld Lang Syne'.

23 DECEMBER   Sunday. A boyhood friend of mine arrived at lunchtime. He is in the Mil Gov Detachment for the Province. He says that Mil Gov officers at that level are mostly men with staff experience with a Corps or in London, and are much more anti-German than the fighting troops or than Mil Gov officers in mere Kreis detachments.

In the evening a brief visit to a newly arrived Salvation Army team. They are very nice, but call each other by their rank. A female Major is in charge, and Captains float around and are addressed as such. [*However, their dedicated professionalism on the job at the grassroots put us to shame.*]

24 DECEMBER   Monday. I took a load of toys to a hospital for infectious diseases. All the children, mostly with diphtheria, were gathered in the large central hall, some in their cots or on trolleys, others dandled on nurses' knees. In a gallery above were some other children from outside. The place was wonderfully decorated, with Christmas trees, lights, and so on, and the show that was put on for them included songs, recitations, a few scenes from the story of Hansel and Gretel, a roller-skating champion, a comedian, a sword-swallower, a fire-eater, and Father Christmas—being one of the Other Ranks of Mil Gov, who did the job very well. Mil Gov officers were there in force, and I acted as a sort of liaison between Coombs and the staff. The eats were supplied from Red Cross parcels which Coombs had obtained from mysterious sources, supplemented by some of the Mil Gov people's chocolate rations. Other FAU people arrived later.

In the evening we sang a few carols at units in the neighbourhood. First at the Town Major, then at the Military Police, then at the 69th Regimental HQ Officers' Mess. There was no reply there, but we found them all at the next port of call, the Officers' Club. We sang outside and then had to sing inside, and then were sat down to eat and drink amid applause. I got involved in a long argument with the Brigade Quartermaster, a slightly tipsy Major who wanted us to sing more carols and in the attempt to persuade me got round to the expression of deeply Tory sentiments and the narration of his life history.

25 DECEMBER Christmas Day. Chris and I slipped away as soon as we had finished breakfast and got into the cellar of the ruined church a quarter-mile away, just as the service was beginning. The crypt made quite a good church, although of course not large enough, and it was packed. The sermon, by a youngish pastor, was good, and at the close of the service the congregation sang the Christmas song 'O du Fröhliche'.

[*The Schauffelberger family lived at Unna, some miles to the east. When stationed with the Free French in Alsace a year before, I had met some relatives, hence the invitation for lunch today.*] The meal was excellent. Being Swiss they have the privilege of a car; and having a well established dye factory and laundry, they have many country connections (by the time you are in Unna you are almost out of the Ruhr). Being Plymouth Brethren, Mr S. read an extract from the New Testament after the meal. Evidently life in Switzerland is getting back to normal, with more and more things unrationed, and visitors (Poles, French, Americans) bringing money into the country. He had found it most depressing to come back to Germany from Switzerland. Mr Mertz [*see p. 143*] was enjoying his job, of getting the Mainz schools going again, but the French occupation was getting more and more severe and that he did not like.

Back to the Section for the evening. Chris carved the goose, candles on the table provided the lighting, the cook found by her plate a bunch of grapes brought for her from Brussels by Diana, Bernard poured out the wine, Brenda brought in a flaming pudding. Afterwards singing, home-made light verse, and much laughter.

26 DECEMBER   Wednesday. Brenda and the Kings went out to invite children to a party in the afternoon. They invited ten from some of the families we had seen living in cellars, and eight from the worst of the refugee hostels. The party began at 3.00 and lasted nearly three hours. The children started off by playing musical bumps, then had tea, then Alfredo 'the funny man' did some conjuring and made funny faces for them and made them do recitations themselves (at which they were very good); then with Chris at the piano we sang songs with them and Brenda read the tale of the Pied Piper of Hamelin. Finally, Bernard, a passable Father Christmas, gave them presents from the tree. It was a great success, except that the poor kids could not do justice to the tea that was there for them; however, they went away with lots of mince pies, a toy each (saved from the Coombs party) and much apparent satisfaction.

At the officers club in the evening we were at one of four or five large tables. Towards the end of the meal, one of the officers of the largest table (about 20), proposed a fraternal toast in the form: 'The Officers of the 90th City of London Field Regiment, Royal Artillery, will take wine to the officers of the umpteenth Independent Searchlight Battery', etc. This started a ball rolling and sooner or later a table drank wine to us. I had to rise and reply. By that time our glasses were low. I said: 'Members of the 4th Friends Ambulance Unit will take ... dregs...' A gale of laughter let me go no further.

27 DECEMBER   Thursday. John Tovey and Valerie are beginning the systematic delousing of the refugee hostels, with a team of Germans whom they instruct and supervise. Our power duster (for delousing) is a small petrol machine with ten compressed air jets to blow the powder.[2]

Over the weekend preceding Christmas, I was depressed about the work; feeling that one is only a drop in a big bucket, and that all one can do must seem from certain angles quite ineffective. This is only a phase, but all relief workers must sometimes feel, as Brenda said: 'It's wrong to try and do relief work; one would be far more useful back in London influencing public opinion.'

A Swiss team is coming here which will feed 1000 × 1000 × 1000 calorie-children-days and bring baby food and clothing too. They want to be attached to a German organisation and we have selected the Arbeiterwohlfahrt for this, but we will have to do a lot of preparation before they arrive and help them a lot when they do.

Two visiting VIPs. The BRCS Commissioner for NW Europe, a General Lindsay, who came down with Colonel Agnew, Deputy Commissioner for Germany, reading my reports on the way. I showed them round the railway station, an air-raid shelter, and cellar dwellings. Also Dr Audrey Ellis [*see p. 100*] who is a charming person with whom we have had a most interesting time.

[*There appears to be a gap in the letters extant, covering most of January. Again, other documents can be drawn on.*]

On the evening of Friday, *28 DECEMBER*, a fierce gale came up and showed how flimsy the tottering fabric of the city was— from the dislodging of an armful of roof slates to the collapse of a building with thirty shoppers inside, or the blocking of main roads by tremendous heaps of masonry. By the time the wind had died, an hour or so before midnight, about 15 deaths had been reported, and it was not known how many people were buried.

I visited the Fire Brigade at 11.30 p.m. and they were coping, though all ambulances were still in use. The roads were sprinkled with falls of brick and stone, sometimes forming a barrier right across, sometimes lightly scattered so that your vehicle crunched and jerked as you drove over. Great sheets of rusty iron, so frequent a sight on the house-tops, lay limply folded and bellowed like thunder as the truck wheels crumpled them. A bridge over one of the principal streets now lay across the tarmac, a mass of twisted ironwork and broken bricks.

The next morning the main falls provided a hunting ground

for those gleaners who get their only firewood by poking around among these dangerous ruins. Wood is needed because despite a monthly ration of 2 cwt coal being 'available' to each householder, it lies at the pithead and is a waste product called 'schlamm', a slimy muck which emits only 40 per cent of the heat of hard coal, and has to be burnt along with something more combustible. Though Dortmund is a town built on coal, householders in tree-lined streets have sometimes had trees allocated to them for felling and burning.

I wrote on *29 DECEMBER* to Mil Gov reporting arrangements for the Section's ambulances to be on ten-minute call at night, and our other load-carrying vehicles being available too, and suggesting some precautionary steps, partly based on FAU experience with emergency accommodation ('Rest Centres') in the London blitz.

Our Boxing Day party had been for especially needy children, so on *NEW YEAR'S DAY* we took 16 children from Plettenberg-strasse to the country. They played football till lunch had been prepared in the mobile kitchen, and then sat down in a long straight line to eat it [*Plate 21*].

On Friday, *4 JANUARY* I stood in for Penelope Torre Torr, our BRCS Liaison Officer, at a meeting in Düsseldorf called by a Colonel Donnelly, the PHO for North Rhine Province. It was attended by two other Mil Gov officers, Audrey Ellis for COBSRA, and representatives of five FAU and two Salvation Army teams working in that Province, together with their LO. Donnelly's idea had been to let the teams ferret around for a few weeks on the ground before calling such a meeting, and then make it regular, perhaps fortnightly. It was useful to exchange experience, and useful also to hear Donnelly's ideas about what we might and might not do, but at under two and a half hours was too short for fruitful discussion.

On Saturday, *5 JANUARY* I wrote to Penelope with suggestions for improving the use of transport. Army regulations prevent military petrol being used in a vehicle driven by a German, prevent a German driving any army or requisitioned vehicle, and prevent a German-driven vehicle being used for 'military purposes' (i.e. for British personnel). Relief sections possess load-carrying vehicles used largely for getting individual members around, but no staff cars, whilst the Germans have cars but need trucks. Penelope forwarded this to BRCS HQ to take up with the Control Commission, but the rationalisation implied stands little chance.

The following week we had a visit from Audrey Ellis and discussions took place with Dr. Spengemann and Arnsberg Mil Gov about children's health and nutrition. Much of this turned on the specific needs and relative priorities of different age groups. The greatest need for more milk was for babies under six months whose mothers became prematurely unable to feed them—which they thought might be met by mothers receiving babies' rations from the fourth month of pregnancy. Spengemann had found that two-thirds of the babies at a mothers' advice clinic had signs of incipient rickets, but Ellis thought a cod liver oil distribution about to begin would be effective against it. The high infant mortality rate was largely due to chest troubles—there was no resistance, so bronchitis easily became pneumonia.

As to older children, Spengemann felt the three- to five-year-olds needed help most, since damage done then is hard to repair. Of six-year-olds entering school, 25 per cent were testing TB-positive. Ellis was concerned about the ten- and eleven-year-olds who were just over age for cod liver oil and school feeding and who were losing weight, but it was agreed that final decisions should depend on weight and height surveys.

Other public health issues concerned adults, and on Tuesday, *8 JANUARY* I reported to Coombs on the possible public use of school showerbaths. The army was interested, since although they had VD and lice among the troops under control, scabies was a problem. Sixteen schools had showers, but only seven of these could easily be put in order, none of which was in the town centre. If fuel were available for this, other difficulties could be overcome.

The second meeting of the Welfare Committee took place on Friday, *11 JANUARY*. There was a new DRK representative, Dr. Spengemann was co-opted [*Plate 22*], and Brenda and Diana, besides myself, attended from the Section. In line with Spengemann's concern for two- to six-year-olds, kindergartens were the main agenda item. It was noted that kindergartens allowed medical control and supplementary feeding under adequate safeguards, but only one-fifth of Dortmund's 25,000 children aged between two and six at present attend. The meeting addressed aspects of this problem, including shortages of accommodation and furniture, and the fact that some children were kept away for lack of clothing and footwear.

The coordination of the German voluntary societies was discussed on Saturday *12 JANUARY* at a meeting of teams in the NW Arnsberg Public Health area, attended by Coombs and Hobbs for Mil Gov, Penelope as LO, and the Leaders of the Salvation Army teams in Herne and Hagen, and of the FAU teams in Dortmund and Bochum. A meeting was fixed for 26 January of all leaders of voluntary societies in the area, and 4 FAU were asked to lay the groundwork for this in Unna and Lünen as well as in Dortmund.

My fortnightly report dated Tuesday, *15 JANUARY* welcomed Audrey Ellis's visit and reported on work arising. By now we had visited no less than 18 British subjects, who get Red Cross parcels. Arising out of the storm (and my memo of 29 December) we are involved in contingency planning for 'storm groups' to turn out automatically at strategic points.

The mobile kitchen we fetched from Brussels had begun taking a nutritive drink to 15,000 schoolchildren a day. The Dortmund Schools Department contracted with a German Grossküche or large-scale kitchen to undertake the cooking and distribution, and we have contracted with this firm for them to use the vehicle. This was exceptional (see pp. 114–15), and I drew up strict conditions. All the same I felt the proprietor might have bitten off more than he could chew. (Penelope later wrote to Vlotho about the vehicle's legal position. 'It is in theory a WD (War Department) vehicle, which can be driven by a German, by personal permission of Col. Agnew'.)

On Wednesday, *16 JANUARY* I had a talk with several officials in the Stadthaus, including the Oberbürgermeister, Dr Ostrop (see p. 148 n.8) about the 'storm groups', and the influx of refugees from the East. He was keen to limit Dortmund's population in present conditions, and the previous summer had issued an appeal to Dortmund evacuees to stay where they were and not to come back so long as the shortage of accommodation was so severe (Stadtarchiv Dortmund 1985: 43). He thought that where refugees had 'Dortmund' written on their cards as destination as they passed through official transit camps, surely they could be held there until it was certain they could be accommodated.

On Thursday, *17 JANUARY* Audrey Ellis wrote to Dr Spengemann about Maltavena, a malted wheat flour and soya food for infants, to be produced experimentally as a milk substitute at the Union Brewery at Dortmund. The idea was to break down the starch in wheat, so as to make it digestible by babies, using a process of fermentation similar to that for brewing beer. It had been tried on babies at Great Ormond St. and the London Hospital, with satisfactory results. It could be used as the sole source of nourishment over short periods, otherwise as a supplement. She sought his advice in selecting children to whom it could be given, and in the supervision of large-scale production.

On Wednesday, *23 JANUARY* I met with Penelope on a number of points. All food stores must be guarded. The Swiss LO, a Dr Lötscher, will be around some time to see to preliminary arrangements. They would like to be attached to us for all their worries, such as rations.

[From 24 January, letters home take up the story again.]

24 JANUARY   Thursday. A meeting at the Union Brewery on
the Maltavena preparation. The experiments being carried out
here, largely under our direction, should have results of importance for Germany and all other stricken parts of Europe next
winter. It has been a hard job explaining (on behalf of the
Control Commission) to the local children's doctor that it is
more important that babies should be weaned on it, to see the
results, than that some of the two to six years age group should
benefit from it as an addition to their diet. He is very concerned
about the 2–6s, but now agrees with us about the use of
Maltavena, especially since the 2-6s will get 350 calories per
day from the Swedes.

In the evening two guests came to supper. One was an interpreter of the German transport company working with the 69th
Field Regiment. He had been in Greece during the German
occupation. He brought out an English sovereign, and said that
the English put sovereigns in the pockets of the uniforms they
dropped by parachute for partisans, and that these became the
only reliable currency, used alike by Greeks and Germans. I
have never heard this before and I should like it authenticated.
But there was the sovereign, and absolutely unworn.

The other guest was the lady pastor who used to be in Alsace.
She had been trying, in the French zone, to get permission to
go to Alsace to look after people who were interned there now,
in very bad conditions At one of her interviews at Baden-Baden,
a Frenchman had said: 'Those who wrong, throw the fact away
as down to the wind; those who are wronged, engrave it as on
stone.'

25 JANUARY   Friday. We had a meeting yesterday morning,
with the usual members of the Welfare Committee, plus, at my
invitation, the Swedish LO and the head of the Ernährungsamt
(Food Office). The Swede was very pleased with the meeting
and its results. The Swedes can at the moment only feed 15,000
of the 25,000 two- to six-year-olds in Dortmund Stadt Kreis.

But the Kreis covers a large area, some of which is country and untouched, and I suggested they choose the areas in which the children were worst off. We had for the meeting the necessary information—i.e. the boundaries of the various subdivisions by which ration cards are given out, and the numbers of children in each of them. So the Germans, with their expert local knowledge, selected the most hard-hit areas, and the Swede was pleased that his food would go where the need was greatest.

Seventy tons of Pacific packs, some of many released by the War Office for relief work, are coming our way, and we are to be responsible for the breaking-down and distribution of them. This will be a big job, and Tony is going into it with his usual carefulness and thoroughness. We are trying to get hold of a German mechanic to relieve him of the job of looking after our vehicles.

We had a burglary one night, when two of our bicycles and a hunk of meat and some sausages were stolen from the cellar. The Major at Public Safety set the Kriminalpolizei on the job but I don't suppose we shall ever hear anything more about it.

A visit from another old school friend, a German refugee, now an interpreter corporal at the Province Food Office at Unna. He came over with a Control Commission official who controls dairy products in the Zone. They had just been to a factory where they are making butter out of coal. They said it was rather tasteless, but seemed all right.

The Section was briefly down to four but we are now up to nine and will be twelve again at the end of next week when others return from leave. Then we shall continue full strength till March.

The Colonel in charge of the Mil Gov Detachment here, came to supper. This was a result of the visit of the MPs. He is very good company, but has fixed ideas. He seemed rather shocked that we knew more about some things in Dortmund than he did himself. We mentioned Maltavena, he said of course nothing had yet been done, a special investigation commission was awaited. We told him that the Union Brewery was already producing on an experimental scale, that the Control

Commission had been to see us about it the previous week and again that afternoon, and that the Provincial Food Office at Unna was supervising the experiments. He concluded that the investigation commission had come, in bits and pieces, but hadn't called on him.

On another occasion I had been impressed when a Colonel was reeling off to a visiting Brigadier the statistics about Jews and ex-concentration camp victims in Dortmund. I later found that he had asked Penelope what the Brigadier was interested in, and she had secured these figures for him from Brenda's files in 4 FAU.

26 JANUARY Saturday. The German Red Cross is weak, according to my theory, (a) because it depends so largely on voluntary part-time helpers; (b) because very rarely do welfare organisations have 'push', if they depend entirely on humanitarianism for their motive power. A Protestant, Catholic, Socialist, or pacifist relief or welfare organisation gets its kick from its particular spiritual background and the application of that to reality. The DRK, like the WVS in England, got its kick from the sort of shallow patriotism that flourishes in wartime, 'helping our brave boys', and when the Nazi structure, to which it was so bound, collapsed, it was left with an insufficient *raison d'être*, in contrast to the religious bodies. So the best way for us to 'reactivate' the DRK would be to give it, not organisational efficiency in itself, but the sense of purpose out of which enthusiasm and efficiency would emerge. This cannot be done directly by us, but only by explaining the matter to a German, who could apply this theory (if correct) to the situation as a German sees it.

The cutting you sent about 'An Administrative Staff College' was most interesting and I shall hang on to it. [*This refers to an article in* The Times *on 7 November 1945. The proposal was later realised at Henley, where I was a course member in 1951.*]

We have had a night of high winds. Demolitions are now taking place on a large scale, with a gigantic grab, and dynamite has been applied for.

27 JANUARY   Sunday. Five of us went for a picnic to a place near Altena, in the Sauerland. After having our meal in the shelter of a rock we went for a lively walk over upland country, very high, and finished by having (ersatz) coffee and waffles at the home of the cousins of Hanna Schauffelberger's brother-in-law, the Bernings, who are what one would call gentleman farmers there. A grand change.

Just received *Shall Our Children Live or Die?* (Gollancz 1945). I understand it is to be printed in German and Brenda's father will sell it.

28 JANUARY   Monday. A conference in Mil Gov between the Food and Education Departments of the City, the Food and Education officers of Mil Gov, and Penelope, Marjorie and me. For all children attending school between 6 and 14, there is to be a 300 calorie soup meal. This is excellent, but the cooking and transport arrangements are very difficult. We are to keep an eye on them for Mil Gov.

29 JANUARY   Tuesday. To Unna for a meeting in Mil Gov with the heads of the voluntary societies, plus the Landrat, the chairman of their Welfare Committee, and the head of the office for former concentration camp victims. It was interesting to compare the situations in the two towns, Unna and Dortmund, but how far an area conference, or inter-Kreis co-operation, can be furthered, is still doubtful. I went on to the Province food office to discuss Maltavena with the Major in charge of Beers, Wines and Spirits.

31 JANUARY   Thursday. A conference of all headmasters to make arrangements for the new school feeding scheme. In the afternoon, to Iserlohn with Diana. We saw the BRCS LO at Corps. She told us about short leave facilities in the area. She is a horsy Girl Guide of great age, and not so competent as Penelope, but a model of efficiency compared with the UNRRA District Welfare Officer, to whom she introduced us, and with whom we tried to talk about ex concentration camp victims.

This UNRRA woman seemed to be sitting in a daze without the capacity to grasp the simplest situation, and excusing herself for being interrupted, 'but we are fighting against time here, you know'. We told her that UNRRA had agreed to supply food and POL (petrol, oil and lubricants) for a rest home for ex concentration camp victims in Bad Pyrmont, and would it be possible here; and that 'Joint' was distributing food for Jews and in view of this would it be possible to get the same for the others. She had never heard of either and seemed hardly inclined to investigate either, since 'channels are so tedious'. But she was grand at introducing red herrings.

Then we saw a Major at Corps 'Q' Branch, who was efficient and charming and promised to do his best to get us two staff cars. This was the real object of the visit. I have high hopes of success. He even told us to ring him up if we got depressed and thought the thing had been pigeon-holed. Diana had come at the unanimous suggestion of the Section, to lay on charm if necessary; it wasn't needed, though no doubt her presence helped.

After all that we had tea and rich cakes in the Lagoon Club for Other Ranks, overlooking a beautiful lake. A short knock-up on the pingpong table and home.

We need the staff cars because our transport is in a bad way. The Fordson has sprung a main bearing. Some weeks ago John Tovey, who is usually conscientious to excess, allowed an ambulance just out of REME (Royal Electrical and Mechanical Engineers) to run without water and it became red-hot. Then two days ago Tony Trew, the most careful driver you can imagine, skidded the Dodge into a wall and bent the chassis. The ambulance we got recently from Brussels has a broken main spring, so we are reduced to one which needs a top overhaul so badly that you can only get into top gear at about 35 mph.

So yesterday Tony and I put one more vehicle on the road by changing springs between the new ambulance and the one with the cracked cylinder block. Tomorrow he is changing the heads of that one with the one needing top overhaul, which will stop it coming off the road. The other three will take months to repair, since there is a long queue for Brigade work-shops; but these two jobs will save the situation, and if we get the staff cars it will return to normal. Tony wants to give some-one a pleasant surprise with the new head, and is pretending to go to Hamm for spare parts while really carrying out 'operation transcapitation' in the 55th Anti-Tank garage just a mile away.

In the event, Tony went on working far into the evening, and Diana and I went out to haul him in, found him deter-mined, so brought a Tilley lamp, hot coffee and YMCA slab cake, and helped. The next morning at breakfast Ken was very peevish at being 'fobbed off' with the ambulance that struggled, of which he thought he'd had enough, but got a tremendous surprise when it started straight away and ran perfectly.

FIVE

Acting Liaison Officer for Westphalia

1–18 February 1946

*Collaboration with Mil Gov. Visiting other
Ruhr sections. An FRS Conference.*

1 FEBRUARY Friday. Penelope rang me up and asked me to
take over her job for a fortnight, while she went to Paris on
convalescent leave. She has been quite off colour for the past
week, not able to do a thing. So now for two weeks I am British
Red Cross Liaison Officer for German Welfare Work in Westphalia, with six teams already at work, two more to settle in
during the next week (at Hamm and Recklinghausen) and three
more in the offing. Of the six, three are FAU,[1] one Salvation
Army, one Save the Children Fund, and one British Red Cross
itself. I have to co-ordinate and control them and be a link
between them, the Provincial Administration at Münster, and
whatever else goes on at higher levels.

Penelope was always based on Dortmund, which means I still
live with the Section and can keep an eye on it, but Chris Smith
is taking over the day to day running, and Brenda will be going
to all German conferences connected only with Dortmund, which
I have covered hitherto. I have an office in Mil Gov here, and
a German secretary, who is quite competent and speaks English.
The first week will be quite full with meetings, and visits to
Münster and Vlotho, but in the second week I may get a chance

to get round some of the other sections in the field, and learn from and advise them. The Province is divided into three Regierungsbezirke or administrative districts, each of which has a Mil Gov detachment controlling it [*see pp. xiv–xv*], and I have also to keep in touch with the relevant officers in those detachments about the work the teams are doing.

The Swiss representative came to lunch, a Herr Lötscher, and we talked over the arrangements for his team and feeding scheme. I am to write him a letter giving full details of how we propose to use them. They will of course have to be closely coordinated with the Swedes. A pity the latter have been first on the ground; it would have been simpler if they could have started together. It is not quite certain how far the Swiss will mind being absorbed into the more comprehensive Swedish scheme, and so one will have to advance warily.

Lötscher was very nice, competent, and full of ideas. Very emphatic that there should be no discrimination—'even if the child is the son of the Gauleiter [*a Nazi official in charge of an area*], he remains a child to us'. The Swiss are sending in books and I am to receive a catalogue shortly. He also left with me plans for a 'village' for refugees, to be built with prefab hutments; so that they can settle and integrate themselves once more into a community. These plans are being translated and typed by 'my' secretary for the Public Health and Refugee officers at Münster.

In the afternoon I briefed Major Battersby, the Assistant Public Health Officer at Province, for the Monday meeting, and was introduced to the officers for German Welfare there, Captains LaBrosse and McHale. Battersby is a sound Scot: reliable, businesslike, and friendly. LaBrosse is an excitable French Canadian with whom it is hardly possible to negotiate logically. McHale is taking over from him and will be very good, I think. The Monday meeting is the one for this Province corresponding to the one for North Rhine at Düsseldorf which I attended, and arose out of my report and recommendations on that. Battersby introduced me to the Landeshauptmann, a man who comes second only to the Oberpräsident, and knows everything there is to know about welfare work in Westphalia. He will be a most valuable contact.

I walked into a discussion in LaBrosse's office between him, the two officers, and the Jewish representative at Province. LaBrosse was scorning an interpreter and trying to carry on in his own execrable and comic German, with great excitement. The Jewish representative was objecting to having to deal with the Welfare Department, since this carried the stigma of 'charity'. In connection with the Anglo-American Commission on Jews, a questionnaire has to be completed in very short time, with details of all Jews in the Province. The telegram said 'HQ realise this is a Herculean task'. Anyway, it had sent the Welfare Department into a flat spin.

One gets a new light on the Section in this new job. Penelope's last report: 'Alarm felt at first by 918 Detachment (our Mil Gov) at the number and variety of problems stirred up, has given way to appreciation of the way in which they are being handled'. This impression was evidently culled by her from 'comments in the Mess'. Then in came the Major who was Public Health Officer for Münster Regierungsbezirk. I introduced myself as having been leader of 4 FAU. 'Ah,' he said, 'a team with a very good reputation.' 'Among whom?' 'Among us all.' I enjoyed repeating this later to those who had deserved it, of course.

4 FEBRUARY   Monday. The meeting of all section leaders, with the Public Health and Welfare officers from Province. It went off quite well and it was decided it should be held monthly. Mike Rowntree, who had been with us on Sunday, stayed for the morning session. So did the two Guides, who are bringing a kitchen/canteen mobile team for work somewhere in the Ruhr, and we arranged that they would probably divide their attention between Hagen and Bochum. They will be much needed with all these new feeding schemes, and the shortage of stoves, containers, transport, etc. Major Battersby is an excellent man, sensible and decisive. We kept more or less to the agenda I had made [*including Public Health, Feeding, the Voluntary Societies,*

Refugees and Youth Work] but it was obvious that other teams had not covered so wide a range of activities as we. The best team (apart, of course, from 4 FAU) was Harold Thrift's 133 from Bochum, but 142 Salvation Army was not represented, and they are understood to be pretty go-ahead.

The officers from Province seemed pretty interested, at any rate Major Battersby made notes furiously the whole time and promised to take several matters up.

5 FEBRUARY Tuesday. To Münster to see the various officers at Province Mil Gov relevant to our work. Lunch with Major Battersby in his mess. He let me have a good dose of his views— he is a real Glaswegian man of the left, and doesn't think much of the 'military caste' who are running the Province—'They still think in mediaeval terms—they've none of them any idea of the meaning of the atomic bomb—they won't even get down and look at Dortmund'—and of the way Mil Gov is run—'I'm a Public Health civil servant, and we find out what the people want, and send it up to Whitehall, and there's a row if it doesn't get done: here the C-in-C has the idea there's going to be an epidemic, and has lots of equipment held in reserve which could perfectly well be used, when there are no signs of an epidemic at all.' And again, 'of course, I am very sympathetic to Friends' views, but you don't want to have any illusions about the Germans. All they're sorry for is that they lost the war. If they'd the chance they'd atomise London in a jiffy. *They're no whit better than our own people if they're as good!*'

Later, the officer for German Welfare (mostly the Voluntary Societies at Münster) repeated in practically the same form Battersby's complaint that the coal allocation was ridiculously low, that the Commission had the coal but wouldn't release it, that France's demands were ridiculous. One feels very much at home. On our suggestion, Welfare are going to apply to Property Control for a house in the country for ex-concentration camp victims.

The officer for Refugees told me his branch are asking for a BRCS team for each of the three Regierungsbezirke, to be mobile, and meet trainloads of refugees at the detraining points. The big stream is about to begin, and Westphalia's allocation is about 500,000, which is like bringing in a city slightly larger than Dortmund and spreading it over all the country areas. If only the people at Potsdam had known what they were doing...

Chris was also at Münster for a Youth Conference with some visitors from England, from the National Association of Boys' Clubs, and together we saw the education man, a Canadian Colonel.

6 FEBRUARY   Wednesday. To Hamm in Penelope's car, which is an extraordinary little thing, a two-stroke two-cylinder. The cylinders are semi-opposed—i.e. it is a 'V2'.

It is said that Hamm is built on very soft sandy soil which much diminished the effects of the bombing [*its extensive marshalling yards had been a frequent target for the RAF, as all British wartime radio listeners were well aware*].

It is good to have a secretary. Even so, what with one thing and another, I didn't arrive till noon. My purpose was to see the two-person advance party of a BRCS team coming to Hamm, to explain to Mil Gov their position, and to deal with any difficulties.

The CO of Mil Gov had been a little startled to get a team dumped on him rather suddenly, and didn't quite know what he would do with it. However, the second-in-command of the team, a most capable girl, had already set his mind at ease, and I talked some more on what other teams had been doing (mainly the celebrated No. 4, of course), and told the CO to whom civilian relief teams were responsible and what was their relationship to Mil Gov.

We had lunch at Mil Gov, where the two of them were living for the moment. A visiting Green Lizard [*the increasing numbers of civilians in the Control Commission wore a uniform with green epaulettes*] from Food and Agriculture was having difficulty persuading the other officers that it was a good thing for him to kill the horses being kept for them to ride, to save fodder for the scraggy beasts who were working. They were being pretty conscienceless but he was firm and evidently had the final word.

7 FEBRUARY Thursday. Tony and Valerie and I went to Vlotho for the Section Representatives' meeting. We took the Brummagem Belle, dropping 25 kids at a place near Bielefeld on the way, for a country holiday. Undernourished children are given a month's country holiday with families chosen by the Innere Mission, and we supply the transport.

The cab of the Brummagem Belle is now very much more comfortable, having doors and a windscreen. Valerie was in the back with the children, a Fürsorgerin (carer), and a large urn of cocoa contained in a home-made hay-box with blankets instead of hay. We turned off through Bielefeld and delivered the children at a village seven miles beyond. The pastor had got the news only that morning and had had difficulty in arranging accommodation, since the place was already very full with refugees. However, all were left there and we were confident they would eventually get settled in families for their month's stay.

The meeting at Vlotho was handicapped by the fact that sections are now split between those working with DPs and those working with Germans.

8 FEBRUARY Friday. Tony loaded up with stores and returned. I spent the morning visiting a family friend at the 23rd Scottish Hospital. I got a lift to Bad Oeynhausen in the post truck, and hitched from there in one go right into the hospital. I found our friend in the Red Cross Room, where she was surrounded by the most extensive stock of all sorts of occupational therapy and recreational materials. I was closely questioned about our work, it seemed they felt themselves shut off in that hospital from the civilian life around them, and were full of unsatisfied curiosity about it. She comes under the BRCS HQ at Brussels and not at Vlotho, which is concerned only with Civilian Relief and not with Army Welfare.

Back to Vlotho in three quick lifts, for the Liaison Officers' meeting in the afternoon, but in time to do a little business before lunch with the Advisory Officers of the other agencies represented by teams in Penelope's area—BRCS, Save the Children Fund, Salvation Army.

The LOs' meeting was quite a large affair, with all the LOs—representing different geographical areas—and the Advisory Officers—representing different relief organisations. Also, the people attached to various Corps Districts for British subjects or claimants for British nationality; and representatives of UNRRA, of the International Red Cross (a Swiss), of the Control Commission's Welfare Branch, and others.

Colonel Agnew laid before the meeting his 'appreciation of the situation as at April 30th, 1946', which he was going to present to the Voluntary Societies in London, where he was flying the following day. He envisaged the withdrawal, after that date, of six teams a week, which would wind up the whole operation in a further two and a half months. A COBSRA HQ with wider terms of reference would replace the present BRCS HQ and administer specialists working singly, attached to Mil Gov units. The discussion showed that the team system would be desirable over the summer and, if personnel were available, throughout the next winter, and Colonel Agnew decided to modify his plans accordingly.

Afterwards Graham Wood and I, as LOs for North Rhine and Westphalia, discussed with Colonel Agnew's Personal Assistant the question of Pacific packs and school feeding, and with the Colonel and the International Red Cross representative, the draft agreement for the Swiss teams. This developed into a wide-ranging informal discussion. Colonel Agnew, from a most unlikely background—having been a regular soldier all his life until 18 months ago—has absolutely the right spirit for his position, and is always quoting a passage from a book by Max Huber, President of the International Red Cross, on the need for humility [*The book was* The Good Samaritan, *London, Gollancz, 1945*]. And I had been struck by how the whole tone of the conference, which included representatives of the most 'patriotic' English bodies, was hardly to be distinguished from the tone the FAU would desire.

9 FEBRUARY Saturday. Vlotho is on the banks of the Weser, and my room, in the grand and luxurious house where I slept the night, looks out over it—at present a swollen, turgid river, racing down. Floods have made telephone communication very bad—I could not get through to Dortmund all morning.

I returned to Dortmund after lunch with the Swedish Feeding Team, just arrived at Vlotho. The Swedes were in two lorries and one staff car, and since the cabs and car were full, I had to travel on the back of an open lorry—however, I had two jerseys, battledress, American jacket, leather jerkin, and Swedish leather coat with fur-lined collar, as well as blankets and raincoat, so I was not badly off. The floods were phenomenal.

It is nice to come back home from Vlotho or other places, in the evening, and sit among this section which everyone has been talking of as a 'crack' section, and find that it has been going on using its own initiative and progressing on the now familiar lines, handling the fresh things as they turn up.

10 FEBRUARY Sunday. Diana and I went to the Schauffel-bergers for tea and supper. Herr Berning, the eldest brother-in-law, has a factory in Wuppertal which makes metal buttons which are sold to a firm making working suits for miners. He said (I don't know how these things are found out) that the amount of money now in Germany was seven million marks, of which three million were used in the black market, and the amount needed to run the country was 0.3 million. Therefore, as soon as all was ready (and new notes were already printed), and the rate of exchange had been fixed (this would depend on reparations decisions, I imagine), all money would be called in and people would receive in the new currency only a proportion of what they gave. The black marketeers would be forced to destroy money in excess of their income declared for tax purposes. This would mean money would regain its value as a medium of exchange, and it would be possible once again to make people work for money instead of only for goods which they can barter.[2]

It is certainly true that every German one meets says that people have too much money and that no-one will work. He said that there was a run *to* the banks at Christmas time, when the news came that this was being done in Austria and that money in banks fetched 40 per cent of its value and money outside banks only 10 per cent. The example of bartering he mentioned must occupy many workers: a man, living in the Ruhr, goes to the country, gives a farmer a suit in exchange for butter, returns, keeps some of the butter to supplement his rations, gets another suit with some more of it, and sells the rest of it and is able to live on the proceeds for several months before needing to repeat the process. Berning said that all the time, Germany was getting poorer and poorer, and that only such financial measures, coupled with reactivation of industry, could save her. I have often thought what a Gilbertian position it is, when Germany exports coal to France free of charge instead of using it to make things which could be exported to Britain to recompense the British tax payer for the herrings he is paying Norway to send to Germany because Norway needs the money and Germany cannot pay for them.

Having just written that, I turn to the *New Statesman & Nation* just arrived and read: 'Meanwhile, the Occupying Power had got to foot the bill for the substantial imports of food required to keep the population alive in the British zone—a farcical situation in view of Britain's own shortage of foreign exchange.'

11 FEBRUARY   Monday. To Düsseldorf to represent Westphalia at Graham Wood's North Rhine Province monthly meeting. The fiery Irish Col. Donnelly had been on a 'Brains Trust'— 'Silly questions they ask you—"What is going to be done with all the Nazis not at work?"'

I came back partly along the autobahn, which had been completed, even at the detour by Duisburg, but during the floods the detour has again to be used. The river Ruhr near where it joins the Rhine was enormous.

12 FEBRUARY   Tuesday. I started out on my tour of the Ruhr sections—hitching, since transport was so short. Our driver took me as far as the Salvation Army team in Herne, and dropped me at their home for undernourished children.

The Salvation Army team is a good one, including three pacifists, and they seem to be very good at getting German workers of a similar type to themselves. The leader was at Vlotho, deputising for their Advisory Officer, but the two who were sharing the leadership in his absence were first class men. They have great energy and get things done, but I think do not always consider whether they are not just robbing Peter to pay Paul. They were most hospitable, and grateful for all the information I brought them (I was hawking round a specimen Pacific Pack which made me welcome with the inquisitive in every section).

After lunch they set me on the autobahn and I hitched fairly easily to 126 FAU, north of Gelsenkirchen, where I spent the night. The Section includes two old friends from the Hadfield Spears [*the mobile hospital with the Free French*] one of whom, a nurse, had just got engaged to another member of the Section, a fact which had only been revealed the previous evening, so I came in for the boisterous exhilaration usual to a small section in such circumstances.

After tea I went down to the scene of a flood. Nothing had yet been done, but I heard later that the Swedish team nearby have got extra supplies sent down to help in the feeding.

13 FEBRUARY   Wednesday. They drove me into Gelsenkirchen and set me on the Bochum road, where I got a lift in a German lorry to the Bochum Rathaus, where I got out and joined 133 FAU in their office. Led by another old friend from Hadfield Spears, they are a thoroughly alive and vigorous section. They lent me an ambulance to visit Hagen, which is near their billet.

119 BRCS at Hagen live in great luxury, English country house style, with an open wood fire in the drawing room, but did not strike me as particularly energetic. John Tovey and Tony, coming back from Siegen with a load of children in the

Brummagem Belle, took me home. We off-loaded the children
in mid-Dortmund, and John and Tony said the difference in
health and spirits between those they had taken and those they
had returned with was so tremendous that it made these trips
seem very well worth while.

14 FEBRUARY Thursday. To Münster with an ambulance from
133 FAU, driven by their building specialist, who was enquir-
ing about release of building materials. We had to go via Hamm,
the way through Lünen being impassable due to floods. I saw
the head of Refugee Branch, and Major Battersby, now acting
head of Public Health, chiefly about the new teams. We got in
late, having to spend an hour in Münster looking for a petrol
point.

15 FEBRUARY Friday. Dortmund Welfare Committee Meeting. Mostly a discussion on the right use of Pacific packs, but
also on the attitude to be taken to three hundred communist
ladies who wanted to be absorbed into the Arbeiterwohlfahrt
but to retain their own cohesion. Decision not taken but the
feeling of the meeting was that attempts to infiltrate another
organisation should be resisted, but that they should be encouraged to form themselves into their own welfare organisation and then be admitted to the Committee on equal terms to
others. They call themselves the Freiwillige Frauendienst (or
WVS!), or Rote Hilfe (Red Help). The latter seems more appropriate!

16 FEBRUARY Saturday. Chris and I start early for Bad
Pyrmont, for a Friends Relief Service conference there.[3] A talk
on the 'Re-education of German Youth' was to be given by the
Deputy Director of Education from the Control Commission, a
Colonel Horwood. He arrived to find a mixed bunch of British
and German Quakers and others, listening without interpretation to a contribution in German by a German Quaker, and
including a well-known German educationalist who, he was
aware, knew more about German education than he would ever

know. He had expected to find greenhorns ('I thought I would have to tell you what a Regierungsbezirk was', he said ruefully), and came ill-prepared for what he found. He gracefully withdrew, promising to come back better prepared the next day.

In the afternoon Mary Friedrich took some of us for a walk to Friedensthal, a 'Quaker village' with a most interesting history.[4] The group included an IVSP (International Voluntary Service for Peace) team leader, who hopes to come to Westphalia for the new refugee reception work.

17 FEBRUARY Sunday. Not only was Horwood's address fully prepared, but he came backed up by a female Green Lizard who was the Information Officer of his branch and would be able to answer any questions of fact that he couldn't! He actually gave an excellent address, on the Control Commission's attitude to youth movements, and adult education, with a short reference to the problem of those in internment camps, over which he said no policy was yet framed, though he assured us it was exercising the minds of those in authority, and that the basic idea for the inmates must be 'educational not penal' [*see pp. 171–2 and Appendix*]. We were all impressed by his breadth of outlook.

Three members were present from each FRS section in the field as well as HQ staff, so it was a moderately large conference. Other participants included Maurice Webb,[5] now in FRS uniform as Travelling Commissioner in NW Europe, as fat and as charming as ever; and Maude Brayshaw, Clerk of London Yearly Meeting,[6] also theoretically in FRS. She is staying at Cologne and visiting FRS and FAU sections. German Quakers there included August Fricke of Kassel, Leonhard and Mary Friedrich, the Yearly Meeting Clerk from Berlin, and several others. Also present was an American Friend attached to UNRRA, and three of us from the FAU.

I admired the masterly way in which the conference was handled by Roger Wilson, the FRS General Secretary (who by all appearances is going to be a very big name in the Society of Friends[7]), and the general spirit in which it was conducted.

18 FEBRUARY Monday. To Vlotho, having been asked to speak that afternoon to members of five new BRCS teams not yet deployed. There was one FRS team, one Salvation Army, one Save the Children Fund, and two BRCS, so it was a fair audience. I led off, describing the Mil Gov set-up and what should be the attitude of teams to it. Then the FAU Section Leader from Bochum talked about how his team went to work, and so did Capt. Preece of the Salvation Army team at Herne. There were questions after each contribution.

What a contrast there was between Harold and myself, who both spoke for about fifteen minutes, in moderately quiet tone, and Preece, who gave a forty-minute speech in evangelistic, rhetorical style, and approached the high-pressure salesman technique in 'selling' his youth booklet: 'if you want to know how to start a youth group—here it is; if you want to know what the functions of its officers should be—here it is; if you want a specimen programme of suitable activities—here it is; if you want a spiritual appeal—here you have an epilogue, containing a little spiritual appeal...' Miss Roberts, a wise old bird, had evidently known what to expect, since she wanted us to 'set the tone', and refused to allow my last-minute attempt to back out of setting the ball rolling.

After tea Richard Ullmann [*see p. 147*] gave a very fine address on the German psychological situation and its relationship to the relief worker, which aroused great interest.

SIX

Dortmund Developments

19 February to 18 April 1946

The food shortage. A mine disaster. A visit to the French and US Zones. Montgomery's talk to the Section Leaders' meeting.

19 FEBRUARY Tuesday. Back to Dortmund. Penelope had arrived back from Paris over the weekend. After lunch Ken King and I went to Mil Gov to talk about school feeding and Pacific packs. We saw the Deputy Director of the Food and Agriculture Branch of the Control Commission, who was passing through, and had with him a major from the Provincial Food Team at Unna.

The question of Pacific packs was rather overshadowed by what he told us of the general food situation. He, and all Mil Gov food men, had always said they could feed Germany till March but no longer; it had been known that potatoes would run out, but the answer had always been that increased bread ration through imported wheat would keep the calorie content of the rations up. Now, stocks were dangerously low, and his chief had just returned from England, having been told that he could not have more wheat since it was not available. Today he had been at Düsseldorf to meet a nutritional expert who had come up from Vienna, and might have some idea, such as 'kill all cattle' or 'catch more fish'. But his opinion was that only a miracle would save the situation, and he was talking of all industry closing down, and the normal consumer's ration being maintained by the cessation of all heavy and medium-heavy workers' and miners' rations. Since all potatoes would be needed for seed, it would shortly be a punishable offence for Germans to sell them. Food and Agriculture had promised Education to do the school meals, and Pacific packs might be needed in order to ensure that. If it were possible to ensure it. Why such drastic changes may have to be introduced so suddenly was not explained except by implication that the Control Commission had expected further wheat imports.[1]

He had spent some time in Berlin last summer. He thought the Western Allies would have to admit that quadripartite administration didn't work, and get out. Berlin was a shop front that had cost the British zone far too dear. People in Berlin were well fed now, he thought they looked far better than they had done last summer. He said the Russians were making a desert of the great fields of Pomerania and Mecklenburg.

I asked them how they liked the prospect of another two million mouths to feed in the British zone by summer. They both replied, seriously, that they thought it would be nearer ten million—that we should not be able to stop all the people coming over that would want to come over. They said that we had supplied potatoes for the American sector of Berlin, the Americans agreeing to provide potatoes from their zone for North Rhine Province; they had hummed and hawed about fulfilling their part of the commitment until frost was on the ground and now he doubted if the British zone would ever see those potatoes.

20 FEBRUARY Wednesday. Shortly before supper Penelope rang to say there had been a mine disaster near Kamen and could we send our ambulance.[2] The ambulance was at Bochum, the Kings having taken it there to inspect a babies' home with a view to using Maltavena, so I got through to FAU 133, the section there, and the Kings' and one of the 133 ambulances were able to leave practically immediately. We heard no more till about 8.00, and I got a Mil Gov car to take four people out to relieve the Kings and the drivers from 133, and bring them back for some supper. However, shortly after they had gone the others arrived back. Ambulances had rolled up from all over and the rescue squads could only get a few people out at a time, so they had not been used. The British were there and everything was being laid on in a big way. Evidently 500 people had been trapped by an explosion, and the mine was burning, and many of those so far brought up were dead. Some British officers had gone underground about five minutes beforehand.

FEBRUARY 21 Thursday. Penelope again rang up and said Colonel Graves had put a car at our disposal in case we wanted to go over and see whether any relief or welfare work outside the official scope should be carried out. I went, and interviewed the German doctors and one or two British officers. I went with five preconceived ideas:

(1) Nourishing drinks from the food parcels for those brought out in a state of shock and exhaustion, and for the night shift of the rescue party. This was willingly accepted, the first aid room having nothing of the sort, and the night workers getting meals at midnight and 6.00 but nothing in between.

(2) Extra helpers from Dortmund voluntary societies for overstrained medical services. This was unnecessary, since the services were at the moment only standing by, and there was plenty of personnel in reserve.

(3) Evacuation of cases from nearby hospitals to free bed space. As such this was unnecessary, but the German doctors did not know where they would put a hundred cases if they were got out suddenly, and we were able to clear this point with Hobbs (the Public Health Officer of the district) and tell them.

(4) Clothing for those caught in the explosion or burnt. This was unnecessary, since the mine itself had stocks.

(5) General investigation. This found (a) that there was no reserve of morphia known to the Germans, a matter we clarified with Hobbs; (b) that soap was badly needed in the first aid rooms, since patients came filthy out of the mine; we got this

through Colonel Graves, and Ken and Marjorie took it down the same afternoon, with drinks and information.

Hobbs had been going on short leave—was actually going to get married [*see p. 162*]—and eventually went off, leaving with Ken and Marjorie all the relevant information that he had. An RAMC officer I talked to was only there in case the British officers were got out and was not interested in the general treatment of casualties, so I am glad we were able to do something in a different spirit, even if only as a gesture. The final position seems to be that about a hundred men were got out alive, by different ways, that a second explosion followed on the first, and that slightly under 400 were left down there and were not saved. One would have thought that with floods on top of everything else, Germany, and the Ruhr, had had about enough. But troubles never come singly.

You mention survival of the fittest—a grim conception. I think of the Balkans where rations in big cities are under the 1000 calorie mark, of Bengal where famine threatens again and the FAU has had to start orphanages on a big scale, and of here where cuts threaten, the population will suddenly increase, and our supplies are already like gold in that some people would do anything for them.

In the afternoon a couple of BRCS drivers arrived with a three-ton load of Red Cross parcels for the British subjects in the Ruhr area, which other sections will collect from us as needed.

In the evening we had a section meeting to discuss the future in view of my possible departure to take up Penelope's work as a permanent job, when she leaves at the end of next month. I was offered the job, provisionally, last weekend. The section said it would let me go and would like to see Tony Trew as my successor. We also considered the situation in view of the return to the UK, within the next two months, of Brenda, the Kings, Chris, and Bill Judd—the whole 'top layer' of the section, with the exception of Diana. We decided the rump could and should continue, here, with reinforcements. Consciousness of all these changes has rather depressed people.

I am undecided about Balliol. The fact that the FAU is closing down on June 30 does not of course affect my conditions of exemption under the National Service Act. With possible promotion here, and great unity with the aims and spirit of FRS, it looks as if I could be very well employed in Europe till my time is up.

22 FEBRUARY Friday. It is snowing. This morning there was a committee meeting of the German welfare societies with the Swedes, in our dining room.

This evening we received two new 15 cwt Fordsons as replacements, which does ease our transport position. Our German mechanic is a first class fellow, and keen on the job, which saves a lot of work for John and Tony.

23 FEBRUARY Saturday. Count Bernadotte has changed his plans and didn't come today. He will be in Dortmund tomorrow, but only to pay a quick visit to the Swedish team.

24 FEBRUARY Sunday. After snowing furiously, it has now stopped, and all is still, and each twig has its little covering. We went out ski-ing with Brenda's skis, but the snow was wet and hardly thick enough, and it was difficult to find steep enough slopes. However I ski-jored behind the ambulance at 20 mph, and we had quite a good time among the woods and fields. Tony and John Tovey have made a toboggan with some sheet iron and an old pair of steps, and a snowball fight with the local kids is at present in progress.

27 FEBRUARY Wednesday. To Vlotho with Penelope and the Swedish LO, with the latter's car and driver. The autobahn was clear of snow and we arrived about 10.00. The morning session was marked by Sir Raphael Cilento's exposition of UNRRA's plans for the repatriation of Polish DPs from the British zone. It was done with method and clarity. He reckons that 80 per cent of the Poles will want to go home, and that by stepping up repatriation eventually to 6000 a day by rail, road, and sea routes, it will be possible to clear this lot out in two-and-a-half to three months.[3] Then UNRRA *might* help with the rehabilitation and eventual settlement of the hard core.

Other matters were mostly detailed. Twenty-five representatives of the National Association of Boys' Clubs are to come out from England, and the Societies for the Blind, and for Physiotherapy, are interested in helping to develop their opposite numbers in Germany. A representative from 'Christian Reconstruction in Europe' is also to visit sections. Some of Chris's photos of school feeding are being enlarged for display at the Control Commission exhibition in London. At lunch I sat next to the representative from the Commission's German Welfare Branch. He is the man who decides on applications to form welfare organisations for the whole zone, but he is a Green Lizard dug out of the Civil Service whose only topic of conversation is what he did in Iraq during the 1914–18 war.

1 MARCH   Friday. Diana and I started out on short leave over snowy roads via Wuppertal and Cologne and into the French zone to Mainz. After calling in on the Mertz couple, we decided to go on to Diana's friend Wolfgang Jacob at Heidelberg and return to spend the next afternoon and Sunday morning with them. We went straight on without checking the oil level with the result that on the autobahn we developed a big end knock with loss of pressure. We got towed into Mannheim with some Americans. After some persistence on our part, they offered to tow us through Mannheim to the Heidelberg autobahn, and while waiting we were given Coca-Cola and toasted cheese sandwich in their recreation room.

We went through Mannheim behind a ten-tonner breakdown truck, flashing a red light on and off as it went, and blowing a siren. It was midnight by the time we found the house and a young man came running downstairs delighted to see Diana and crying 'Du! Du!'. We unloaded the stuff and parked the truck and took an essential part out of it and I put up my bed in the office/library.

2 MARCH   Saturday. Wolfgang is studying pathology (he is already a doctor), a fellow lodger is studying art, and the landlady is a Frau Professor, so it was a very scholastic atmosphere.

Wolfgang took us for a walk over the shoulder of the hill, across the Neckar, and up to Heidelberg Castle, then back through the town. We talked hard all the way and he is a remarkable man, with liberal and original ideas. And a captivating personality. The scenery and old buildings and views and whole atmosphere were beautiful and peaceful.

3 MARCH   Sunday. Back at Mainz, with Georges and Ruth Mertz. Georges is an Alsatian. Ruth is Swiss, related to the Schauffelbergers. I met them at Hohwald, Alsace, when I was with the Free French. Georges, as a French citizen, works in the Mil Gov of Hesse-Rhenane. They live at Gonzenheim where all the French officers and their families live together in houses built for the French—in 1919!

4 MARCH   Monday. A walk with Ruth, down into Mainz, then through some pine woods back to the 'Zigeunerlager' (Gypsy camp) as the Germans call it because the French just throw all their rubbish out in heaps and never get it cleared up.

In the afternoon we went into Mainz in the old bus that takes the officers to their work, and then walked through the city to the place where the *Don Suisse* people have their hutments. We went into the sewing room where Germans were busily at work, and on to the station where they had a hutment being used by the German societies for the reception of refugees. However there are only about 20–30 a night and we thought this grand hutment was wasted there. But the Bahnhofsmission (Station Mission) compares favourably with Dortmund's.

Then back to Gonzenheim. Georges' work is now progressing, since they are starting a University in Mainz,[4] and he told me interesting stories about French Mil Gov. He is a wonderful man—witty, wise, honest, tactful, charming, intelligent and concerned about the right things. They make a wonderful couple.

The Germans say 'The British zone is badly fed and well administered, the American Zone is well fed and badly administered, the French zone is badly fed and badly administered'.[5]

5 MARCH Tuesday. The big end means we have to drive at only 25–30 mph, though we got thicker oil at a service station, which keeps the pressure up. It has knocked out a plan to ski at Winterberg, and we will have to overnight with the FRS section at Cologne. Off down the Rhine Gorge, past the Lorelei and the Deutsches Eck at Coblenz. A beautiful journey, close to the river all the way. Our only delays were a puncture where one crosses from the US to the French zone, and a big detour where the bridge of the mouth of the Lahn is blown and one has to climb high into snow and go through Bad Ems. We gave a lift to someone who worked for Coblenz radio, and to a 'British subject' getting her things to Detmold from the French zone. We also gave a tow to a French car for several miles. Remagen Bridge,[6] which we turned off to see, is mostly sunk beneath the river, but work to rebuild it seems to be starting. I was vividly reminded of the newsreel of its collapse. It is a two track railway bridge. The Rhine was full and fast.

We arrived at the FRS section just as they were having supper and there was plenty for us. They live in a most beautiful house.

6 MARCH Wednesday. We saw over the Ford works at Cologne—very interesting, but we failed to get them to mend our big end or replace the engine. We lunched at the Düsseldorf Yacht Club and arrived back at Dortmund in time for Chris's party of Youth Movement Leaders in the evening. It was a most pleasant, lazy holiday, full of change and new interest, particularly through being in the French and American zones.

[*The letters do not cover the week before home leave, but other documents are available:*]

On Sunday, *10 MARCH* my fortnightly report noted that 'Maltavena III' was the most satisfactory yet, that the Mil Gov school feeding scheme was about to start, and that the Swedes were feeding their full 15,000 and had started footwear and clothing distribution.

On Monday, *11 MARCH* Bernard Jackson rendered his report, requested by Mil Gov, on German reactions to the lower ration scales (see p. 138 n.1). He had done this incidentally, in the course of house-to-house visiting to survey housing accommodation, but warned that responses might be neither representative nor frank. People felt the old scales had been just enough and wondered when they could be restored. It was felt that children and working men would be worst hit, particularly those in the city centre or with long distances to work and no access to garden produce. However, he recorded much resignation and some fortitude: 'better than air-raids'; 'we lost the war, and must expect to suffer'; 'we must just bear it'.

The middle class were less stoical and some said the Communists would be able to make capital out of this. (In another comment reported at the Welfare Committee: 'Geben Sie uns genug zu essen, sonst können wir Hitler nicht vergessen'— 'Enough to eat we must get, or Hitler we cannot forget'.) But any solution was seen as in the hands of America or the Russian zone; most people realised and appreciated that England had shipped potatoes and grain to Germany, and none blamed Mil Gov. The danger is apathy rather than active discontent.

[*At breakfast, just before departure on home leave, Diana and I announced our engagement—to an apparently unsurprised Section. Return was overnight on:*]

28–29 MARCH We had a good journey. The Channel was absolutely calm, a lovely crossing. At Calais camp we waited long enough to have a meal, but no longer, and then got a cushioned compartment on the train to ourselves right through to Dortmund. A midnight meal at Brussels and a morning one at Krefeld were our only stops. We arrived at Dortmund station at midday on Friday.

I have had to write testimonials for all members transferring to FRS, and estimate the work the Section is likely to be doing after June.

This summer weather makes an immense difference to life here—doing paperwork in the garden instead of indoors, sitting in the sun instead of round the stove, etc. And it's splendid for the Germans for whom heat is such a problem. The current phrase among them to describe any waste of energy is 'throwing your calories out of the window'.

31 MARCH   Sunday. In the afternoon we were in the garden, having just finished giving out cocoa and *butterbrot* to the neighbouring kids, when a RAF sergeant came in saying he'd like to take some photos of it. He spoke fluent German, having been in Switzerland and Austria before the war, and was in the intelligence section of the RAF. They have plain clothes men who travel in German trains to hear what people are saying—spying without risks. We hope to rope him in for the Youth Movements, as we do all Englishmen who speak good German, but he didn't seem over keen.

It was depressing, getting back to Germany, with its manifold problems of immense, insatiable, ubiquitous need for the essentials of life, looming up all over the place, and the difficulties of turning people away or ignoring them, of eschewing favouritism, and so on. No doubt we shall settle down.

In the evening Miss Dean, Penelope's successor, paid me a visit, partly for advice, being a little scared of the job. However, she will settle down all right. She has studied at the London School of Economics and was a Probation Officer.

It was a grand leave, and thank you for making it so good, and for taking so well the shock of suddenly having a future daughter-in-law thrust upon you.

2 APRIL   Tuesday. This evening at Chris's request I visit a pingpong youth club.—he says they are the most cynical he has come across and would like a good discussion. They were nearly all in the army and many in the Hitler Youth and have had no other background and are now cynical and disillusioned.

4 APRIL Thursday. Richard Ullmann is visiting us till Sunday. He is a German, Jewish by blood but Christian by upbringing, and now Quaker by conviction; by profession a professor of history. After several months in Buchenwald he got out to England and worked with Friends throughout the war, latterly visiting PoW camps in Britain and lecturing to budding relief workers. Then, a month or two ago, he came out to Germany in the FAU and has been in the section at Essen.[7] His deep understanding of the inner situation in Germany, of past political developments and the present psychological situation, his keen interest particularly in youth work, and his absolute willingness to put himself at your disposal, make him invaluable.

6 APRIL Saturday. An unexpected visit from the Colonel in charge of Mil Gov, who burst in saying: 'I've brought Kingsley Martin to see you.' And not only the editor of the *New States-man*, but the editor, and a reporter, of the *Manchester Guardian*. You may remember several excellent articles on Germany, some you have sent me, which this reporter had written. He took voluminous notes on our Maltavena file and the history of Ken and Marjorie King. Kingsley Martin is a fine person with most untidy hair. He whispered to Diana 'What's the Colonel like?' and 'Smoke? No? Well give 'em to the Germans'.

7 APRIL Sunday. I visited youth groups with Richard Ullmann on two evenings, and there was a meeting of representatives of all the movements at our house on the Friday. He has given us, and the Germans we deal with, the benefit of his advice and insight, at the meeting of Welfare Societies, at the Lanstrop settlement [*see p. 148 n.9*], and in visiting the concentration camp victims Welfare Office and the Jewish representative.

8 APRIL Monday. A visit from a friend who had trained with Diana at St Thomas's Hospital, London. She is in charge of physiotherapy in British hospitals in the zone, and spent the night here, between visiting hospitals in Wuppertal and Iserlohn.

9 APRIL   Tuesday. Off went the Kings, after six months with us, of excellent work on the Public Health side. Another big loss. Their last evening was spent checking over Kenneth's report to the Commission on the coal distribution situation.

In the evening we had the Oberbürgermeister to supper.[8] He is an old Social Democrat, had to leave Germany (and his wife and four children) in 1933, and has only now seen them again. He spent the pre-war years in France, Belgium and Holland, and was in France, working with the Resistance movement, till 1942, when he went to Switzerland. Before 1933 he was Landrat of Dortmund-Horde, now he is back as Oberbürgermeister of Dortmund. He is a large and expansive fellow and I think he enjoyed being with Englishmen on social terms.

I was out this morning at Lanstrop.[9] We gathered together the representatives of all relevant welfare workers, municipal departments, etc., in the town, bundled them into an ambulance, took them out there, let them talk their heads off about it, and brought them back again. I think something will happen as a result.

I received the book *Twilight of Civilisation* and have now passed it on to Stadtvikar Luig of Caritas Verband. Could you please order *Problem Families*? We have a copy belonging to Cologne section, it comes in useful in talking about Lanstrop, etc.

11 APRIL   Thursday. The youth movements are sorry to be losing Chris, and had planned a secret farewell 'do' for him. It took place this evening at our house. After a song or two, Paul Schwitteck called on Stadtrat Levermann to make a speech about the progress of youth organisation in Dortmund since the war. At the end of the address, Levermann thanked Chris for the work he had put in, and the message of goodwill he had brought, and presented him with a beautifully written scroll with the crest of Dortmund on it.

Chris then made a wonderful speech of thanks, saying how much he had enjoyed his work, and what had led him to do it. It was an expression of faith which deeply moved the company, although many could not share it. Then Schwitteck made a short speech and presented Chris with a book of songs, hand written in Gothic lettering, illustrated with whirls and pictures, in many colours, beautifully done. It had *'Dem Freund und Förderer der Dortmunder Jugend'* ['To the friend and patron of Dortmund youth'] on it, and the signatures of the leaders of all the movements. Finally we had more songs. Later in the evening there was a discussion to decide the form in which these evenings should be continued. A different person each week will introduce a subject for discussion, and another person will be master of ceremonies.

12 APRIL Friday. The Section Leaders (Westphalia) meeting with the Public Health officer from Arnsberg. The usual exchange of ideas was useful. In the afternoon the meeting discussed youth problems with the youth officer from Arnsberg. He evidently knows the German background well, and has given himself to his work with great devotion, travelling round the Kreise, attending German committees, and putting forward ideas, and there is not much he doesn't know about the essential character of each movement and the way in which things ought to be moving.[10]

13 APRIL Saturday. Dr Köhler called. He is one of Erna Rosier's Göttingen circle, but lives in Bochum, being a mining engineer, a pioneer in his line which is something to do with earth vibrations. He is one of the few Christian Socialists to be found in Germany. He spoke interestingly at supper of present conditions among the miners.

We have received the *Manchester Guardian* with the Maltavena article in it.

14 APRIL Sunday. In the afternoon Diana and I had a walk in upland woods, with views south over the Sauerland. This is wonderful country very near at hand, and it was a perfect spring day. The trees are coming into leaf and blossom and everything looks very green. In the evening (summer time having started) four of us had our first game of tennis at the Club nearby, one court being now in use. Afterwards the Gruppe Gartenstadt came to say farewell to Chris, and this meant (after devotional), songs of all sorts till curfew time.

15 APRIL   Monday. Michael Tarrant has taken over youth work from Chris, and Leslie Richards, a Welshman, is to interest himself in education. They will settle down well, I think. Leslie has been in university teaching in Wales, and Michael is hoping eventually to become a missionary.

17 APRIL   Wednesday. Group 40, I see, will be partly out at the end of September.[11] Groups will then be being released at the average of one per ten days. One can therefore expect group 42 for soldiers (which is the same as 41 for COs) to be partly out on October 20th. I shall therefore go up to Oxford at the beginning of term ten days earlier and hope that I don't get prosecuted. I have applied for a job with FRS in London from July till October, in connection with their work in Germany or elsewhere in Europe.

   I saw at Vlotho the *Economist* of April 6th, with five excellent articles on Germany.

18 APRIL   Thursday. At Vlotho. The meeting was quite interesting. The leader of the Cologne FRS section led off, on the subject of youth work, most competently, and a Major who is the youth expert from the Control Commission was there to answer questions. The outstanding event of the day (Monty's visit included) was the address given on 'German Psychology' by a Colonel Sedgewick, in charge of Religious Affairs in the Control Commission. He has known Germany intimately for twenty years, ever since being a student at Bonn after the 1914–18 war, and also knows about psychology, so was well equipped to give it. He has the deepest knowledge of Germans, and the clearest appreciation of their faults, of anyone I have met in the Control Commission; and yet he was the most progressive in his views on their treatment. He said he would, if he had his own way, wipe the slate clean, and start again with them; he condemned reparations, the harping on the guilt clause, and the zonal system. This is only extraordinary when you know in what terms he mercilessly exposed the bad side of the German character.

The discussion which followed his address was an excellent one showing great unity of outlook between all sections of opinion represented, e.g. FAU, BRCS, CCG. Montgomery himself, that afternoon, also in his speech condemned by implication reparations, condemned in private the zonal system, said in public how much the cut in rations made his efforts difficult, and echoed the cry of others: 'If only we could give the Germans something to hope for.'

By and large, however, Monty's speech was a great disappointment. He was not at all *au fait* with the situation in Germany as expounded, for example, by his subordinate General Templer,[12] who had a far better grasp of things; his words were correspondingly woolly and platitudinous. He made such obviously untrue statements as: 'Without you fellows I don't think we could have done it.' His description of how he bucked up the Home Guard in 1940 was just a hoot.[13] It left one wondering how he got where he was. Surely a good general must have a precise mind?

Easter at Einbeck

19–22 April 1946

19 APRIL Good Friday. Diana and Tony arrived at Vlotho with Bill Judd. We drove to Bad Pyrmont and dropped Tony at the BRCS Rest Home to have a quiet weekend and get over his boils. We visited Leonhard and Mary Friedrich and the Rest Home being opened by FRS for three-week stays by victims of persecution. The two hostesses had just arrived from England— one of them, Elizabeth Fox Howard, about 70 but as sprightly as they make them.

We drove to Einbeck and arrived mid-afternoon, parked in the Marktplatz, and Diana and I went straight over to the Ohnesorges. They were both there and delighted to see us and to put us up for these two days. We unloaded stretchers, food and kit, and the word went round among bystanders that the Ohnesorges' house had been requisitioned, much to her amusement. Herr Ohnesorge is now quite better from his typhoid, and is absolutely loving being back home. He is an economist and was most interested in a textbook prescribed by Balliol which I had with me.

We had tea and talked for an hour or two, and then went out. They said, invite people round this evening, whomever you like. We said, well, let it be mutual friends, whom you like, whom we know! So we invited the Urbanczyk brothers and Herr and Frau Gies. Brian Clapham of the Guides team, a lawyer of 32 who wants to join the FAU, came too, and Frau Köbberling dropped in.

When we called on the Gies's, they had visiting them the youth worker for the Kreis, a nice young man whom I had met before but did not know. So they showed interest in the youth position in Dortmund. Herr Gies used to run the welfare work for Einbeck but now does only journalistic work, principally for a journal in the American zone. We called on Herr Voges and arranged to come round the following evening. He also said, 'Are there any other of your friends you would like me to invite round at the same time, since I know you have such a short time here.' I said I would be interested to meet Herr Borowski again.

There is now a new regiment in Einbeck, the 2nd Essex from Berlin, and they are bored to tears after the gay life of Berlin and take it out of the Germans by assaulting the men on the streets after dark. Both Herr Gies and Herr Ohnesorge have been attacked in this way without any provocation whatsoever. They are rumoured to be a Strafregiment (penal regiment) but of course there isn't such a thing in the British Army.

This, and the fact that the Poles are now getting such a lot of clothing and food that it all finds its way into the Exchange Shop and is swapped for the Germans' household goods which they cannot replace but are prepared to give up for food and clothing, has slightly altered the Einbeckers' morale since we were here. And then everyone knows that the liberal-minded men in the Guides' team are under the thumb of the leader and dare not tell her when they go out to visit German houses and so on.

The 'separation of function' [*see p. 148 n.8*] is now in being, so that the former Landrat is now Oberkreisdirektor, and the former Deputy Landrat, Borowski, is now Landrat.[1] The Urbanczyks are still on the Council, but were busy now with their law practice. The younger said everyone was worrying now about whether the Ruhr and Rhine would be annexed, because 'if we have to pay for our own coal, then it's all up'. I think there's some faulty economics in that, but one can see his point. The Volksbildungswerk, or Adult Education course, which had just finished, had been a great success and a bigger one was being planned for next winter. Most of our friends had been lecturing on it. Dr Köbberling now works in a hospital at Holzminden. Another child is on the way, and they were thinking of leaving the Baptists.

20 APRIL Saturday. We talked with the Köbberlings. He showed me the programme of a conference for doctors in Stuttgart, with topics such as 'The boundary between medicine and psychology', and 'The duty of a Christian doctor'. He gave me the address of the Slavonic Christians in Holzminden since I could find out whether their friends in America could send them parcels. He said he had to come to Einbeck each week to see the diabetic patients, who were now getting *just* enough food and insulin to keep alive.

We drove to the stud farm at Erichsburg and rode with the Polish Captain and one of the Guides. At one point Diana shot past me shouting 'stop' and when the horse stopped at the end she fell off. I came racing up expecting to find her with broken bones but she was chiefly worried about having dirtied her face. I was so relieved I got quite angry with her for worrying about *that*.

After a late lunch we visited the Sohns who now have rooms in a nice house beside the chalk works. Sohns is a quite widely known painter, and both are refreshingly colourful persons. We found how impossible it is to give any idea of a place like Dortmund to someone, even with imagination, who hasn't been there.

Then a brief visit to Frau Dr Matthas, the dentist. Her husband is back from being a PoW in American hands, and runs the practice, he being a dentist too, while she prepares to have a baby. They are two (and, as she said, soon three), living in one room in the house of her parents; the only other room they have is the surgery. Still, she was very happy.

Supper at six and then with the Ohnesorges to the first

meeting of the 'Goethe Society', to hear Dr Janssen speak on 'Goethe's *Faust*'. A most difficult lecture to follow (even for Germans, I was told), but notwithstanding, I found it most interesting. I was pleased, after the lecture, when someone had asked if Voges knew someone else, and he said yes, they had already met—at our house (4 FAU) 'wo die Einbecker sich kennengelert haben'—'where the people of Einbeck got to know each other'!

Then to the Voges's house for an evening's chat, with the Ohnesorges, Borowski, a younger man, and Herbert Voges's mother and sister in the background. Borowski related how difficult it was to find people to sit on the denazification committee, because people who committed themselves had not come off well, either in 1933 or in 1945. The opinion was expressed that some day denazification must come to an end, because its continuation meant that no-one knew where he was and this stultified the life of the country. I asked him what he thought of the opinion expressed in the *Economist* that the British should openly support the Social-Democratic Party (he is a Social Democrat himself). He agreed that the Communists were a great threat to democracy, asserted that the SPD was the only democratic party in Germany, but thought that it would be able to gain strength on its own.

21 APRIL   Sunday. Bill Judd was staying at the home of Erika, who had cooked for us in Einbeck, and we paid them a visit and then went to the Landjagerkäserne/Sikorski Polish camp. Matysiak was out, Theresa was back in Poland, but we met the other three who were with us in that picture [*Plate 13*]. None of them wanted to return yet. Then we visited Mrs Künkel. She had been once to the Dutch border, and is able to go over to a village to meet her son (who lives in Amsterdam) to arrange details of getting to America. The difficulty had been that the Dutch authorities would let nobody in whom the Americans would not guarantee to admit to the US; and the necessary formalities with the Americans could not be gone through unless you were in Holland![2] However it looks as though all the red tape will eventually be overcome. She was looking very pale and thin and she has heard that the Americans won't allow ill persons in and I think she is giving all her food to the weaker of her two children for fear of that. However she has now had a lot of parcels which ought to help. She was lively and in very good form. She has been giving some lectures on psychology in the Adult Education Course.

Then we went with the Ohnesorges on a picnic up behind Einbeck, in the sun in a field in the woods on the top of the range of hills in which the town nestles. A nearby inn heated up tins of stew for us and we had cold potato salad, etc. Tea with the von der Ropps. The Baron is as keen on his work as ever but as far from getting premises for his school.

We then drove to Göttingen, and after supper met again with Erna Rosier's Quaker circle. I was asked to give an account of our present work, and this was followed by questions. This developed into a discussion on the general state of morale in the Ruhr towns. Besides the two of us, Dr Köhler from Bochum, and a woman who had been in Gelsenkirchen, had first-hand knowledge of the Ruhr.

Göttingen is said to be a hotbed of Nazism, accentuated by the large proportion of students. The large towns are more in touch with the workers' parties and therefore think of the world tension in terms of Communism versus Social Democracy, rather than of Russia versus the West, which is the way it strikes Göttingen, less in the real world and therefore thinking in larger terms, and also lying on the Russian zone frontier. The Ruhr towns have a tremendous job of reconstruction to do and are buckling down to it as far as the rations, etc., allow them. This means that in spite of everything their morale is probably higher than that of intellectuals who realise the implications of reparations and so forth.

22 APRIL   Easter Monday. We picked up Wiebke Türke at Moringen. Her father had just returned from being in a Civilian Internment Camp in the US zone, in a very weak state, old and white and thin. He is going to the FRS Rest Home for a few weeks. They had not told him yet of Wiebke's husband's death, for fear it might be too much for him. He had been head of a sort of concentration camp in Moringen which he had made a very nice place to be in, and ex-inmates of it and others who knew about it have been trying to get him released. Pre-war [*1935*], Brenda had visited it with her mother [*Bailey 1994: 64*], and recently Elizabeth Fox Howard had written to Sir Hartley Shawcross asking for his release, but had had a letter in reply saying that he could do nothing as it was in American hands.

On the way back to Dortmund we called on Pastor Mensching and his little church near Bückeburg. He has recently been to a meeting of the International Fellowship of Reconciliation in Stockholm, including leading Christian pacifists from Britain, other West European and Scandinavian countries, Czechoslovakia and the United States. He gave an epic description of the journey there, without pass, without money that was any use, with nothing but faith. If any official asked him why he was going, then he 'had to start to tell them about the FoR'... And there was an official who said: 'Do you really think you will get through?' 'Yes.' 'Very well, I'll give you my stamp, then.'

He spoke of the way all difficulties were overcome, and of the tremendous co-operation that had been given him by all sorts of people, but balanced it by saying how much the Germans were hated, not only in the land through which he had travelled, but in the lands of whom he had met representatives in Stockholm. There were further discussions on a forthcoming youth week in Bad Pyrmont, on the possibility of community service in the manner of the IVSP, and on 'Wie kann ich ein besserer Versöhner sein?' ('How can I be a better reconciler?').

SEVEN

Final Weeks

23 April to 9 June 1946

*The refugees from the East. Bremen. Martin
Niemöller addresses a hostile audience. Visiting
internment camps for Nazis. A weekend in Berlin.
The Russian repatriation mission. A youth
conference.*

23 APRIL   Tuesday. The representative of the *Don Suisse* (Swiss
Gift) has arrived and is living with us. He is a very nice chap.
and we get on well together. The main thing is to get the
barracks up as soon as possible. They will serve as Kindergarten, Feeding Centres, Youth Club rooms, Sewing and Mending
Rooms, a kitchen and dining room for refugees, and other things,
and look like being pretty well used throughout the 24 hours.

24 APRIL   Wednesday. Yesterday evening Diana and I went
round to Mil Gov No. 2 Mess. The officers there said they
thought that many Mil Gov officers like running Germany, and
do the Germans' jobs for them, which does not help the Germans
to stand on their own feet. With this I agree. They gave some
amazing examples of how the Germans do exactly what you ask
them to, no more and no less, if you give them exact instructions, and of how to handle them to make them do things their
way when that is the best way. Then in came two Lieutenant-

Colonels, one the former head of Dortmund Mil Gov, and now head of a division at Arnsberg, for the Regierungsbezirk, and the other the head of the Political Branch for the whole zone. They had been seeing one of the leading Social Democrats of the zone, who lives in Dortmund. The discussion turned on the supply of reading matter to Mil Gov officers and the Germans, on the Swiss and Swedes, and so on.

25 APRIL Thursday. To a meeting of the Flüchtlingsausschuss, or municipal committee for dealing with refugees. They are just like Mil Gov, trying to make the best of the crass things that are done on the highest level.

Alfredo is at last leaving us for Switzerland; he has been thinking of it for a long time, and required the final push. This came when his standard of work, which has been steadily falling for a long time, became such that I had to tell him it must get better or we would have to part company. It is a good thing in many ways: his southern temperament does not mix well with those of our hard working German cook and helper; he is a man who needs frequent changes of work and he has been with us a long time; and having to fend for himself again and make his impression upon new people will raise his standards once more, I think. Moreover, he will have a far better life in Switzerland than he would have in Germany if he stayed here when we went; he is a waiter by profession, and will get four months hectic work in summer, four in winter, and a holiday with bags of money in between.

Now we have to help him on his way with guidance through red tape and so on.

When in Einbeck I bought some stamps from the Russian zone—three depicting *Wiederaufbau*, or reconstruction, showing housebuilding, bridge building, and locomotive building; and two, printed on cigarette paper, showing *Bodenreform*, or Land Reform, with a man ploughing. All are *Provinz Sachsen*— i.e. a special issue for Saxony. The Wiederaufbau ones are marked with the price in two parts, e.g. 12 + 8, the extra 8 pfennig being a tax for reconstruction.

I shortly go on the Swill Round—to collect uneaten food
from army messes. This is likely to be a great success. They
are doing it very well, dividing up porridge plus rice, meat,
bread etc., in different containers, and we deliver it to Homes
for Old People, Volksküche (People's Kitchens—usually for
people with no cooking facilities), and refugee hostels. One
evening we collected three sacks of beetroot which 'would go
bad if they weren't taken'. It is not worth calling at a unit of
less than 300 men, but we hope shortly to collect from nearly
3000, in about half a dozen different regiments.

This evening a Youth Meeting at our house, when someone
gave a talk on 'Wanderungen' (rambling). The Germans make a
science of everything, and the speaker's idea of a ramble was a
regimented activity in which you learn about the countryside,
and such points as when and how long you walk, talk, rest, eat
and play are points for 'technical discussion'. Luckily for my
peace of mind there were some more independent spirits in his
audience…

26 APRIL   Friday. The latest joke: 'Die Deutsche haben Rasse,
die Russen haben Masse, die Engländer haben Klasse, die
Amerikaner haben Kasse'. To which one might add 'die Franz-
osen haben Hasse' [*'The Germans have Race, the Russians Mass,
the English Class, the Americans Cash—and the French Hate'*].

1 MAY   Wednesday. Promised to be a nice quiet day (a public
holiday for Germans). However, Mil Gov had interfered in the
getting of a house for the Swiss, and there was a frightful tangle,
not to say schemozzle, which I spent most of an irritating day
straightening out. The Swiss seem to think they can arrive
without papers, warning, authorisation, agreement, furniture,
transport, or cooking equipment, and find everything laid on.
Mil Gov seem to think that such complicated problems cannot
be solved by the FAU on a mixture of what rights there are in
the case and what is called the 'old boy net', and we have to sit
in their offices while they throw their weight around on the
telephone complicating the issue.

FRS want me for the 'Germany desk in Friends House'—as from yesterday! But I can't be spared till the Section is settled down on its new course, i.e. when three new people have replaced five leaving (new total being eight), and Michael Tarrant has got the hang of leading it. The plan now is that I shall go on continental leave on June 1st or thereabouts, and come home in mid June.

2 MAY Thursday. To Münster for a Province Welfare Committee. Before the meeting I was involved in a discussion between Province officers and Information Control people from Hamburg about a proposed visit of American and English press representatives to black spots of the Ruhr, with an adverse report in view, to get the farmers of the Middle West to feed less grain to cattle [*see p. 138 n.1*].

I found officers at Münster full of the Internment Camps (of Nazis) which have just been handed over to Mil Gov from the army, with conditions in a pretty bad way. They are getting the inmates to work so that they can have heavy workers' rations, getting more food for the hunger oedema cases in the camp hospitals, combing Westphalia for welfare goods for them, and trying to get a hue and cry raised. I think Richard Ullmann is likely to get in, to do his lecturing.

The meeting was just like our Welfare Committee, only at Province level. Although Captain McHale is an excellent chap, straightforward and concerned, he has to use an interpreter and approaches everything from a completely English standpoint, without much realisation of the complexity of the problems involved. It would be better for CCG to consist of fewer and better men, working from higher levels through Germans, than to be an army of mediocrities.

The application of the Communists to form a welfare organisation came up. The straightforward Englishman says: 'welfare must be kept free from politics'—an excellent sentiment, but not realistic, welfare in Germany, like everything else, being shot through and through with politics.

Back just in time for the Swiss–Swede meeting with our Welfare Committee, but much enlarged. A tense time until at

last the concession came from the Swedish side. The problem
was simply that the Swiss barracks are best used in the town
centre, but the Swiss feeding not, since that would destroy all
the Swedish lorry routes and be costly in transport. But the
Swiss, wanting each barracks to be a tangible symbol of all
their activities, could not agree to receive Swedish food in them!

6 MAY   Monday. Captain Hobbs is the local Public Health
Officer [*see pp. 139–40*], a sanitary inspector in civil life, not
very bright or cultured, but sound and straight. He married an
Estonian, a DP, young and charming and very intelligent, who
studied philology during the war first at Prague and then at
Berlin. She speaks fluent Russian and German and will soon be
speaking perfect English. They have a flat to themselves and we
had a most pleasant hour or two chatting of this and that. The
flat is by courtesy of Colonel Graves, who might have followed
the rule for service marriages and said they must live fifteen
miles apart (this rule assumes that if a pair live together the
result will be detrimental to their work!). I understand Kingsley
Martin spoke of Graves as 'energetic and paternal'. Mil Gov
officers would agree with the second epithet but not the first.
     A party at our house, partly to celebrate Bill Judd having
passed a test in a 30-ton tank transporter of the 55th Anti-
Tank Regiment who give us our rations, and so having received
a driving licence for very heavy vehicles, valid in civil life ('it
might be my bread and butter some time', he says).

7 MAY   Tuesday. I am now convinced that a principle which
plays a very large part in the *Don Suisse* organisation is that of
advertising Switzerland and her good works; everything points
to that and Herr Lötscher has said so in so many words. The
team leader knows it and is desperately trying to serve two
masters; the rest of the team are as shocked at the idea as I am,
particularly one, who is as straight as a die. However we have
reached a *modus vivendi* which serves the interests of Dortmund, our relationship with the team remains good, and we
know exactly where the organisation stands.[1]

Practically everybody has mixed motives, of course. Take the case of me who went abroad partly believing that it was to serve a greater need, but partly because it was a more comfortable place for a Conchie in war-time; in so far as the FAU in its publicity neglects the second factor in the building up of its overseas work, it is guilty of the same deceit (and self deceit) as the *Don Suisse*. And in such a situation of mixed motives, spiritual salvation is only to be found, for the individual at least, through complete inward honesty, i.e. a lack of self deceit.

10 MAY Friday. This evening Leslie Richards and I had a talk with Dr Leonhardi (in charge of secondary education), and Schulrats Schleef and Wagener. Schleef is fat and jolly, a raconteur who is able neatly to point the moral of every tale. Wagener is thin and earnest with an intense hatred of the Nazis and a sound appreciation of and unshakeable attachment to the principles of Christianity and peace. Leonhardi is a good thinker and a well read man but apt to be disheartened by the many difficulties and become rather a 'granny'. All are Westphalian born and bred and had much to say about the differences in mentality between them and the refugees from the East, whom they described as the militaristic type. The difficulties of settling these Easterners into the population of Western Germany are enormous, and this conversation was limited to the difficulties that arise in the educational sphere and with farmers.

The other topic we discussed at length was the relationship between East and West, and my thesis, that Germans too have a part to play in bridge building and reconciliation, met with different reactions from each of them. Leonhardi said little, but grasped it; Schleef could not understand the danger of arming the West against the East; Wagener realised that, but had little faith that it would be possible to come to terms with atheistic Communism.

11 MAY Saturday. The next morning I heard the other side of the refugee question from Dr von Reinbardt, the leader of a refugee organisation at Schwerte which I visited with John

Tovey and John Haines. He is a land-owning aristocrat of the same type as Baron von der Ropp; and I should imagine that he has the same sort of militant Christianity. He sees the danger of refugees becoming radical, and therefore keeps his organisation un-political; he knows Russia well, having studied their agricultural methods, and he wants Western Germany to be oriented towards England; he, again, realises the dangers in this which I pointed out to him, and realises that a bridge must be built, and an idea found which both sides can grasp, but he does not see such an idea ever being found.

He realises that the British zone, with millions of superfluous population in an area deprived of industry, is an economic impossibility, and hopes that the British will give the expellees the possibility of emigration. What a hope! So his organisation, though it has the best of intentions, is not really directed at settling the refugees in, and should therefore be banned by Mil Gov if they continue their present policy.

Leonhardi & Co say Easterners came after the last war, worked their way into the best positions, kept alive associations which proclaimed their desire to return, and when the chance came just hung on. Dr von Reinbardt says the West Germans do not like the Easterners and try to keep them out of everything, and that the Mil Gov policy of refusing to permit refugee organisations was inspired by the West Germans who did not want them to have a fair chance. Leonhardi talks of the militaristic, humourless type; von Reinbardt of the more intense and energetic type, of the Easterners. Just one more instance of the countless chasms which split this country from top to bottom. How are they to live together, now that they must?

After an early lunch Tony Trew, Diana and I set off to spend the weekend in Bremen. We went through Osnabrück (which is destroyed, and which I had not seen before) and Vechta. At Calveslage we had tea with the Kathmanns, who gave us fried eggs and ham and black bread and coffee, and pressed us to return on the way back. Their children are grown out of all recognition since we last saw them. In Bremen the superb

Rathaus and Cathedral now present a sorry spectacle but still retain much of their grandeur.

Some way out of Bremen, at Vegesack, in the country, we found Dr and Frau Kurz, who live in an exquisite little farmhouse-type house. Diana had stayed with them in the 'thirties, and they seemed terribly glad to see her, and we did not get to bed till after midnight. Two sons are PoW (one in England, now resigned to staying there for a year or two as slave labour), their daughter Helga is studying at Marburg (and has called in on the Section once or twice) and the fourth child, a son of about fifteen called Bernard, is with them, half-days at school, the rest helping his father with the garden or his mother with the house.

Dr Kurz is the typical German Professor, with a little beard and white hair fluffing out backwards and a most kindly face. Though prepared to compromise enough to retain his post as Director of Schools throughout the Nazi time, and now relieved of it, his attitude to life and the world is far deeper and gentler than that of any real Nazi could be. He is a mathematician and scientist and now, when not at work in the garden, he spends his time studying the American method of teaching mathematics from books which he had brought back with him from the USA. This is part of a study of which the theme is that Germany should seek to benefit from the close contact which she has with the foreigners now on her soil. He was impressed with the account of our work that Helga had given him, delighted that the links with England, so long broken, were being taken up again, and most anxious that German youth should not, as a result of the crash of everything it had been taught to believe in, become bewildered and cynical and without faith or hope. He has been thrown back, by his enforced idleness, on the 'things that endure', has been reading Goethe and living in the realm of great men and supra-national culture.

12 MAY Sunday. In Bremen again we filled up at an American filling station (Bremen being the 'Enclave').[2] We then had lunch with Diana's friend Ursula, her three children, her mother, and

Dorothea Jacob, Wolfgang's sister. Ursula is the breadwinner, often leaving the house before the children are up and returning after they are in bed.

I should think there are very few families with their own house in Germany now who do not have someone billeted on them, except for the very lowest income classes who were living several to a room anyway. The expellees are quickly filling up all country accommodation to what Mil Gov calls 'saturation' point and still there are hundreds of thousands of them to come.

14 MAY Tuesday. With Richard Ullmann, who had come over from Essen, to hear Pastor Martin Niemöller give an address to all Pastors in Westphalia. He knew of our presence (the only lay people there), and had approved. He spoke for two hours without a note, his address entitled 'From Treysa to Geneva'. Treysa was the first conference of Protestant Churches in Germany since the occupation began. It had elected a council of twelve (with Niemöller as a member) to represent them. Geneva was the recent conference of the World Council of Churches, the first to be held since the war.

Niemöller dealt largely with the Stuttgart declaration [*a declaration of German churches confessing their share in Germany's guilt*] and the question of guilt, and subsequently with his experiences as one of the two German representatives in Geneva. After hearing the address, Richard thought he was moving towards pacifism. The second part was similar to Pastor Mensching's description of his journey to Stockholm, but not so enthralling. One might say that Niemöller is a clear-sighted, honest, fearless, earnest Christian, a great preacher and a human personality; but that Mensching is a saint.

There were, however, great moments in his address, particularly in his defence of his attitude with regard to the guilt question, and his account of the first meeting with the Bishop of Chichester. It is difficult for us to understand the furious opposition which his preaching of national repentance, and about the Church's share in the guilt of Nazism, has aroused, since it seems so clearly the correct Christian attitude in the circumstances.[3] It is perhaps easier when we try to imagine what the popular reaction in England would be if the Church laid the same emphasis on repentance for the part we British have played in bringing misery to the world. People don't realise that what goes for an individual (with regard to casting out the beam in his own eye before the mote in his neighbour's) goes for a nation too.

Permission has been granted for Richard Ullmann to visit Civilian Internment Camps. He will advise them on education and welfare questions and outline the tasks which will be before William Hughes when he comes out again from England to be concerned with them.

In the afternoon a meeting to prepare for the visit of twenty-odd press representatives (from UK, US, and, it turned out later, from Denmark) to the Ruhr, coming to Dortmund on Friday morning. They were chiefly concerned with food questions (CCG's idea in letting them in and taking them around is that public opinion may be stirred up to send over more food). They want to see school feeding, Swedish feeding, old people's homes and kitchens, and private dwellings. We and the Swedes and several Mil Gov officers and the Public Health man from Münster and the Provincial Food man from Unna were at the meeting, the outcome of which was that from 10.00 to 11.30 they should see those things (excluding dwellings) in two parties, to a route mapped out by us, and from 11.30 to 12.30 private dwellings. Diana and I mapped out the programme which was cyclostyled for them the next day. We were to provide guides and also to lunch with them.

15 MAY Wednesday. Herr Figge visited us in the evening to give most members a second German lesson. He starts off a lesson with a few remarks about the use of capital letters for nouns, is off (in German) talking about a new practice of writing nouns without capitals, how he doesn't like it, since there is too little variety in the printed line, one falls asleep, it's like driving along a straight road, and so on... A curious way to learn German, but captivating.

16 MAY Thursday. An uneventful morning meeting. The welfare representative from Münster announced that Communist welfare organisations would be permitted (a coincidence, *or* a result of a report I submitted recently on the question).[4] One or two other questions, largely of supply and of public health, were discussed. The Colonel in the chair began with a nice little speech welcoming the Swiss. He then remarked that the work we were doing knew no distinction of caste or creed, victor or vanquished, that difficulties were bound to arise, and could be overcome by co-operation from everyone, and that he was sure that in future the Swiss would be good co-operators! Miss Vichser was left to take that how she liked... [*see pp. 161–2*].

In the afternoon I went with Leslie Richards to a Youth Hostel half an hour's run away, at Hohenlimbourg [*between Iserlohn and Hagen*], in beautiful country, where the Falkens [*the Social Democrat youth movement*] were having a leaders' course. The warden of the hostel is a member of the Versöhnungsbund, a pacifist therefore, a fine colourful middle-aged man, running a bookshop there. He gave me a copy of *Die Gegenwart*, which appears in the French zone, and showed me copies of magazines from the US and Russian zones; certainly we are far behind any other zone in this respect, due to the lack of paper here.

We were there to hear Fritz Henssler, one of the most prominent Social Democrats of the zone, address them. He was not inspiring, for so prominent a figure, and this indicates how poverty stricken the SPD is in this respect.[5]

The swill round for me that evening. Next week we include in it the fourth and last regiment, and our daily haul might average four to five cwt.

Afterwards Heinz Junge, leader of the Free German Youth in Dortmund, spoke on 'Separatism and the Future of Germany' to our group of members from all four movements. The FDJ is really but not openly Communist inspired, and his address was most persuasive, very clever, anything that might look like propaganda most carefully hidden, yet definitely quite tendentious. Separatism refers to the various movements, e.g.

of 'Rhinelanders', 'Hanoverian Guelphs', etc., who would like one region or another to split away from the rest. The group has been greatly rejuvenated in response to our appeals, with the result that the discussion was less deep but more lively, and with a greater number of participants.

MAY 17 Friday. The Press arrived, and two of us took round each of two parties. Things went moderately well, they saw the cooking and then the eating in a school, then the eating in a kindergarten, then a municipal home for old people. We visited a cellar dwelling and then a goodish middle class one, and interviews with the locals took place right left and centre with us interpreting. Then both parties together streamed off in a long line of green Volkswagens to the Club where lunch was ready. One Yank was already tapping away at a typewriter, and a Despatch Rider was able to take off some 'hot stuff' immediately after lunch, but a writer for the *Reader's Digest* said he was in a position to let it 'cook for a generation or two' and work it into a book.

Over lunch I talked with a Dane, whom we will visit in Berlin next weekend, and the *Times* Correspondent in Moscow ('lent' to Germany for several weeks). The *Times* man had been in Moscow the whole war—that is, for Russia, since 1941—and got on well with the Russians. He was settling down there to make a specialist study of the country, since he said there were many things about them one could not understand during the war, and one would have to wait for the return of normal times to see how they behaved then, before one would be able to get to the bottom of it. He said Churchill's Fulton speech had made them very despondent.

Off they went to Recklinghausen. We went on to a hotel reception 'in honour of the Swiss, Swedish, and British Red Crosses'. Those present included Col. Graves and two other Mil Gov officers, three of us, three Swedes, three Swiss, and about 30 town dignitaries, ranging from the Oberbürgermeister and Oberstadtdirektor downwards. The Oberbürgermeister and Colonel Graves made speeches. The new Oberbürgermeister,

Dr. Scholtissek, is a member of the Christian Democratic Union (CDU) party and seems a fine man.

The Captain of the Swedish Red Cross was most interesting in conversation about the Russians—he saw communism (although he was very far from sympathetic to it) as a dynamic force which will sweep Europe, by virtue of the fact that it knows the value of work and therefore appeals to workers. Socialism in Sweden, he said, was definitely destroying the initiative of the individual and being bad for the soul of the country—it was going too far in the direction of the Government fulfilling all needs from cradle to grave, so that workers did their bit and then were done with it, apart from their grumbles, exactly like the soldier. He spoke of Russia as the most conservative state, and this takes a bit of thinking out to me.

After a quick supper I visited the Pastor who had invited us to hear Niemöller. He wanted to discuss his address. We discussed the guilt question, the position of the church in Germany past, present and future, and its relationship to Nazism, Socialism, and Communism.

18 MAY　Saturday. I got notes written [*Plate 23*] on my visit to the refugee organisation in Schwerte, since on Tuesday the discussion on refugees will be opened by the man in charge of the Control Commission branch, and the deep problem of their integration into West Germany can then be discussed with him. Then a girl from Corps came. She has to do a survey of youth movements, particularly interested in evidence of more than local connections between various branches of the various movements, and in their connections with political parties.

After lunch Diana and I drove to Wuppertal, and found the Kochs' beautiful house without much difficulty [*the Kochs were a couple known to my parents before the war, the link having been more probably Rotary than grocery*]. The house is full of bombed out relatives and others, but in fact they still live a life of incredible luxury, lacking nothing since Herr Koch is a grocer and they have enough food. And he who has food has everything. The eldest son is interned in South Africa, he was evidently anti-Nazi and fled the country before the war. His mother said of him: 'He was against Nazism—he didn't understand it...'! The daughter's husband had returned a fortnight ago from being a PoW in US hands. He had been captured at the end of the fighting in Tunisia (he knew the country there just as I did!) and had spent three years in America, living very well till the end of the war; then on starvation rations (he fainted twice); then, put to work on cotton-picking, very well again.

There is no doubt that they were typically Nazi. Herr Koch is a business man with a definite business morality, but no Christian or Socialist background to make him immune from Nazism, and he would be much impressed by the prosperity the Hitler regime had brought to the country, without going into it very deeply and seeing the evil in the system. He is however no fanatic (he believes for example in giving up a war that is obviously lost), and is now ready to learn. Essentially a follower and not a pioneer, except in his business; a judger by results. Frau Koch thinks even less than he does and now wallows completely in the unconscious assumptions of neo-Nazism, but is very good good-natured and would follow her husband into any new ideology into which he might be drawn.

It seems Balliol are prepared to try and get me out on class B release.

22 AND 23 MAY Wednesday and Thursday. Visiting Civilian Internment Camps with Richard Ullmann [*see Appendix*]. Things are far better than they were and the English staffs do all they possibly can, but suffer from the lack of definite directives and help from above. It is noteworthy that even when it is a question of pure Nazis the Englishman on the spot is completely free from the 'take it out of them' spirit, is purely constructive and tries to make the best of things for the people in his care. The Commandant at the CIC at Recklinghausen said: 'If there had never been such things as concentration camps, that would be sufficient reason for avoiding creating them; but since there have been and we have made such a fuss about them, we must be doubly certain not to do the same ourselves.' But it is characteristic of British policy in Germany as a whole that no positive guidance towards a new ideal is forthcoming from above, the idea is rather to create a vacuum and play safe. We were welcomed, though chiefly in hope of the necessary materials for activities, which of course are very scarce. But the English officers there were also keen on getting higher levels stirred up.

Our chief interest (or mine at any rate) was in finding out from actual contact with the internees what their outlook was. This was not possible in Paderborn where we were accompanied by the Adjutant and had to speak in English and keep to business; but in Recklinghausen we had a long talk with two of the internees which was most interesting. However the internees there were not half so Nazi as in the camp at Paderborn, being largely the Ruhr industrialists, and also people who had joined the party from self interest rather than fanaticism. The interpreter officer at Recklinghausen said that people who used to be in the Gestapo were the best at reporting what was going on in the camp, since they gave objective and full information.

A 'Frau Joyce' was on the programme at Paderborn as giving English lessons and Richard asked if she was Haw-Haw's wife.[6] She was.

24 MAY Friday. I have been keen to visit Berlin, partly because it will probably be the last chance of visiting anywhere on the Continent so far east for many a year to come. The leader of the FAU Section there is Nev Coates, a Geordie formerly in our unit with the Free French, and a good friend.

So, Diana and I set off to Berlin after lunch. Valerie took us to the autobahn, and with hardly a moment of waiting, we got a lift in the magnificent open tourer of a Major-General. It had a flag in a bag on the radiator, only flown when he was in it. Diana tried to get the driver to take the bag off, by claiming to be a Major-General herself, but he wasn't having any. He sat back nonchalantly chewing gum with only a little finger on the wheel, going along at 80 mph, and definitely enjoying himself! We were in the back, being blown to pieces.

Our train went overnight from Bad Oeynhausen. I was able to stretch out over most of one side of a compartment and we both slept fairly well.

25 MAY Saturday. The next morning before arrival we observed the countryside and noticed the railway lines (including sleepers) which had been taken away by the Russians, so that the one we were on is now only single-track. Several goods trains (containing stuff looking as if it had been turned out for reparations) had Russian guards.

Nev Coates met us and drove us to the FAU section billet in time for breakfast. The section is full of fun and was most hospitable, very ready to give us information and place transport at our disposal when possible or even run us places.

The terrible damage in Berlin is less noticeable because the streets are broader and the ruined houses are set farther back. And with higher rations there is a noticeable difference in the people. Later we took tram, tube, and bus to Unter den Linden and the old city centre. Kurfürstendamm is the best shopping street in Berlin but there are few real shop windows and many articles bear the label 'made up out of your own material'. A good exhibition of 'Life in England Today'—mostly photographs.

We rode in a rickety old bus through the Tiergarten [*zoo*] and the Brandenburg Gate, passing the gigantic Russian war memorial and the Reichstag, and getting out at the far end among the famous buildings. It was very hot, and students were reading in the grounds of the University. It is under Russian control and a new one has been started in the British sector.

Nearby we went into an art exhibition which was a staggering revelation of the state of chaos and depression of the German mind at present. There were paintings of ruined cities, of air raids, of rubble-clearing, of mis-shapen or sorrowful-looking people, of poor thin horses, of allegorical representations of Nazism and the ruin it brought—which all added up to a tale of horror and downfall and nothingness.

We took the Underground back for lunch, reading some Russian sponsored newspapers, which gave a quite different picture of things from those of the West.

After lunch we went boating on a lake in the French sector, in the North West; Nev and his half-Swedish friend Inge got out a motorboat with outboard motor in which one of the section had some sort of an interest, whilst Diana and I walked along the side of the lake and finally got an old lady to lend us a canoe, in which we paddled out to meet the others and tied up to each other in the middle of the lake to have tea. It was very pleasant and corresponded to what one has heard is typical of some Berlin recreation.

In the evening we drove into the American sector, the residential part of Berlin, to meet the Danish journalist who had visited Dortmund. The Press Club was in the house of Funk, the Nazi Finance Minister; one dined upstairs in what used to be the bedrooms, each holding two or three tables. Downstairs was bar, orchestra, dance floor and two sitting rooms, and later there was a very feeble cabaret followed by dancing. Our Danish friend heard much from the British in Berlin against the Russians, and found among the Russians much mistrust of the British.

26 MAY Sunday. A morning concert from the Berlin Philharmonic. The audience were very smart and you might have imagined yourself in quite another country than present day Germany.

In the afternoon we went to the Olympic stadium which is a series of vast buildings in concrete in a very totalitarian style. The victors of the 1936 Games for which it was built are commemorated on a plaque. We got chatting to some Russian officers with their wives and a child, one of the wives speaking quite good English which she had learnt at the Institute of Moscow. They were very friendly but her husband did not wish to prolong the conversation after a certain point. He wrote at her dictation a letter for me to my Liaison Officer friends of Vechta days; goodness knows if it will ever reach them.

27 MAY Monday. Booking a passage back to Bad Oeynhausen was quite an affair. 'Your application has to be signed by a superior officer.' 'My only superior officer is himself not in Berlin. I came up on a Movement Order which included the return journey.' It would have been troublesome, though possible, to take the form away for Nev Coates to sign and bring it back again, so I then suggested that I might sign Diana's and she mine. The Captain looked at me, said 'You up on a Charlie?' 'Yes', said I, not knowing what a Charlie was. 'All right then; but you chaps, taking up seats needed for people on business…' The next thing I knew, he had given us sleepers!

31 MAY Friday. In the evening Diana had several Dortmund ladies in for coffee to discuss the formation of a women's organisation similar to the Women's Institutes.

1 JUNE Saturday. We have two FRS people staying with us this week; they are making a film of conditions in Germany and the work of BRCS teams. This morning they filmed a meeting of the Welfare Committee [*Plate 20*]. They have still to do a 'housewife' story and some other subjects before they go on Monday. [*The film was produced as* While Germany Waits *and was later deposited in the Imperial War Museum.*] It's glorious weather, and one is tempted to lie and sunbathe in the garden or even to go off and swim somewhere.

3 JUNE Monday. Colonel Gidley-Kitchin, Col. Agnew's successor as Deputy Commissioner for the British Red Cross Civilian Relief in Germany, is visiting, and I took him round the Swedish kitchen, the warehouse where the Pacific packs are being opened, and a pair of Swiss hutments where he met the leader and a member of the *Don Suisse* team. The electrically driven circular saw which Tony designed and had made for opening the aluminium tins of the Pacific packs is now working better than any tin opener, you just swish each rounded side of the bottom of the tin over it, then do the same with the corners, and whole bottom then 'comes off in your hand'. The Swiss hutments are nearly finished, needing only the wiring and similar minor matters.

I left the Colonel at Miss Dean's office and went on with John Tovey and Michael Tarrant to Iserlohn. We saw the Lieutenant-Colonel in charge of the Mil Gov Detachment there, about the refugee association in Schwerte. He was glad to see us, had suppressed the organisation once and had not known of its reappearance, and thanked us for details. What he said, namely that von Rheinbart only represented an aristocratic clique of refugees, is probably true, and there was no occasion to discuss the general principle of refugee organisations. He did however branch out into an account of his dealings with Russians—DPs, journalists, and Liaison Missions. 'Britain and the US must be BIG—realise how mistrustful the Russians are and do all they can to remove the occasion for it.'

We had lunch with Mr Parker of *The Times* at the Press Club. After asking about the youth movements in Dortmund, he turned to his experience in Russia. He said that as a journalist he had complete freedom to talk to any 'man in the street', although Soviet officials were difficult to get to. In Moscow during the war he had been tied to his work and unable to travel the vast distances necessary to see the rest of the country. The population of Moscow had grown from the usual four millions to 6.5 millions, so that housing space there was about three or four square metres per person. This is just below the average of Essen, but Moscow did not have other problems of Essen, e.g. the breaks in the sewage system.

He said Russia was very short of trained negotiators and was therefore generally outplayed by Britain and America, whose negotiators were cleverer, particularly where business interests were concerned—and as a result Russia tried to make up very clumsily what she had lost through lack of skill. He compared the case of Russia in Persia and America in the Belgian Congo. In the Congo, complete rights over uranium had been obtained without the American, Russian, or even Belgian man in the street knowing anything about it. In Persia, no greater an imperialistic step had been taken, but America and England had been able to play it up tremendously—and, in the end, wilfully (where doubts had been cast in the press on the word of the Persian Government in saying withdrawal was going according to plan).

He also said that one could not speak of a solid Eastern bloc. The Russians themselves were very frightened about the countries bordering their frontiers; Poland might jump any way any time, and the Balkan countries were so volatile and uncertain that you never knew where you stood with them; the whole area was in a state of flux and not at all as regarded by the West.

I asked him about the Russian Mission here. He said they were a repatriation mission and also dealt with the proper burial of Russians killed in wartime captivity. (The most die-hard Nazis from Hemer Internment Camp were being used to undertake the exhumation; one of them had recently run away from the working line, and was fired at by the guards before it was found he had only run away to be sick.)

4 JUNE Tuesday. In the morning Michael Tarrant and I visited the area north of the station where there is a whole collection of cellar, wash-house, home-made and emergency dwellings. The man with one leg, whom I had earlier visited with an Australian journalist, now has a room at the top of a nearby building, but his two neighbours are still happy in their wash-house, and at the back of it, in a coal-hole certainly not big enough to swing a cat in, lives another old man who waxed lyrical about the flowers springing up on the rubble, and hopes this summer to put a roof on three walls adjoining his coal hole and so get a little more room. All could go into an old people's home but prefer their work and their independence. All are real old philosophers in my opinion, and I like them.

Round the corner, houses are springing up, from the bricks and slates laboriously reclaimed, scraped and washed, by the future inhabitants themselves (since professionals go only, as they say, where there is butter and bacon to be had). One house, of which John Tovey took a photo some months ago when snow was on the ground, is now double in size (and a two-storey one at that). Every little bit of ground among the rubble is planted—there are even vegetables growing on a heap of bricky earth four feet high from which they look like falling off.

The new Regional Commissioner for Westphalia was in Dortmund today, and may move his base here from Münster. He is a short grey-haired man, wears civvy clothes, speaks good German having been here before the 1914–18 war and also in the Occupation Commission after it, worked with the FAU during the blitz (presumably was in the London County Council or the Home Office), told me he had always condemned our bombing policy, and was most sympathetic and sensitive towards the Germans we visited. He is quiet but is all there, and I should think he considers very deeply before coming to a decision, but once made it is the right one.

He wanted to see housing conditions, and we first saw the cellar dwellings and the reconstruction going on around them, then an upper-middle-class house of six rooms with seven people living in it, and then an upper-working-class flat with ten people (eight children!) living in three rooms, the man a miner on night shift. Both these were picked at random. In both families there had been a recent bereavement. Afterwards over tea we discussed how to reduce the volume of money in circulation, and he said it was difficult to call it in because no one knew how much the Russians had printed, and he thought they didn't know themselves.

We also discussed potato supply. How would you deal with the farmer who keeps back potatoes either because he thinks the value of money will drop and he prefers to have goods, or because he wants to exchange them rather than sell them, when there is nothing to buy? Either you can search all cellars and turf-covered heaps (claimed to be of swedes) in the fields, which demands almost Gestapo methods and a regular army of incorruptible policemen or soldiers. Or you can stop people coming from the towns, so effectively that no one gets to the farmer to enable him to black market his wares, which might induce him to give them up when next officially requested (but this too would require an army of police to make it effective, if indeed that were possible). Or you can allow people from the cities to travel into the country and buy or exchange freely, in which case the farmer trades.

In the evening the Oberbürgermeister (Catholic and a lawyer) and the Oberstadtdirektor (Social Democrat and civil servant) came to supper. [*See p. 148 and n.8. The latter was Hansmann. The former was Dr. Herbert Scholtissek, who served from April to October, when the first elections took place and Fritz Henssler took up the office (Stadtarchiv Dortmund 1985: 109).*] The latter we have had before, but the former we had only previously met at the reception given to Swiss, Swedes, and the English some weeks ago. They had just been having a meeting of the Town Council where the question of Confessional schools had been debated, and whether religious instruction should take place in school hours. The new system, whereby one of them is like a mayor and the other is like a town clerk, they find difficult to grasp, I think.

5 *JUNE*   Wednesday. Diana and I, with Michael Tarrant there too, spent the whole morning briefing the two new women members about the German voluntary societies, the Swiss and Swedes, Maltavena, etc. Michael and I had made another allocation of jobs, since Bernard too is now returning home, being able to study as a result of the new Class B orders, and we have been getting people to hand over to other people these last few days in our presence so that I could add comments where necessary and he could get the grasp of everything.

In the afternoon we went to see Colonel Graves so that I could introduce my successor; he was told: 'If you do half as well as McClelland we shall be very pleased.' The stopping of the swill round, about which you will have read in the papers, has started having repercussions at our level, so later I typed a letter for Brenda's husband, if he agreed, to forward to Victor

Gollancz. You can imagine that I had some comments to make on: 'The food will be of more use if fed to animals; there are financial reasons for the decision.'[7]

6 JUNE Thursday. With Fru Palme of the Swedish Red Cross to see the Russian repatriation mission. A most delightful evening. There were two colonels, one a charming man with a very fine aristocratic face, the other more bull-necked; and one young soldier, a former student of architecture in Moscow, who spoke excellent English and acted as an interpreter for me. Fru Palme spoke fluent Russian and that, coupled with mention of the *Times* correspondent, soon broke down their initial reserve, and they said time and again that having no other Russians to speak to they felt very cut off and were glad to have visitors and hoped we would come again.

We talked about everything conceivable, except that politics was lightly skirted around.[8] They were tickled at a new Paris fashion called atom-bomb clothes. They said repeatedly that we lived in very interesting times (possibly, according to Fru Palme, with something of a fanatical glint in the eye), but never that we lived in terrible times. They mentioned the next four-power Paris conference and said that the last had made some progress and they thought this one should make more. A great difference from my friends of last summer occurred when about halfway through our stay they asked me if we would like to drink champagne, and added that the English said the Russians were always drinking and therefore they did not know when to ask!

They said five million Russians had been repatriated from Germany since the end of the war, and 500,000 from Westphalia. They were now investigating the deaths, and had found that 10,000 had taken place in Bochum alone. They were having memorials built wherever Russians had been killed.

The first colonel had a medal for the defence of Russia, two Red Stars, one medal for the defence of Stalingrad, one for bravery, and one to commemorate the victory over Germany. He had been in the south of Russia when the war started and had never seen his wife in Moscow since, although they were in regular correspondence; and he thought he would get no leave till the repatriation business was finished. They heard Moscow radio, but got Russian newspapers five days late, since although they were flown to Berlin, they had to come by car from there. There were three officers (we saw another playing with a puppy in the garden as we left) and a number of ORs. The interpreter said that many Russians were now learning English as it was more necessary than it used to be.

7 JUNE Friday. To Volmarstein [*near Bochum*], where Section 133 is closing down, to do a swap with some of their vehicles. I drove a Canadian Ford V8 back, a very nice vehicle running well.

The more one talks to people of neutral or both-sides outlook, such as the Danish journalist, the Swedes, or Mr Parker, the more one realises that it might take years of patient fostering of goodwill (what Bevin calls the growth of confidence) to undo the harm done by Churchill in a few hours at Fulton.[9] He could not have played upon Russian suspicions more effectively, or made them more depressed about the possibility of co-operation with the West. It seems to me that the best safeguard against communism is progressive social and economic reform, and that provided the Labour Government moves fast enough (which it is doing at home though not abroad) it will provide this safeguard.

In the afternoon, to Vlotho and then on to Pyrmont arriving in time for a cup of tea at the BRCS Rest Home and finally bedding down in the Quäkerhaus.

8 JUNE Saturday. Beginning of a one-week conference of youth in or connected with the Versöhnungsbund (German Fellowship of Reconciliation), mostly from the British zone, but some from Frankfurt (US), Stuttgart (French) and one from Berlin, about fifty in all.

The first session, on 'Religion and Socialism', was introduced by Adolf Grimme, who used to be Minister of Education before 1933 and is now in charge of education in Hanover region. He won our admiration by not delivering an address but immediately getting the whole group of young people discussing, and guiding the discussion most skilfully. Considering, as he later said, that these people have not discussed for thirteen years and so hardly know what discussion is, the session was remarkably fruitful; although his must be the credit that it did not degenerate into pointless controversy on side issues or insoluble problems. The participants were not representative of German youth, since with a few exceptions all had pacifist inclinations, but even so it was most encouraging.

After lunch Richard Ullmann and I had a session with Adolf Grimme and Wilhelm Mensching on the Civilian Internment Camps. General Templer's right hand man had indicated to BRCS HQ that this was not a matter in which the Control Commission wanted the BRCS to get mixed up, and that an interview about our report with the relevant officer would not be forthcoming. We therefore had to think of other ways of pushing our recommendations. One of our conclusions had been that the German educational authorities must accept responsibility for the delivery to the camps of a proportionate if not adequate supply of educational materials including books. This suggested that the obvious person would be the German educational adviser to Commission at zone level—which is what Adolf Grimme really is. He said it would be difficult for him to apply for educational materials for the camps since his requirements were already allotted and based on the number of educational institutions, but he agreed later to put forward a petition for the separation of the young people (say, all boys and girls under 17 or 18) into separate reformatory schools of a progressive character.

It remains, first, for Richard to secure an unofficial interview with Colonel Wolfe-Murray, who is going to be in charge of the Camps (and goes birdwatching with Mike Rowntree each weekend); second, to try to get the Münster Welfare Section of Mil Gov to put up our report with recommendations, and do what can be done about it on their level; and thirdly, to raise the matter in the right quarters at home. I understand at least one article (in the *Observer*) and one letter (in *The Economist*) have appeared about these camps.

9 JUNE Sunday. Meeting for Worship, at which the Epistle from London Yearly Meeting was read out. The next session of the Youth Week was on 'Unifying Christianity', introduced by an address from George Carpenter of the Salvation Army at Vlotho, who said: 'Some differences between sects are of belief, others only of method. The method of the Quakers, for example, is a very quiet one; that of the Salvationists, a very noisy one.' We leave the conference today and thus miss hearing Professor Siegmund-Schültze [*co-founder of the FoR through the parting handshake in August 1914—see p. 62*].

ENVOI

'Continental Leave'

10–20 June 1946

Impressions of the Nuremberg trial and defendants.

10 JUNE Monday. Back in Dortmund, and taken by Tony to
the station to begin our 'Continental Leave', consisting of a
visit to the family in Munich with whom Diana had stayed
before the war. We take the 9.15 to Frankfurt via the Rhine
Gorge, arriving at 6.00. There was no over-crowding and it was
a comfortable journey, though on wooden seats over which we
put our sleeping bags. At Frankfurt we had a good supper in a
'Transient Officers' Mess'—exactly like a restaurant—with
Americans, British, French, Poles, Russians. Americans like
coffee in the course of the meal, not at the end. And they eat
a lot of meat.[1]

We got places in the coach reserved for the US army in the
10.15 p.m. Munich train, again on wooden seats but since we
each had one and could lie out and rest our feet on the opposite side of the gangway we both had an excellent night's sleep,
cosy in our sleeping bags. Many American wives were travelling and also, it seemed, some German-American wives. We
talked to a Negro sergeant who said it was easy to get into the
Nuremberg trial. He liked being out here, was a regular army
man, wanted to re-enlist for another eight years.

11 JUNE Tuesday. Arrived Munich 7.30 a.m., got a hitch and a tram and a bus to the suburb of Solln, managing all right with the heavy black kitbag which contained the food and which we carried between us, as well as a back pack, side pack and raincoat each. The house is a big house in a garden in a very pleasant area near the Isertal. We were greeted at the door by the sixteen-year-old son, and a minute or two later by Mutti [*Mummy*], who was very glad to see us and made us feel absolutely at home. After a wash we sat on the veranda overlooking the garden and had a sort of second breakfast of potato soup and toast.

12 JUNE Wednesday. We went to the PX (retail outlet for American troops) and through Diana's pushing tactics did the most incredible thing of getting PX rations—cigarettes, confectionery, drink, toilet requisites, and so on—for a week. An American soldier gets, each week, 240 cigarettes (or 200, plus 8 cigars, or tobacco), 4 Mars bars, 4 chicken lunches (similar to Mars bars), 4 bars chocolate, 4 rolls butterscotch sweets, 2 packets chewing gum, 1 tin roasted and salted mixed nuts, 4 pints tinned fruit juice, 2 pints tinned beer, 6 bars toilet soap (half our size). When we did the same thing later, at Heidelberg, we found fruit juice and roasted nuts and fancy biscuits unrationed. In other words, in the US the supply of goods available equals the purchasing power of the consumer and one can to some extent rely on lack of money being a rationing factor. We could not carry all at once so only took my lot and came back for Diana's later. We also visited the Red Cross Club in the Bürgerbraukeller (the beer cellar where Hitler made a famous speech).

[*The holiday included opera, theatre, concerts and art galleries in Munich, much talk with different members of the Jacob family, and a two-day visit to Garmisch-Partenkirchen, a ski resort currently a recreation facility for American troops. On our return from there to Solln:*]

15 JUNE Saturday. After supper Hannes showed a film made at Trupe near Bremen in 1934 when Diana first visited them. Shots of her on horseback and in a boat with Wolfgang.

17 JUNE Monday. We hitched to Nuremberg, arriving lunch-time. Our enquiries about getting into the trial led us to Americans, British, Americans again, French (who would have been delighted to give us tickets for their imminent celebration of the battle of Bir Hakim[2]), British again and American again. Finally the American corporal at the courthouse pushed back his seat, said there were fifty people who hadn't turned up, and handed over a pair of tickets. We were in by 2.45, for a session which lasted till 5.00.[3]

Hardly had we sat down than Reuter's correspondent, having noticed our shoulder-flashes, passed us a note saying what was going on, and signed it 'Reuter's special service for FAU'. The defence of von Papen was going on, his attorney standing at the prosecutor's stand and asking him questions, and referring the tribunal from time to time to various documents which were before them. Von Papen himself was sitting in the witness box, making his defence as prompted by the questions, speaking at some length on the question of his post in Austria. Occasionally Lord Justice Lawrence would interpose, generally to get something clarified or to keep them to the point.

Von Papen's second defence counsel was his son—a tall young man who had evidently never had much to do with politics. He listened to the English translation and occasionally told the first defence counsel when there was some mistake or imprecision, and the latter then told the tribunal. Von Papen himself also listened to the English.[4]

The other defendants were guarded by US soldiers with truncheons, all very smart with white helmets, belts and gloves; they are relieved from time to time. [*On account of the helmets they were called Snowdrops (Tusa 1983: 147).*] Sometimes the defendants passed notes to each other or to their attorneys (few of whom were present), and once, when von Papen said something about the Gauleiter of Austria, they got all angry and excited.

During the interval and at the end they stood up and chatted together, or with their attorneys, and Goering had something to say (perhaps a ticking off) to von Papen at the end.[5]

We couldn't see the prisoners very well and moved after the recess which occurred about fifteen minutes after we had arrived. Hess then went out, not feeling well. Up till then he had been writhing with head in hands. Goering mostly lounged back in his corner, occasionally leaning forward to say something to Ribbentrop, who sat bolt upright with lips pouting, or to look more intently at von Papen in the witness box, or round at the audience, guards, or us. He looked aged and tired and worried and worn, his face a mass of bleary wrinkles [*Plate 24*].

Jodl and the other army and navy men looked old and not particularly savage, merely unimaginative, efficient servants not very interested in, nor up to, what was going on. Schacht and von Papen looked the Baltic Baron type of well meaning, humourless, earnest person who gets used by others more far-sighted and realistic, and less scrupulous, than themselves. Baldur von Schirach represents, according to the Reuter's man, the capture by Hitler of the university type devoted to Bach and Beethoven and Goethe; he looked it—young, intelligent, serious. Funk looked roundheaded and greasy. There he was, and we had been in his house in Berlin only a few weeks before. Rosenberg was small and narrow and intense. Seyss-Inquart did not look particularly intelligent. Streicher looked exactly like his pictures—horrible. Most of them seemed bored, and three (Seyss-Inquart, Funk, and Frick, I think) chewed gum continuously.

The interpreters are hard put to it and do extremely well. A transcript of the proceedings is made and duplicated copies of the morning's session are ready at the end of the afternoon's. The press have a room in the same building to write their stuff. They put it into another room which sends it to London, New York, etc., within the half hour, and recently sent off the four millionth word.

At the end of the session the Reuter's man, Hamsher, made himself very friendly and offered to put us up for the night in the press camp; we accepted. He had been speaking to the prison doctor who said all the prisoners were bearing up well, except Hess who might have a breakdown. (A German friend later said he had seen Hess about a week before his departure for England in 1941, and he looked like death.) Their clothes were pressed every day to keep up their morale. They are under constant observation ever since Ley hanged himself with his towel from the lavatory cistern bracket.

Hamsher said he thought the trial would have a value, in the example set by Lawrence, in the meticulous and patient and scrupulous hearing of everything relevant the defence had to say. The Russians seemed a bit out of their depth now and then, but having promised to co-operate they were co-operating and were working hard. The Russian counsel occasionally put questions which had to be ruled out of order, e.g. 'And what other crimes did you commit at this time?'—assuming guilt unwarrantedly. But a Czech journalist said he thought the trial was of little use, since non-Germans were convinced already and Germans were taking no notice of it; and that it had gone on far too long. The *Times* man said he found it still absolutely fascinating himself, but very difficult to make news out of it. However he had written 'about a column' that day and was supposed to be writing a book about it. Hamsher thought that Lawrence would recommend to the UK Government that there should be no more international tribunals. General opinion is that if anyone gets off it will be Schacht who put up a good defence.

We went off in the Press bus to their house, the family mansion of the Faber family, the makers of pencils, in a little village on the Stuttgart road. The whole village is to Faber as Bournville is to Cadbury. The mansion was built in 1906 like a castle and is horrible [*it has been described as 'repellent', and 'Schloss Schrecklich' (Tusa 1983: 229)*]. We had a wash and a stroll round the garden and then dinner and then went in to town for our luggage, and round the Zeppelinfeld where the party rallies used to be held (typical Nazi architecture), before returning to the Grand Hotel where we had a drink with a man in charge of the German journalists at the trial, a naturalised Englishman now in the Information Control Office at Hamburg.

18 JUNE Tuesday. We hitched to Heidelberg. We finally landed an American Mil Gov officer who invited us to an excellent supper, including grapefruit juice. Kreis detachments are now only two officers and two enlisted men, and we dined with the two officers, one of whom was a school teacher and the other a farmer. They were tightening up curfew and other regulations in preparation for the arrival of black troops in the area, expecting trouble. Bad to lift one's foot before coming to the stile. They thought the Germans couldn't manage without a larger detachment, and much confusion was caused by higher levels sending down contradictory instructions only through German channels.

On with an English convoy after some waiting; it had been picking up suspected war criminals. It dropped us at Frankfurt station whence we got a jeep taxi to near the autobahn. By this time it was nearly nine o'clock. We had good luck and were in Heidelberg at 10.30, having come most of the way with an American Negro officer. He had studied sociology and was all set to fight the Negro cause, possibly later by a propaganda base in Europe. He thought that Negroes stayed at home too much, they should get out and around more, otherwise other nations would take for granted what the white Americans said about them.

19 JUNE Wednesday. [*We visit another branch of the family in Heidelberg.*] Fritschov's father was a banker and in spite of being anti-Nazi was arrested for having remained in his position and is now interned in Berlin. His mother is Norwegian and is already back in Norway and he wants to leave Germany too. After lunch (during which the mother-in-law expressed her belief in the importance of Hitler being dead, and couldn't understand how Wolfgang had shed nationalism—'but don't you feel yourself a slave?') we four went to buy PX supplies, and I had quite a time getting a hundred military marks, going first to the Bank (Finance Office), then to American Red Cross, and finally with success to Mil Gov. The uninterchangeability of these with Reichsmarks in the US zone has caused a black market in them and any German could make big profits collecting military currency in the British zone and selling it in the American.

After tea we set off, getting by tram to the autobahn, with one lift to Mannheim, and then with an American officer and his wife, at 110–120 kph, to Frankfurt for the night train. The compartment included us, Yanks, Italians, Russians and Germans, and we slept quite well, feet to feet along one bench.

[*On 20 June we visited pre-war friends of my parents at Krefeld, then by various hitches via Dusseldorf and Essen got back to Dortmund. No letter covers the final days in Dortmund before return to the UK. However, they must have included a presentation from the Innere Mission of two booklets, home made with care and taste, dated 18 June 1946. The texts on the dedication pages are in fine Gothic script, and translations follow.*]

> FOR MRS [*sic*] DIANA CLOSE
>   of 4 FAU
> we dedicate to Remembrance
> as a mark of our thanks
> for her friendly service
> to our German people,
> above all to our children,
> these poems by German Christians
> from these years of distress for our nation.

> FOR MR. MCCLELLAND
>   of 4 FAU
> we dedicate to Remembrance
> as a mark of our grateful
> recognition of his friendly service
> to our German people
> these pictures of the former beauty
> of our now destroyed city,
> as we still carry it
> in our hearts and memories.

Postscript

The Section continued work in Dortmund under the Friends Relief Service banner until March 1948 (Kelber 1949: 116). Diana Close and I were married in September 1946 and two weeks later I became an Oxford undergraduate. In the early post-war years, we had visits in Oxford from Wilhelm Mensching and Rohtraut Fricke, and in Newcastle from Jacob Köbberling and Herbert Voges. In 1950 we visited Fru Palme (see p. 180), who gave a small dinner-party for us in her flat in Stockholm, including her daughter Catharina, who worked at the Karolinska hospital and took us to see round it the following day, and her son Olof, later to become his country's prime minister and a highly respected international statesman, before his early death by an assassin's hand.[1]

Our contacts with Germany gradually dwindled except for the Jacob family, where intervisitation has extended to our and Wolfgang's children and even one granddaughter. However, in 1961 I spent a week in Berlin for British Quakers, with Eric Tucker, Secretary of the British Friends Peace Committee. The Berlin Quaker office was in the East, but travel was still then possible to and from this sector by the U-bahn or Underground (the Berlin Wall went up only a month or two afterwards). Amongst other themes, the Quaker group shared with us their concern with the difficulties for Quakers and others of living under communist rule. Margarethe Lachmund was a particularly impressive figure, active in interceding with the authorities in the same spirit and with the same courage as had been shown by Corder Catchpool in Berlin in the thirties. I was also delighted to encounter Aktion Sühnezeichen, an organisation providing opportunities for Germans to undertake work projects abroad in a spirit not simply of reconciliation but of expiation, thus expressing an acceptance, as Germans, of joint responsibility for the past crimes of their fellow-countrymen. Its work continues today.

In 1973 I was appointed by the British government to be one of the first trustees of the Anglo-German Foundation for the Study of Industrial Society. This body had been proposed by the Federal President, Dr Gustav Heinemann, in a speech in London, and was financed for its first five years by an annual grant of three million German marks from the Federal Republic (subsequent funding has been shared by the two governments). It was the counterpart of a similar initiative vis-à-vis the United States, the German Marshall Fund, in recognition of Germany's inclusion in the Marshall Plan. The initiation and financing of the Anglo-German Foundation was intended to express Germany's gratitude for the particular contribution of the UK to the post-war reconstruction of Germany.

The Foundation was established by Royal Charter in Britain, and has its secretariat in London with a branch office at the Alexander von Humboldt Foundation in Bad Godesberg. Its objects are to promote the study of modern industrial society so as to broaden understanding in the two countries of its problems and their possible solutions. Its patrons are the Duke of Edinburgh and the President of the Federal Republic, and there are six trustees from each country. I served until 1979 and we normally met twice a year in London and once in Bad Godesberg.

This bilateral organisation brought me back into a much closer working relationship with a group of Germans than I had experienced in more widely multi-national organisations (such as the International Fellowship of Reconciliation, of which

I had been co-treasurer in the 1950s, and the European Foundation for Management Development, of which I had been a co-founder in 1971). The situation was altogether different from that 'on the ground' in 1945–46. The German trustees represented the 'establishment' of an essentially new country, economically the more successful of the two and in many respects the more advanced. In contrast to most of the Germans we met in 1945–46, they were confident and relaxed. After lunch on the day of our first meeting, in Lancaster House, the senior German trustee, a former Federal Minister for Education, encouraged the abandonment of the provision of simultaneous interpretation, saying with modesty and humour: 'Broken English is the lingua franca of modern Europe.'

The Foundation also brought me into contact with the Königswinter Conferences, the vision, creation and passion of the remarkable Frau Lilo Milchsack. They are an annual get-together of politicians, academics and opinion leaders in Britain and Germany, unofficial but influential, based on mutual understanding and respect between counterparts in the two countries.

Diana and I determined to re-visit Einbeck after one of the Bad Godesberg meetings, and beforehand I asked the von Humboldt Foundation if they could track down Herbert Voges. It turned out that he had become the Einbeck Bürgermeister. We found Einbeck restored to its former glory as a real gem of a Hanseatic League town with its rich collection of carved and painted timber buildings (whose fronts had been largely obscured in 1945–46 by fire-protection overlays). The Köbberlings were still in Holzminden, Jacob having retired from the hospital, where he had originally secured a post, we learnt, because Diana had driven him there one day after visiting the Dassel Erholungsheim. Elly Ohnesorge's husband had died, but she herself was flourishing and spent a day walking in the woods with us.

In 1995 we were introduced to a German student of linguistics at Tübingen who had written a seminar paper on 'Tyneside Dialect in Situational Context'. The parallel with Herbert Voges was striking, and we were able to put the two in touch, Herbert having by then moved to southern Germany.

In January 1996 the *Stille Helfer* exhibition (see p. x) was opened in the German Historical Museum in Berlin by the Federal President (who 'will never forget Quäkerspeisung, because I got half an hour off school each day to help to distribute it'). Brenda Bailey, Neville Coates (see p. 172) and I were amongst the former relief workers from Britain and the USA who attended the opening. We felt ourselves to be living exhibits. I was impressed by the readiness of Germans to revisit their darkest hours, and acknowledge the help that had come to them then. The exhibition later toured a dozen or more locations elsewhere in the country.

Diana and I were asked to help introduce the exhibition at its opening in Dortmund in September 1966, and took the opportunity to visit Vechta and Einbeck as well. The proprietress of our hotel in Vechta happened to know the Kathmanns, and my former German teacher, and in no time at all arranged for us to visit the eldest Kathmann boy, Ludwig, and his wife at Calveslage. Ludwig (then a teenager, now retired) remembered the family being evicted into the incubation room (see p. 33), but also 'good relations with the Quakers'. The family business had grown enormously and its offices now take up the whole of the original building. They introduced us to Professor Joachim Kuropka, a historian with a special interest in Vechta's experience after the war, and we spent two hours with him the same evening. As to my German teacher, she now lived elsewhere, but was due in Vechta the following day for a school reunion, and we were able to meet her over lunch at the home of her brother and his family.

Einbeck maintains its attraction for tourists but has also expanded with factories and other businesses, often built up by 1945–46 expellees from the eastern territories. The Landjägerkaserne, which had been owned even pre-war by a local family business, had been extensively rebuilt. Huhnesrück is still a horse stud farm. The Erholungsheim at Dassel, one of our largest DP camps, is now run by the YMCA, largely for people with learning difficulties. In casual conversations around the town, when we dropped the names of Frau Ohnesorge or Dr

Voges, we found that more likely than not people would say: 'My English teacher—the best you could have.' Elly Ohnesorge was now 87 but as vivacious as ever. She lives opposite one of the Ammermanns (see p. 153 n.1), the family whose business owns the Landjägerkaserne. Frau Ammermann is a daughter of a British intelligence officer with Quaker connections who, when with Mil Gov in 1945–46, had been able to help Leonhard and Mary Friedrich at Bad Pyrmont—so a chain of coincidences comes full circle.

We found central Dortmund completely rebuilt, but the Gartenstadt remains, and Plettenbergstrasse is largely unchanged—though the trees are larger. Our Quaker host told us she plays tennis, as we had done, at the former officers' club nearby. Some of the organisations we worked with are still flourishing but we were unable to make contact with any individuals we had known. However, there is a small Quaker group in Dortmund, who looked after us well. The old Stadthaus still houses the main municipal departments but across the new Friedensplatz from it is a new Rathaus for the Oberbürger-meister's and Oberstadtdirektor's departments and for weddings and occasions, and it was here that the *Stille Helfer* exhibition was mounted. Our loans for it included the booklets given to us by the Dortmund Innere Mission (see p. 190). The municipality provided every support for the exhibition, the Oberbürgermeister formally opened it, and we were interviewed by press, radio and television. Here, as in Berlin in January, the principal questions the media asked us were: 'What was your motivation? What were your feelings? What did British people think of your helping your/their recent enemies?'

Looking back at the experiences of 1945–46 from the perspective of fifty years later, a number of issues call for comment. They are related to three themes: refugees and displaced persons, the administration of the British zone, and the emergence of the Germans from Nazism, war and defeat.

(1) *DPs and Expellees*

The German expellees from the East had been uprooted by the wholesale shifting of Poland westwards, agreed by the Allies. This was rough justice for the German nation, but that was small comfort to the individuals concerned, who were victims of deliberate ethnic cleansing, to use a later term—'There will be no mixture of populations to cause endless trouble...', as Churchill put it in the House of Commons on 15 December 1944. (Grosser 1971: 27). However, they were still in their own country and able to use their own language, though their presence accentuated desperate shortages and they faced some hostility (see pp. 163–4). Their presence was bound to stimulate revanchism, and for years the Federal Republic, supported by public opinion, refused to recognise the Oder–Neisse line. It is remarkable that these refugees have become so fully integrated in West Germany, and that the 1945 territorial settlement of Eastern Europe has finally been unreservedly accepted by the new Germany.

The DPs were even farther from our picture of typical refugees as being forced to flee from an oppressive regime in their own country. The DPs had been induced or forcibly transported from their homelands by an occupying power, to work in that power's own territory, in order to release its own nationals for other service, mainly the armed forces. The closest parallel is perhaps the transshipment of Africans to work as slaves in American plantations in the sixteenth to the nineteenth centuries, though in that case generations were to pass before they were liberated, and hardly any of them, or their descendants, ever returned (the reverse migrations to Liberia being negligible). Once Germany had been conquered in 1944–45, most DPs from western Europe got home almost immediately, only a few remaining as a result of special circumstances of one sort or another (see, for example, pp. 50–51). The substantial minority of East European DPs who refused to go back became refugees in the usual sense, of being unwilling, through a well-founded fear of persecution, to return to their country of origin.

In the short term all that could be done on the ground was to make their desperate situation a little less dire. Mil Gov and the COBSRA teams did this, materially and in the case of the teams, sometimes psychologically or spiritually. FRS was better than FAU, as I reluctantly recognised (p. 57), in understanding the fundamental plight of DPs of having to live in camps without privacy or security, after experiences of being uprooted and treated as sub-human over a period of years, of not knowing what would happen to them next or what was happening at home or to loved ones, and of not knowing, if a time of decision came to them suddenly, how they should decide. Preferential treatment from the Allies would keep body and soul together for a few years, but uncertainty about the future was all-embracing and debilitating.

As responsibilities were transferred from the Western allies to the new democracy in West Germany, the privileged status of DPs was gradually eroded and it became increasingly urgent to help them get out of a country in which they could play no useful role. Emigration and resettlement had to be the aim when repatriation was out of the question and integration into German society impossible. But many countries for some years offered entry and work only for able-bodied males without families, an unacceptable price for most to pay. Members of the FRS teams who had worked to serve the DPs' interests in Germany and had come to know them well, became convinced that emigration represented the only reasonable solution, and that, painful as it was to part, they could serve their friends' interests better by trying to open wider possibilities from the outside (McNeill, in Kelber 1949: 104–5).

The international community was conscious of the issue. UNRRA had been set up in 1943 primarily to assist in repatriation. It ceased operations in 1947 as a result of disagreement with the USSR over forced repatriation, and was followed by the International Refugee Organisation, which managed to resettle over a million refugees in the four and a half years from mid-1947, leaving a 'hard core' of 175,000 (Marrus 1985: 344–5). The office of the UN High Commissioner for Refugees was established in 1951, also initially with only a three-year mandate, though it has continued ever since (Ferris 1993: 6–7).

I remember thinking in 1946 that another couple of years should see the back of the refugee problem. That was not a good prophecy. Instead, the creation of refugees has proved to be an endemic disease of twentieth-century humankind. Some progress has been made since those years by the international community in recognising obligations to those who have to flee from oppressive regimes or genocidal enemies. But side by side with measures to succour the outcast must be moves to secure recognition of human rights world-wide.

(2) *The Administration of the British Zone*

It would be easy to underestimate the difficulties faced by the British administration. They were operating initially in a context of overwhelming devastation and the breakdown of civilian communications and supplies. 'Trains crept over improvised bridges: only 650 out of 8000 miles of track were operating' (Annan 1995: 148). They had to prevent or handle major movements of people—of DPs going home, of evacuees returning to cities from as far away as Czechoslovakia, of the newly surrendered Wehrmacht being released to save the harvest, of Nazis and suspected Nazis being interned, of refugees before or from Soviet occupation, and later of 'expellees' from the eastern areas which were being incorporated in the new Poland.

They had also to be ready, possibly for underground resistance and all manner of sabotage, and at least for a sullen non-cooperation. In fact, as Bölling describes, the occupying forces and the German population encountered each other with mutual surprise. The former had expected sabotage by 'Hitler's vaunted Werewolves' or at least a fanatical wall of hatred; they met only vacant stares and boundless exhaustion. The latter had been told that the invaders would show them no mercy (Bölling 1964: 4–6).

The British had to maintain public order, not least amongst liberated DPs and others out for revenge. The extirpation of

Nazism was a cardinal objective, but they had to rely on Germans for ordinary civil administration at the grassroots, and they were ill-equipped—perhaps not even Solomon would have been well-equipped—to sort sheep from goats. Not allowing them to stay at their posts would present a Hobson's choice: 'if middling officials ... were expelled, they would have to be replaced by British officials, and the British taxpayer would foot the bill. If they were not replaced, life in the British Zone would become nasty, brutish and short' (Annan 1995: 204–5).

Certainly, mistakes were made, for example in imposing the British system of divided responsibility in local government. The relief worker's worm's eye view made us conscious of confusion and of measures that were counter-productive. Some shortcomings arose from the fact that many matters had to remain unresolved whilst relations between the Western allies and the USSR gradually demonstrated that a united four-power administration of the whole of Germany would be impracticable and a unified western Germany inevitable. It took time for it to become clear that coal-mining and heavy industry in the Zone would have to be rebuilt, not for reparations but to pay for essential food supplies, the cost of which would otherwise continue to burden the UK economy and taxpayer.

In terms of quality of personnel, combat units had had preference over civil affairs units. After VE Day and particularly VJ Day, demobilisation was unstoppable and the first call-up groups to go were those with most experience. Civilian 'green lizards' coming out for the Control Commission were those who could be spared from a civil service stretched by the tasks of reconstruction at home. There were strong pressures to cut costs and avoid the Zone being a drain on UK resources. Unfavourable comparisons were drawn at home with the per-capita cost of ruling India (Thies 1979: 41, drawing on Hansard vol. 426, col. 533, 29 July 1946).

Given all these considerations, success depended on a widespread commitment to good, indeed dedicated, administration. The official historian quotes the Political Adviser to the CiC, who spoke of the 'single-minded devotion' and 'the skill, good

humour and common sense' of officers in Mil Gov detachments, often operating 'with inadequate staff, working long
hours and without the requisite instructions'. He quotes the
'warm and clearly genuine' tributes from leading German ad-
ministrators to the 'competence and integrity' of their Mil Gov
counterparts. And he describes how many Mil Gov officers,
after initial reservations, 'found themselves engaged in work of
great value and absorbing interest', finding it 'the most reward-
ing work they had ever undertaken' (Donnison 1961: 465–6)

Time and again I too was struck by these qualities in the
majority of Mil Gov officers at the levels which I encountered—
working hard to discharge the responsibilities of the occupying
power to the civilian population. For every official like the
woman at Iserlohn (pp. 121–2)—who anyway belonged to
UNRRA—there was a Dickson (p. 79), a Coombs (p. 102), a
Battersby (pp. 125–7), a Wallsh (p. 149) or a Horwood (pp. 134–
5). My own appreciation of this was heightened by the mild
surprise of a conscientious objector, at the end of a long war,
finding that faced with manifest human need among the former
enemy population, FAU members and army personnel saw very
much eye to eye.

(3) *The Germans*

'I do not know the method of drawing up an indictment against
an whole people.'

> Edmund Burke, *Speech on Conciliation with America,*
> 22 March 1775

The Nuremberg indictments were unequivocal and detailed, but
they were against particular individuals and organisations. Outside those defendants (and even amongst them) there was every
conceivable variety of guilt and innocence amongst Germans,
from 'willing executioner' to heroic resistance. The relatively
guilty, having completed the Fragebogen (see p. 109), went to
CICs for further examination, some degree of re-education or
just reflection, trial and sentencing in a few cases, and release
in the rest. The relatively innocent (and the great mass in the

middle) took up or continued positions of responsibility in local government or in business and the professions, and worked hard in reconstruction, pursuing particular political, commercial or other interests whilst recognising to a large extent the need for all to work together.

These were necessary distinctions, externally assessable, in the process of trying to give a whole nation a new start. The relevant questions are practical and societal—did it work? In the event, defeat, if nothing else, discredited Nazism; the behaviour of the Allies showed that there was another way; their measures provided the opportunity for a new start; and a commitment to democracy and reconstruction on the part of the vast numbers of Germans in positions of responsibility and leadership in the new situation did the rest.

Many Germans whom I met in 1945–46 were disoriented, had lost all self-confidence or self-respect, or were consumed with self-pity. But most were people such as I knew to exist at home—enlightened or narrow-minded, idealistic or self-interested, open to new ideas or fixed in their ideas, principled or weak, courageous or cowardly, energetic or lazy. If a gang of maniacs had somehow won power at Westminster, it is terrifying to think how readily middle England might have succumbed. Many of the neo-Nazi ideas, particularly in respect of the threat from communism and what it might justify, would have played well amongst solid respectable people in Britain. We British should congratulate ourselves more on being luckier than on being better.

Individuals had clearly to examine their past actions, involvements and attitudes, and ask what was their own responsibility for the evil of Nazism and the catastrophes that had claimed so many victims. We may only guess at the internal struggles or the Houdini-like rationalisations that may have occurred. Whilst a counsellor or priest may be able to assist a process of acceptance, repentance, purification or renewal, an outsider cannot easily judge another person in this domain.

As mentioned in the Introduction, Quakers believe in 'that of God' in every one (see also the quotation from Corder

Catchpool on p. 63). Something similar was finely expressed by the very architect of Nazi defeat, in an earlier and quite different post, when he referred to: 'a constant heartsearching by all charged with the duty of punishment, a desire and eagerness to rehabilitate in the world of industry all those who have paid their dues in the hard coinage of punishment ... and an unfaltering faith that there is a treasure, if you can only find it, in the heart of every man.' (Winston Churchill as Home Secretary in 1910).

Whether we were concerned with Displaced Persons or with the people of Dortmund who had stayed put, we were trying to do what little could be done for some of the victims of war and oppression. Material damage and deprivation had been accompanied by psychological trauma. The first requirement was for relief, the provision of food, clothing, shelter. The manner in which that is provided can help to restore, or further destroy, self-respect and hope. But relief must quickly be succeeded by rehabilitation, resettlement and reconstruction, which alone can restore confidence and any sense of purpose, individually or communally. Members of relief teams are well placed to see the need for these further steps, but know that they are far beyond their own resources.

People engaged in relief work are driven also to consider the fundamental causes of the suffering they are trying to alleviate, and to try to tackle them. First-hand knowledge of dire need can provide the motivation to do this, but cannot of itself provide the answers to intractable problems, such as how to moderate or erode an oppressive regime, to develop alternatives to war or to resolve conflicts. Nonetheless, the Society of Friends has engaged in unofficial diplomacy and in single-issue politics, finding its justification often in the relief and service work it has undertaken. Members of the 1939–46 FAU have given later service to Oxfam and other non-governmental organisations, which live with the dilemma of whether to emphasise immediate relief in situations of need or to tackle its causes and prevention.

In an age in which graphic images of distress in trouble-spots around the world appear in our homes daily, it may be thought hardly necessary to be reminded of human suffering. But for me at least, to think back to the embers of the Second World War is to re-focus my attention on what can be done to tackle the causes of avoidable human suffering—oppressive regimes, the resort to war, the inhumanity of man to man, and the social structures and value systems that too often promote, but could inhibit, these evils.

Die Rückkehr der stillen Helfer

350 Jahre Quäker: eine Ausstellung des Deutschen Historischen Museums

Stille Helfer vergißt man oft zu schnell

1938 die Carter, es ner Wohlhr Unwegen wurlig haste-te er zum Büro der Quäker in der Nähe des Bahnhofs Friedrichstraße. Der ganze Hof war voller Menschen, die Zuspruch und Hilfe suchten. Carter führte das Büro zusammen mit einem Amer nem Deutschen. Sie solchen. di-

hört die Feindesliebe. Sie gab den Impuls für die Hilfsinitiative der Quäker unmittelbar nach Kriegsende, als es in Amerika und England noch extrem unpopulär war, den besiegten Deutschen in irgendeiner Weise beizustehen. Auch an der Gründung von CARE waren sie beteiligt.

Im August 1945 kam Helen Ad— nach Berlin. An das „No-Fra— bot hielten sich di— waren ni—

... ertigte einen Bericht ... Elend an,

Im Nachbarschaftsheim Mittelhof engagierte sich die New Yorkerin in der Kinderbetreuung. Die deutschen Betreuerin kannten die neuen pädagogisch lungen noch gar ni auf diesem

... nachb— ... der Historiker ...on University of Alabama. ...gnam, erläutert, eine wichtige Selbsthilfefunktion. Es gab Räume zum Tischlern und zum Schuheflicken, Wärme- und Waschräume, und es gab Gesprächskreise. Tent weist darauf hin, daß während der Nazi-Herrschaft deutsche Quäker ebenfalls verfolgt ...den Auch der

Sie kamen, als die Not am größten w...

...g Trümmer, Not und Elend erlebt

...ist de... kommen. De... stellung „Stille Helfer — Nachkriegsdeutschland", die b 12. März im Deutschen Historisch um zu sehen ist. Es ist dies ein Rüc die 350jährige Geschichte der Q Fotodokumenten unter anderem fen, auch solchen voller Dankbai die Hilfe, die diese Gemeinschaft nach den beiden Weltkriegen nach Deutschland brachte.

Die „Religiöse Gemeinschaft d— entstand Mitte de— land al— f—

Mit der Quäkerhilfe ins Nachkriegsdeutschland – Nach fast 50 Jahren jetzt wieder...

Berliner Ausstellung gibt Überblick über die Quäkerhilfe im Nachkriegsdeutschland

Stille Helfer mit politischem Einfluß

sollten ... te Entscheid... ... aren vielen noch aus der ... ersten Weltkrieg bekannt

Zu den Prinzipien der Quäker

... die Kinder gehen zu Di h Helen Adamson.

sind, sondern eine ... ment aus gelebtem Glauben herrührt. Immerhin haben sie, wie Bundespräsident

Ausstellung über Quäker im Rathaus

Erinnerung an „Stille Helfer"

An die „Stillen Helfer", die in den Nachkriegsjahren die hungernde und notleidende deutsche Bevölkerung unterstützten, erinnert eine Ausderausstellung im Rathaus. Die Wanderausstellung, die im Januar dieses Jahres von Bundespräsident und Schirmherr Roman Herzog in Berlin eröffnet wurde, berichtet über das Wirken der Quäker.

Der Titel „Stille Helfer" erinnert an die Verleihung des Friedensnobelpreises 1947 an das amerikanische und englische Quäkerhilfswerk für die „stille Hilfe von den Namenlosen für die Namenlosen". Die umfassende historische Dokumentation zeigt ...

„Stille Helfer" voll Liebe und Toleranz

Quäker im hunger den Nachkriegsdeutschland

Quäker: „Stille Helfer" in menschlicher Not

Selbstbewußte Bescheidenheit

Eine Ausstellung in Berlin erinnert an die Quäkerhilfe im Nachkriegsdeutschland

Germany remembers Quaker help (1996).
German press headlines on the *Stille Helfer* (Silent Helpers) exhibition referred to the 350 years of Quaker history; to Quakers coming to underfed postwar Germany when the need was greatest; to their experience of ruins, hunger, need and suffering; to the return of some of them 50 years later; to their selflessness, their modest self-confidence, their political influence, their love and tolerance; and to the Quaker principle of loving one's enemies.

APPENDIX

Educational and Welfare Needs in Civilian Internment Camps

[*See pp. 171–2 and 182–3. The following boils down our report to a fifth or a quarter of its original length. The report was dated 25 May and signed by Richard Ullmann on behalf of himself and myself. Sennelager is 5 km north of Paderborn.*]

We visited No. 5 CIC at Sennelager on 22 May and No. 4 CIC at Recklinghausen on 23 May, to report on the educational and welfare situations, and make suggestions for improvement. Sennelager held 10,766 inmates, including 761 women, and Recklinghausen 3500.

The Sennelager camp consists of seven compounds, of which one is a hospital, one is for women, and one for criminals or otherwise difficult cases. There is practically no communication between them, because of a shortage of guards for escort. Each compound has a Leader appointed by the Commandant and responsible for discipline, and three subordinate levels of elected leader.

There are thirteen inmates under the age of 18, including a girl of 16 said to be there for having thrown potatoes at a British airman. About 160 cases are investigated per week, but the number of releases is not constant and morale varies with releases and rations. Only three cases of suicide have occurred in nine months, each of them while the order for release was practically ready. The rate of release for those over 65 (only 53 left) and for women is being speeded up.

A great variety of educational and training courses are run by the inmates themselves. Agriculture is the most popular subject, followed by technical and chemical subjects, but English literature (and Thomas Carlyle) are covered too. The programme has to be approved. No active guidance is given, but history, politics and other controversial subjects are forbidden. In the compound we visited, out of 3500 inmates, about half were taking part in one or more courses, and since September 1945, 460 topics had been dealt with in over 6000 lectures. Eleven courses in handicrafts were about to begin, and people were learning English, French, Russian and Spanish. We saw an exhibition of arts and crafts of considerably higher standard than in similar exhibitions in PoW camps in Britain. There is a lack of musical instruments, but some plays are staged. A Protestant and a Roman Catholic padre live in the camp and are said to do much good work.

The British MO, and the internee doctor in the compound we visited, said health was improving though there are still cases of hunger oedema, both chronic and temporary. Three-quarters of the inmates work, and receive workers' rations, but no pay. Only 5 per cent work outside, owing to lack of escort.

At Recklinghausen we were not expected, but were given all facilities, including a long talk with the Commandant, and an hour and a half alone with two internees responsible for the camp's cultural life. There are eight compounds including one for young people and one for war criminals. The compounds are overpopulated and crowded together, with one central cook-house, and 2–3000 leaving their compounds daily to do work, so there can be no strict separation by compound. Internees under 17 are normally released, but there is a 'war criminal' of 15 said to have thrown stones at a British PoW some two years ago.

There are regular visits from a Catholic and a Protestant padre for services and bible classes (but a great shortage of bibles and hymnbooks). Lay representatives of the Innere

Mission and Caritas Verband are expected but have not yet turned up, and the British officers are confronted with marriage troubles and other problems with which they cannot cope.

Educational provision is similar to Sennelager, with 3000 studying English but little interest in other languages. The teachers are vetted and some with appropriate technical qualifications are nevertheless not allowed to take classes. Chess is played (with home-made boards and pieces) but there is little opportunity for sport. Choice of plays to perform is dependent on books available, but there have been productions of *Taming of the Shrew*, *A Midsummer Night's Dream*, and Aeschylus's *Persians*.

The Commandant is keen on improving camp conditions, and water-flush latrines are being constructed and cellars converted. Workshops provide welding and other metal work, and a saw-mill may be used for pit-props and other saleable products. Working party foremen are carefully vetted, as are hut- and block-leaders.

Needs and Recommendations

Considering that many internees are in the camps under allegations for which, if found guilty by a normal court, they would have received a shorter sentence than the time they have already spent in the camps, the Commandants are right to offer as much occupation and education as possible. This should be supported. Practical work and occupational training are greatly handicapped by shortage of tools and materials, many of which could be found in ex-Wehrmacht salvage depots or British army dumps. British Red Cross Society sections could find and transport such things. Stationery is so short that toilet paper is used in classrooms and officers and NCOs of 4 CIC buy pencils and paper with their own money. German voluntary societies could help in this provision. Books are also short—700 books for over 10,000 people in 5 CIC, and six English grammars for 3000 students in 4 CIC. Newsprint might be diverted for CICs, at the same rate as for the civilian population (one newspaper for every five people). Internees might be allowed to authorise collection by BRCS sections of sports equipment they possess at home.

There are enough medicines for hospital use, but a shortage of materials for dentistry, and a need for adjustments to artificial limbs made necessary by lower rations. At 5 CIC, these could be done inside the camp if leather were available.

In many cases there is prejudice against the churches, and a false pride hindering return to them after years of other loyalties. There might be scope for a non-denominational lay visitor with special concern for spiritual case-work.

Each internee may write 25 words every fortnight on a special buff card, half of which is returned by his next of kin, who may send 25 words in reply. The prohibition of other correspondence should be made more widely known, as many relatives send letters to internees who are not allowed to receive them. But an early increase in the number of words and the frequency of correspondence, and permission to receive letters, should be considered. The present regulations are less favourable than those in many Nazi concentration camps,[1] and an improvement would help to end unfriendly rumours about CICs among the population. There are no restrictions on parcels, but the requirement to send via Bonn causes delay and deterioration.

The educational efforts at present are primarily technical, and it is hardly possible that internees themselves are suitable for introducing a humanitarian outlook. Carefully screened lecturers from outside should therefore be admitted. Some German-speaking British officers might be included. The policy of avoiding controversial subjects should be reconsidered. Education for democracy is intrinsically dependent on the discussion of burning questions. The Foreign Office scheme for re-education among PoWs in Britain has been a remarkable success. The Interrogation Officer should first advise on the general atmosphere and special difficulties in different camps. For example the 5 CIC compound we visited seemed to harbour a large number of die-hard Nazis, whilst 4 CIC has a greater number of opportunistic Nazis now trying to dissociate themselves. Young internees should be separated from the rest as soon as possible since they are much more critical of Nazism than is generally assumed, and ripe for active re-education.

We recommend that the Branch of the CCG responsible for the camps should seek the cooperation of Educational Branch in tackling education in them. 'We would further recommend that Educational Branch should seek to bring home the great need for camp education to the German educational authorities, who naturally are not inclined to give preference to Nazi internees while they have to wrestle with the problem of education for the bulk of the German population. It should be made clear to them that at a future date German society will have to incorporate again most of the present internees...'

[*William Hughes, an older British Quaker who had worked for victims of Nazi persecution in Germany in the thirties until he was expelled, and who had lived on the Isle of Man during the war so as to be of service to the interned aliens there, devoted himself to visiting CICs in the British Zone from September 1946 to November 1947, providing educational opportunities and in some cases helping individuals out of a profound loss of faith. Quakers were concerned about the prolongation of indiscriminate internment, and in early 1947 representations were made to British ministers. Segregation of different categories into different camps took place in the summer of 1947, and all but a few internees were released by the end of February 1948 (Wilson 1952: 258–61).*]

Notes

Prelude: Into Germany

1. Both these items were lacking amongst civilians in the newly liberated countries of Western Europe—Italy, France, the Netherlands—in which I had spent the previous year.

Chapter 1: Vechta

1. In particular, numbers of men, women and children by nationality, name of leader, extent of overcrowding or unused accommodation, water supply and other living conditions, size and source of food rations, supplies of soap and utensils, access to health services.

2. It was Mil Gov policy to concentrate DPs in larger camps, specialised to each nationality, pending repatriation. See p. 4. Vechta was to remain for Russians only. There were transport and other limitations on the speed of repatriation eastwards by way of exchange with the Russians for westbound DPs in their area (Donnison 1961: 350–51)

3. Once the fighting had ceased, the British army became an army of occupation, and its ordinary regiments were stationed with a view to ensuring law and order. Civil Affairs and Military Government was a separate Branch under Major-General GWR Templer. It assigned Mil Gov detachments to German Kreise and other administrative areas, with the different task of running the occupied country or at least ensuring that it was run in accordance with British policy. (See diagram on p. xiv and map on p. xxiii). Though the two structures were separate, there was effective cooperation at local level, as in this case of the provision of transport, and

for example in Einbeck (see p. 39), where until the arrival of a DPACS (part of Mil Gov), the Intelligence Officer of the Sherwoods, the local regiment, was nominally responsible for DPs.

4. The other side to this is illustrated by the fact that, as I was to report on 15 June, 'the garrison troops at Goldenstedt are disheartened by the release of the Langforden Russian commandant, whom they caught red-handed, charged with possession and discharge of weapons and attempted rape, and put in Vechta gaol. Mil Gov could do no other than hand him over to the Russians, as only they may deal with him, but this means that now troops intend only to shoot people caught out after curfew, and are not arresting any more Russians.' Curfew at this time of year was 10.45 p.m.

5. I have a detailed note of this meeting. The Russians claimed that in large camps the rations would not be so good, and that in small camps they could buy things from the farms where they had worked. They added that, 'when people were hungry they plundered and ran amok. This was bad, but they were determined to live well in this land where they had been slaves for so many years.' We discussed food rations, the clothing currently being distributed, for which they expressed appreciation, and plans for concentration prior to repatriation, on which they promised to convince their Red Army Lieutenant and then to 'tell all Camp Commandants to be ready to move when we said'.

6. In other situations Quaker relief teams were more directly involved, or more principled. At Goslar the team leader made forceful representations at a high level in Mil Gov, and a new directive was issued (McNeill 1950: 120–21). In Austria FAU members were instrumental, through a successful challenge to an Army order, in saving 6000 Yugoslav refugees from forcible repatriation—and many more later (Corsellis 1995).

7. Donnison (1961) records 'Camp' as the penultimate word, making DPACCS.

8. A member had expressed his frustration in a letter to Gerald Gardiner dated 30 June. Gerald's three-page reply had been formidably well marshalled, detailed and trenchant but reasonable—of a piece with his (earlier and later) legal achievements in England.

Chapter 2: Einbeck, First Period

1. There had been German Quaker groups at Minden and Bad Pyrmont from the late eighteenth century, the Bad Pyrmont meeting house having been opened in 1800. These two groups were defunct by the early twentieth century, but a number of 'friends of the Friends', with connections from before the First World War, became active in the 1920s, with 26 groups by 1925, and some of them founded a Yearly Meeting with its

first full session in 1926 and a membership of 100. Leonhard and Mary Friedrich had founded a meeting in Nuremberg in 1924 and resuscitated the centre at Pyrmont in 1933. The Nazi years were difficult for the few small groups of Friends in Germany, but memories of Quäkerspeisung gave them some protection and with their Anglo-Saxon connections they were able to give some help to Jews, particularly the 'konfessionslosen Juden' who had neither remained Jews by faith nor joined a Christian church. (Greenwood 1977: 80–84, 162–170; Greenwood 1978: 254–273; Bailey 1994: 4–5; Halle 1980: 12).

2. Hamilton Mills led the FAU Section with the Free French 2nd Armoured Division. This had been formed in 1943 when General Leclerc led an expedition north from Chad to the coast near Tripoli. It had taken part in the Normandy landings and the liberation of Paris. I had myself been reluctant to be with the French when they entered Germany (see Introduction). One writer refers to 'extensive depredations' and quotes an eye-witness correspondent: 'For many Frenchmen it is a pleasure to see the panic that seizes the civilians who are being suddenly turned out of their houses.' He adds that the French began by being much harsher than the British or Americans. But of course France itself had been occupied and many French people had been subject to atrocities worse than harshness. See Willis 1962 and p. 216 n.5.

3. These letters to my parents did not tell all. To reach her in the non-fraternisation period, I had to cross the road several hundred yards to the south, out of sight of our sentry. She seemed to enjoy teaching me German behind a hedge, and certainly did it thoroughly. But when I first kissed her, she seemed surprised and shocked, saying: 'Aber—ich bin ein *Deutsches* Mädel' ('But—I'm a *German* girl').

4. In fact she had been a trusted friend whom he had asked to look after all his affairs when he realised that his imprisonment by the Nazis was imminent.

5. The initial objective had been 1550 calories for normal German consumers, with seven variations ranging from 1000 for young children to 2800 for very heavy workers. This compared with 1625 under the Germans in January 1945, shortly to plummet to around 1000 at the time of surrender. But that target could not be maintained. The level was set at 1200 for the four weeks beginning 23 July, and 1430 for the following period (Donnison 1961: 328–37). See p. 215 n.1.

6. I recall the largely elderly female congregation with brown wizened faces under peasant caps, listening silently, and wondered what they made of what we were saying. But when questions came, they showed a well-informed and well-thought-out grasp of current issues of religion and politics.

7. Each DP also had a personal identity card, a small rectangle of pasteboard, known in every language as a notapass because the words 'NOT

A PASS' were prominently printed across the front. See McNeill 1950: ch. 6, 'The Value of a Notapass'.

8. This feeling later led me, at the end of a film in an Einbeck cinema, to refrain from standing for our national anthem (not a step I had ever taken or wished to take in Britain). Immediately after the final chord I was gripped by the scruff of the neck by an angry British NCO sitting just behind me and shaken as a terrier might shake a rat. Fortunately my reaction was simply to go limp. I was later summoned by an officer to whom he had reported the incident, who delivered a mild reprimand and told me that the NCO in question had been much affected by the loss in action of his brother.

On another occasion we were at a concert in Hanover and arranged to meet Hans Wieding after it was over. Both he and I, it emerged, had sat for the British national anthem—an act of much greater courage on his part than on mine.

9. The official figure of Poles in camps at the end of September was 483,504. In July it had been agreed that at least there would be no organised influx of German refugees into the zone until 'the bulk of repatriable displaced persons are evacuated' (Donnison 1961: 352).

10. This apparently trivial matter was actually dynamite. The parcels had standard contents, whilst needs differed. Relief workers wished to break open the parcels so as—for example—to provide children with extra dried milk instead of their share of cigarettes. But that did not please parents of children, for whom cigarettes were valuable hard currency. See McNeill 1950: ch. 8, for a blow-by-blow account.

Chapter 3: Einbeck, Second Period

1. Künkel was a psychologist now living in California, his wife having been caught in Germany when the USA entered the war. International postal communication with German civilians was still forbidden, which is why he wrote to me.

2. Much of the talk was on supplies—coal allowances, indenting for 'housekeeping requirements', DDT, paraffin, knitting wool, etc. On Red Cross parcels (see p. 213 n.10), they would support us on any policy we like to follow, having 'tried in vain to get a definite order from higher levels'. The Polish Red Cross was expected to arrive with goods and services. All Balts would transfer to Goslar. Seeking names of Poles and Balts suitable and willing to go to courses at certain German universities—no fees, DP rations, housing arranged.

3. Under the National Service legislation, those with a conscientious objection to taking part in war were required to register as COs when their age group was called up. Each case was considered by a tribunal,

which might grant exemption conditionally or unconditionally. The condition could be a specified form of 'alternative service'. In these cases demobilisation meant that compliance with the condition was no longer required.

The debate (on 9 November) had been on the second reading of a Government bill to provide for COs' release 4–6 weeks after their corresponding army release group. The Minister of Labour said that the purpose was to avoid penalising those whose objection to military service had been recognised as genuine, and that the 4–6 weeks' delay was not intended as a penalty but to give time for COs and their employers to make other arrangements. Conservative (including R.A. Butler), Liberal, Labour, ILP and Independent MPs all welcomed the bill and paid tribute to COs' wartime service. The father of a member of the FAU said the FAU did not seek preferential treatment amongst the '25,000 good citizens' affected by the bill. Several speakers regretted the 4–6 weeks' delay, hoped that pretribunal service could be taken into account, and sought a Class B release scheme (early release for reasons of national need) for COs as for others. The Government reply, in a debate which had lasted about an hour, was cautiously encouraging on all three points. (*Taken not directly from Hansard but from a contemporary report by Sydney Bailey, who was present.*)

Chapter 4: Early Work in Dortmund

1. The Women's (later Royal) Voluntary Service in the UK was predominantly, in my view, an expression of middle-class paternalism—with, in wartime, strong patriotic overtones.

2. A great improvement on the hand guns we had used in Holland the previous May. The fear was still of typhus from the East.

Chapter 5: Acting Liaison Officer

1. This is below the five mentioned on p. 90, but the area excludes that part of the Ruhr falling into North Rhine Province.

2. Currency reform was eventually introduced throughout West Germany in June 1948.

3. The conference was to consider the future policy of FRS in Germany, and the minutes (FRS doc. 2023) make clear that this was done comprehensively and carefully. Fields of service considered included: DPs; German refugees from the east; young people; internment camps for Nazis; prison visiting; contacts with Russians; supplies of seeds and tools; other supplies; collaboration with American Quakers. The conference also considered relations with the occupying forces, and the issue of forced repatriation by British arms of alleged Soviet citizens (see p. 211 n.6).

4. The land had been presented to three Quakers, the Seebohm brothers, shortly before 1790 by two brothers, princes of the small principality of Waldeck-Pyrmont. The Seebohms developed printing, bookbinding, and cutlery manufacture there (Greenwood 1977: 80–81).

5. Maurice Webb was a leading Quaker in Durban, South Africa. The group there had befriended successive FAU parties on their way to the Middle or Far East. I myself had benefited in 1942 from the hot baths they had offered, and had learnt from Maurice about his involvement with race relations and welfare work in the town.

6. The equivalent for British Quakers of the President of the Methodist Conference—or perhaps the Archbishop of Canterbury!

7. Unquakerly phraseology, but Roger Wilson, 1906–1991, later a Professor of Education at Bristol, did indeed become a leading British Quaker, serving as Clerk of Yearly Meeting (see previous note) in the 1970s. He has described this conference as 'one of the creative moments in the life of FRS overseas... Would that our service had always lived up to its inspiration' (Wilson 1952: 275).

Chapter 6: Dortmund Developments

1. As early as July 1945, 21st Army Group had estimated a need for the import of two million tons of wheat into the British zone during the year to September 1946. The US and French representatives on the Combined Resources and Allocations Board had rejected this request. In the event no more than 112,500 tons reached the Zone before December 1945, and by March 1946 there had been nothing more. CCG now had no option but to reduce the standard German ration from 1550 calories (see p. 58 n.5) to the 'desperate' level of 1014. It was only in May that a UK Government mission to the US secured 675,000 tons by agreeing to reduce UK stocks to ten weeks from the 12 weeks' supply maintained throughout the war (Donnison 1961: 338–40).

It was reported at Vlotho on 19 April that two members of the FAU Section at Essen had decided to live on the new German rations for a week. They found they could not concentrate, and reacted and moved slowly; it was harder to get up, load trucks, and finish work.

2. An explosion had occurred at noon in the Monopol Grimberg mine, probably due to 'lowered standards of safety resulting from denazification'. It trapped 498 men, including three British officers, and 418 lost their lives, in a disaster 'unprecedented in German mining history' (Donnison 1961: 416).

3. Official figures for the Poles in camps were 441,364 on 1 November 1945, and 227,746 on 6 June 1946, a decrease of 213,618, so this rate (as an average over such a period) was neither necessary nor achieved.

(Donnison 1961: table at p. 250, referred to on p. 349).

4. The authorisation had occurred only three days before, on 1 March. The two other universities in the French zone could not cope with the student numbers required. Mainz was established with full academic freedom and became a major success (Willis 1962: 175–6).

5. General de Lattre's rule in the first eleven weeks after the cease-fire had been harsh and grandiose, but he was followed by General Koenig, who had further aims than to 'punish the guilty', including 'to lay down with an indestructible firmness the bases of a Franco-German rapprochement...' (Willis 1962: 74–6, 78).

6. The World War Two action here was the subject of a film, *The Bridge at Remagen*, made in 1969.

7. Like other FAU members, he wore British battledress with Red Cross and FAU shoulder tabs. Asked by a German Quaker about his citizenship, he explained that he was actually stateless at this time, having been deprived of German citizenship by the Nazis, and not yet naturalised in Britain. He concluded: 'Ich bin Europäisch—ich lebe im Staate der Zukunft' ('I am European—I live in the state of the future').

8. This would be Wilhelm Hansmann, in his only month or two with this title. Dortmund had been occupied by American troops on 13 April 1945 and transferred to British control the following day. The British accepted as Oberbürgermeister someone the American commander had already, after a 'short interview', appointed as acting Oberbürgermeister, Dr Hermann Ostrop. The British commander appointed a 'supervisory committee' from 27 April 1945, allowed the formation of political parties from 6 August, and established an appointed town council on 14 December 'as truely (*sic*) representative of the citizens of Dortmund as is possible without holding elections'. He had approved on 16 February the appointment of Hansmann as Oberbürgermeister and Ostrop as Oberstadtdirektor (see quotation from Annan 1995, below). On 8 March, however, he had terminated Ostrop's appointment on grounds of his not being free of 'any taint of Nazism', whilst expressing appreciation of his past services and allowing him to retire on pension. Hansmann became Oberstadtdirektor, serving as Oberbürgermeister for a month until a new choice could be made. (Stadtarchiv Dortmund 1985: 99, 103, 107).

On the 'separation of function', Annan observes: 'Professor W.A. Robson of the LSE had popularised the notion that German *Bürgertum* was too authoritarian. He advocated introducing the British system, in which the mayor and council were elected and were advised by the town clerk, a non-political administrator responsible for carrying out the council's policy. The British insistence on introducing this arrangement bewildered the German officials. Hardly surprising' (Annan 1995: p. 157).

Within this large city there had initially been many appointed district Bürgermeisters, for example in Dortmund-Aplerbeck a Communist miner,

Anton Kalt, who under the Nazis had spent time in a concentration camp. As the Americans approached, Kalt and others, at some risk, had hoisted a white flag on the Evangelical church tower, and Kalt had got through to the Americans with the news that (following some sabotage) Aplerbeck would not be defended. These local Bürgermeister posts were later abolished by the British (Stadtarchiv Dortmund 1985: 24–5, 29).

9. Lanstrop was an isolated enclosed housing development with minimal facilities a mile or two to the north east, occupied exclusively by 'problem families' whom others did not want as neighbours—an unfortunate arrangement to which housing authorities in Britain have also been known to resort. It was later subject to 'the gallant attempt of the city authorities and the FRS team in Dortmund ... by means of sewing rooms, a baby welfare centre and the like, to give a sense of community to the assortment of refugee families and old people who resented being billeted there' (Wilson 1952: 250).

10. The speaker was a Capt. Wallsh. My notes on his talk show that he was concerned about the allegiance of most youth clubs to a church or political party, but recognised that Mil Gov should not take sides or seek to impose a united front. He thought there was an opening for clubs that were non-denominational and non-political, and that the youth hostel movement, which had established its first hostel in Altena in 1909, might be a way of drawing different interests together. He was also concerned to promote the role of women on youth committees.

11. The reference is to demobilisation in sequence of call-up groups. My exemption from military service was conditional on my remaining in any one of several occupations, including 'ambulance work under civilian control'. In the event, Balliol College secured my 'Class B' release. Compare the situation implied here with the proposals discussed in the House of Commons on 9 November 1945, as reported in p. 88 n.3.

12. Templer (later Field-Marshal Sir Gerald Templer) had been appointed in March 1945 Director of Civil Affairs and Military Government in Germany, at 21st Army Group. I had been very impressed by him when he had addressed an earlier COBSRA section leaders meeting. Annan calls him 'a ruthless, incisive, dynamic commander' and adds: 'As soon as he took over he sacked the dugouts and failures who had been shunted into Military Government ... Templer's energy transformed the British zone' (Annan 1995: 149, 150).

13. 'I told them: "If Hitler invades, kill a German a day, and two on Sundays".' I recall also that he made great play with his double insignia, representing respectively SHAEF (Supreme Headquarters Applied Expeditionary Force) and Mil Gov. The official text (in the BRCS Civilian Relief News Letter for 4 May 1946) of Field Marshal Montgomery's speech is however sober and reasonable, whilst still characteristic of the man.

Interlude: Easter at Einbeck

1. This refers to the Landkreis. The town went through the same administrative metamorphosis. Einbeck town, like Dortmund-Aplerbeck, had been saved from destruction by one of the townsfolk getting through to the approaching Americans, in defiance of Himmler's final order to fight to the last. It was occupied a month before VE Day. Heinrich Keim has written: 'On the surrender of Einbeck town to American forces on 9 April 1945, the then American commander, Captain Kauffmann, arranged that with immediate effect I should take over the town administration as new Bürgermeister'. Keim then nominated six local citizens for particular responsibilities, and this group met for the first time on the 10th. Einbeck was included in the British Zone from 12 April, and Keim writes that the work of the town administration then consisted essentially in implementing ordinances promulgated by the British Mil Gov (Keim 1984: 142–3). This arrangement lasted until the end of January 1946, when Mil Gov appointed a representative 24-person council to take over. This council elected a local businessman, Otto Ammermann, as its chairman. He then took on the title of Bürgermeister and Keim became Stadtdirektor. The following September elections for the council were held (Keim 1984: 143–4).

2. The term 'catch-22' had not at this time entered the language.

Chapter 7: Final Weeks

1. A detailed account which I sent to Mil Gov and BRCS makes it clear that compromise arrangements were reached only after a series of meetings and conversations during 2–8 May involving ourselves, the Swedes, the Swiss and to a lesser extent Mil Gov, the Welfare Committee, and the BRCS LO. The issue concerned the location of the 'barracks' or building complex which the Swiss had brought for erection and where they would be working, and the distribution of their supplies. At one meeting in particular two features of the *Don Suisse* or *Schweizer Spende* became apparent, their indifference to costs incurred by the town on their behalf, and their express desire that the recipient of everything they had to give should realise that the article was a free gift from the *Schweizer Spende*.

It might be added that within a fortnight the issue of use of the barracks in the evenings by youth groups had arisen, and had to be referred to Switzerland. Questions of supervision and possible damage, and the avoidance of support for political or sectarian interests, had to be addressed in a letter (18 May) which Herr Lötscher invited me to write to him for forwarding.

2. The US Occupation Zone had no other port, so they took in sea-borne supplies at Bremen and across the British zone, as agreed in

September 1944 in Quebec, and in February 1945 by the Combined Chiefs of Staff (Donnison 1961: 188 and 193). US–British arrangements for US control of Bremen and access to it across the British zone had been agreed only with difficulty (Sharp 1975, pp. 108–14).

3. I vividly remember the hostile mood of the audience on this occasion. Compare a description of Niemöller's address to about 2000 students at Erlangen in January 1946. 'His uncompromising formulations did not find a wide response. His audience protested violently when he said: "We talk so much about being hungry... But I have never heard Germans ... speak out against the harm we have done to others..."' (Bölling 1964: 18).

4. The Freiwillige Frauendienst had applied for its members to be accepted into the Arbeiterwohlfahrt, but after the discussion in the Welfare Committee on 15 February (see p. 134), Fräulein Sattler and her colleagues had rejected this. On 5 April a 'preparative committee', which referred to 'the Communist Party, which sympathises with us', applied to Mil Gov for permission to form a new relief organisation. This must have been refused quite quickly, for by 17 April Fräulein Sattler was expressing regret, in a letter to us, that it had been turned down, as they would continue to try to 'seek in other organisations a platform for their agitatory activities'—in the Arbeiterwohlfahrt in particular, because of its 'interdenominational' character—something against which 'We must guard ... with great determination'. On 8 May I had sent a substantial memo to Col. Graves arguing for permission to be granted, on grounds of even-handedness, precedents, and discouraging entryism. I quoted a British Labour Party statement of 27 March asserting that 'the same party which is a negligible opponent in an open contest can be a serious menace as a fifth column working from within'.

5. This seems now a little harsh on a man, then 60, who had been arrested by the Nazis in June 1933 when the SPD was outlawed, who had spent eight years in Sachsenhausen concentration camp from 1937 until the Allies' arrival only twelve months before this date, and who was to serve as Dortmund's Oberbürgermeister from the elections in October 1946 until his death, hastened by his Sachsenhausen experiences, in 1953 (Högl and Lauschke 1986).

6. William Joyce, 'Lord Haw Haw of Zeesen', a British subject, regularly broadcast Nazi propaganda to Britain from Germany during the war. After the war he was tried for treason, found guilty, and hanged.

7. From the messes of four regiments covering 2–3000 men we collected 4–5 cwt. each evening of food that would otherwise have gone to pigs or the black market. The German welfare organisations met the General Routine Orders requirement that regiments' swill accounts must yield 25 marks per 100 men per month. The messing officers or quartermasters were happy to collaborate and the need was great. The first order to abandon was received on June 5 from one of the regiments.

8. Fru Palme, though a Swede, had been born in Leningrad before the revolution. In this connection she called it 'Leningrad'; they courteously or slyly referred to 'St Petersburg'. See Postscript.

9. 'An iron curtain has descended across the Continent.' Winston Churchill in a speech at Fulton, Missouri, USA, on 5 March 1946.

Envoi: 'Continental Leave'

1. An abiding memory of this occasion is of enormous casual waste of food in full sight of undernourished German passers-by.

2. On the night of 10/11 June 1942 a Free French brigade had evacuated Bir Hakim, in the Western Desert, after having made a notable contribution to the Allied cause by holding out for sixteen days against overwhelming odds. FAU mates of mine in the 'forward theatre' of our mobile hospital had been there too, so my being at the party would not have been wholly inappropriate.

3. A photograph of the courtroom (Tusa 1983: 178–9), makes it clear that we were in the press area and not the visitors' gallery above.

4. It was von Papen's second day in the witness box. A Catholic, and an army officer and diplomat, he had been Chancellor of Germany, without a majority in the Reichstag, in 1932, the year before Hitler came to power. He had served as Vice-Chancellor under Hitler, resigned after the Roehm purge, but later accepted the post of Minister Extraordinary in Vienna, where he was made ambassador in 1936. His defence was that he had been ignorant of the Nazi crimes and when aware, tried to mitigate them or dissociate himself from the Nazis. During the rest of the week this defence was to be demolished by Sir David Maxwell-Fyfe's cross-examination, drawing copiously on documentary evidence. Von Papen was ultimately acquitted of the two counts on which he had been charged— one of three defendants (out of 22) to be acquitted. His leading defence counsel, Kubuschok, was stigmatised by Birkett as verbose and pompous, using 'clouds of verbiage, mountains of irrelevance and oceans of arid pomposity'. The record does show him speedily reporting a mistranslation (Tusa 1983: 499, 389–92, 504, 393; Attorney-General 1948: *16*, 305).

5. Speaking of 1934, von Papen had applied the word 'Gauleiter' wrongly (but perhaps not without reason) to Hitler's liaison man with the Austrian Nazis (Attorney-General 1948: *16*, 299).

Postscript

1. The evening is memorable to me partly for a minor retrospective embarrassment. Diana told me afterwards that the family observed an old Swedish custom, whereby a lady at a dinner drank only when the gentle-

man on her left raised his glass to her. Olof had regularly paid this courtesy to Diana, whereas in my ignorance Catharina, on my right, had apparently had a dry meal.

Appendix

1. It was an advantage that Richard Ullmann was able to make this comparison as a former inmate of Buchenwald, just as the reference to the Foreign Office re-education scheme in the next paragraph was based on his experience lecturing to German PoWs in Britain.

References

Annan, Noel (1995). *Changing Enemies* (London, Harper Collins).

Attorney-General, HM (1948). *The Trial of German Major War Criminals (Verbatim Proceedings)* (London, HMSO).

Bailey, J.E.B. (1994). *A Quaker Couple in Nazi Germany* (York, Sessions).

Bailey, S.D. (1993). *Peace is a Process* (London, Quaker Home Service and Woodbrooke College).

Box, Muriel (1983). *Rebel Advocate: A Biography of Gerald Gardiner* (London, Gollancz).

Bölling, Klaus (1964). *Republic in Suspense* (London and Dunmow, Pall Mall Press).

Corsellis, J. (1995). 'Friendly Persuasion: How 6,000 Refugees were Saved in 1945', *The Friends Quarterly*, October 1995, pp. 353–63.

Davies, A. Tegla (1947). *Friends Ambulance Unit* (London, Allen & Unwin).

Donnison, F.S.V. (1961). *Civil Affairs and Military Government in North-West Europe 1944–1946* (London, HMSO).

Ferris, Elizabeth (1993). *Beyond Borders* (Geneva, WCC Publications).

Greenwood, J. Ormerod (1977). *Vines on the Mountains (Quaker Encounters, Vol. 2)* (York, Sessions).

——— (1978). *Whispers of Truth (Quaker Encounters, Vol. 3)* (York, Sessions).

Grosser, Alfred (1955). *Western Germany: From Defeat to Rearmament* (London, Allen & Unwin).

Halle, Anna Sabine (1980). *'Die Gedanken sind frei…'*, *Eine Jugendgruppe der Berliner Quäker 1935–1941* (Berlin, Gedenkstätte Deutscher Widerstand).

Högl, G. and Lauschke, K. (1986). *Fritz Henssler: Ein Leben für Freiheit und Demokratie 1886–1953* (Dortmund, Stadtarchiv Dortmund).

Hughes, William R. (1956). *Indomitable Friend* (London, Allen & Unwin).

Keim, Heinrich (1984). 'Einbeck in den Nachkriegsjahren 1945–1960: ein Überblick', in *Einbecker Jahrbuch*, 35, pp. 142–62.

Kelber, Magda (1949). *Quäkerhilfswerk, Britische Zone, 1945–1948* (Bad Pyrmont, Leonhard Friedrich Verlag).

Kuropka, Joachim (1995). *'Um den Karren wieder aus dem Dreck zu holen...'* (Vechta, Vechtaer Druckerei und Verlag).

Landkreis Vechta (1995). *Eine Geburtstätte der Demokratie* (Vechta, Landkreis Vechta).

McNeill, Margaret (1950). *By the Rivers of Babylon* (London, Bannisdale).

Marrus, Michael R. (1985). *The Unwanted: European Refugees in the Twentieth Century* (New York, Oxford University Press).

Sharp, Tony (1975). *The Wartime Alliance and the Zonal Division of Germany* (Oxford, Clarendon Press).

Stadtarchiv Dortmund (1985). *Dortmund im Wiederaufbau 1945–1960* (Dortmund, Verlag Ruhfus).

Thies, Jochen (1979). 'What is going on in Germany? Britische Militärverwaltung in Deutschland 1945/46', in Claus Scharf, ed., *Die Deutschlandpolitik Grossbritanniens und die britische Zone 1945–1949* (Wiesbaden, Franz Steiner Verlag).

Tusa, John and Ann (1983). *The Nuremberg Trial* (London, Macmillan).

Willis, F.R. (1962). *The French in Germany 1945–1949.* (Stanford, Stanford University Press).

Wilson, Roger C. (1952). *Quaker Relief* (London, Allen & Unwin).

Index

Note: the index covers only pp. 1–221 and the picture section, except that place names included on the map on p. xxiii are so identified.